One Great Game

ALSO BY DON WALLACE

Hot Water

ONE GREAT GAME

Two Teams, Two Dreams,
in the First Ever National
Championship High School
Football Game

DON WALLACE

ATRIA BOOKS

NEW YORK LONDON TORONTO SYDNEY SINGAPORE

ATRIA BOOKS
1230 Avenue of the Americas
New York, NY 10020

ISBN: 0-7434-4621-6

First Atria Books hardcover edition September 2003

10   9   8   7   6   5   4   3   2   1

ATRIA BOOKS is a trademark of Simon & Schuster, Inc.

Manufactured in the United States of America

For information regarding special discounts for bulk purchases,
please contact Simon & Schuster Special Sales at 1-800-456-6798
or business@simonandschuster.com

To my father, Don C. Wallace, Jr., who handed me the ball,
and to my son, Rory Donald Soon Chong Wallace,
who will now carry it.

CONTENTS

The game?

I think it's way overblown.

I think high school football is overblown.

I think our streak and the hype is overblown.

I never asked for it.

It just happened.

—Bob Ladouceur, head coach,
De La Salle High School

PROLOGUE

On a hot afternoon in July 2001, I went back to high school. Long Beach Polytechnic is only a short drive from my parents' house, and not nearly as much of a journey in terms of class and race as it was in 1970, when I graduated. But I still had my heart in my throat the whole way.

Traveling south on Atlantic Avenue from my old neighborhood, Bixby Knolls, the tidy, prosperous storefronts (Alsace-Lorraine Bakery, Jongewaard's Bake n' Broil, Nino's Ristorante) gave way to freeway-handy franchises (Denny's, El Torito). Then, over the river of thundering 405 traffic and through the forest of oil rigs and pipes that divides Long Beach like a demilitarized zone, Atlantic Avenue itself turned gritty. Signs again told a tale: Ric's Smoke Shop, Rosicrucian Lodge, Tacos Cucio de Jalisco, The Church of Summa This & Summa That, Fish Louisiana Best Seafood, Joe's Liquor, African Art Gallery. As I approached the old school's meanest streets, I was surprised to see brand-new duplex homes all in a row, Craftsman-style with open porches and corner pillars made out of river boulders and concrete: an old Long Beach style from the 1900s.

I nearly overshot the school, despite its being as big as an aircraft plant. Seventeenth Street—where I was once mugged by an eleven-year-old, where parked cars lost hubcaps and tape decks inside of an hour, and where the girls in the windows of the whorehouse across the street used to wave at us as we left football practice—had disappeared. The north side of the school had expanded, turning the blocks, formerly some of the city's worst, into student and faculty parking, and a separate federally subsidized housing development called Poly Apartments. An access road, Jackrabbit Way, was bordered by a fence topped with gleaming concertina wire.

The school itself still looked familiar: beige concrete, four-story buildings, frosted-glass windows reinforced with chicken wire, a twenty-foot-high chain-link fence. The most noticeable change was the new single-door side entrance on Jackrabbit Way, which rendered ceremonial the old front gate on Atlantic, a majestic art deco arch with a thirty-foot-tall cartoon of a feisty jackrabbit and school motto: Enter to Learn, Go Forth to Serve.

And then, for the first time in thirty years, I am crossing the asphalt courtyard by the Snack Shack, scene of many maple bar breakfasts for me, and also two race riots.

Walking by a knot of students under a slant-roofed open shelter, I realize I've clenched myself tight: the old defensive posture, circa 1968. Having spotted a hundred boys in white T-shirts and blue shorts running wind sprints, I set off for what used to be the girls' field, a two-block walk. As I arrive, two black men in their fifties swagger toward the field; both have squire's bellies, wear sandals with white tube socks, and sport identical conical straw hats of the kind favored by the Vietcong in 1966. The sea of boys parts in awe of these two, who banter in a growly sort of way with the other bystanders and each other.

One man, with hooded eyes and an abbreviated Fu Manchu mustache, grabs a freshman and yanks him toward him. "You see the way to get separation on a defensive back?" he asks. Now it's the other man's turn. He swings the player, a boy half a foot taller and eighty pounds heavier than he is. "It's not enough to be fast. If all you got is speed, go out for track."

On a hunch, I introduce myself to the second man, whose salt-and-pepper mustache is less intimidating than the Fu Manchu. Herman Davis, class of '64, has an institutional memory of the football program. When he hears I'm an alumnus, that's enough; we're off and talking about Gene Washington, Earl McCullough, Dee Andrews, the stolen CIF championship Herman's senior year. I'm transported into the world of Long Beach Poly sports history: coaches Mulligan and Levy, Oscar Brown, Marvin Motley, John Rambo at the Olympics, Mack Calvin playing basketball, Billie Jean Moffitt (later King) winning the Wimbledon women's doubles title at age seventeen.

The kids lining the wall look over curiously, shrug: more old Poly guys carrying on. They're used to it.

We walk across the asphalt and go down the ramp to Burcham Field, the dried-up, dusty mat of grass that was so bad that even in my day the other Moore League teams refused to play on it. No varsity game has been held here in over thirty years. I stand, take in the scoreboard, still broken, the cars flashing past on Orange, now renamed Martin Luther King Boulevard.

We're strolling through a gap in the fence, toward a field that didn't exist in my day. Fu Manchu, coach Merle Cole II, nods when I mention the fact. "Tony Gwynn Field," he says—named after the baseball All-Star, future Hall of Famer, and Poly grad. "Tony came here with his whole family, cousins, for the dedication." Merle II gives me a hard look. "Where you say you live?" New York, I tell him. "When you graduate?" Nineteen seventy.

Herman makes a face: "Oh, that was the beginning of the *bad* years. You're one of *them.*"

Merle II stares into the distance. "Poly people don't leave. They come back."

"Well, I'm back," I say. Herman hails a tall young man in jeans and blue T-shirt, bulging biceps. "Chris Webb," he says, "back from Montana! Come talk to this poor 1970 graduate, tell him what it was like to be on the first team to beat Mater Dei."

Webb grabs Herman affectionately and says, "I was driving past and just had to stop by."

Merle II turns to me. "See? Poly people always come back."

Herman says to Webb, "Out of football? Haven't you got a year of eligibility left?"

Webb shrugs, grins, takes off his dark glasses. "It's my senior year. Got a lot of classes I want to take."

Merle II turns to me. "See? Poly kids get their degrees. People are always saying we're a football factory, but these kids, after they get through here, are *prepared.*"

We're in a large group now, slapping hands and bumping fists. It comes to me that I knew Merle II, way back when. He was a small but tough defensive back, a senior on the varsity when I was a sophomore Bee. He still has the same irascible scowl and bark, the same hard look I tried to emulate back then. But, I realize, what makes his scowl memorable now is that it stands out: the faces of Poly have undergone a transformation. Everyone I have passed since entering the campus has had a look of openness, not one of rejection, affected indifference—or even threat.

I mention this to Herman, who nods. "We don't get the renegades anymore. Now, Willie McGinest"—currently the New England Patriots' All-Pro defensive end—"he had that old attitude. First day of practice when I was introduced as linebacker coach, big Willie, he must've been 6'6", loomed over little old 5'10" me and said, 'You can't coach me.' And I gave it right back to him: 'But I am!' "

A parade of varsity players comes onto the field, moving slowly, like giant gazelles in flip-flops and loose shorts, many shirtless, shoes tucked into the gold shells of their helmets. There must be twenty-five kids here who weigh over 220 pounds—a couple, like the one with two-foot-long braids and black gloves, must be 300.

"This may be the best defense we've ever had," Herman says. "No running back got over one hundred yards in fourteen games last year. In eight games, teams got less than one hundred yards in total offense. Tell you the truth, I was shocked when De La Salle took us up. That same defense is coming back."

He asks me if I've had a chance to see the Spartans of De La Salle High School, and I tell him that I'm heading up north in a couple of days. "I know De La Salle took the challenge with Mater Dei and beat 'em three times," Herman says, "but I never thought we'd see them in my lifetime."

The players have begun working out, seemingly without a signal or even supervision from the coaches. Besides the lack of street-hardened affect, I notice the lack of regimentation; everything flows, with little of the tension that infused every minute of practice in the 1970s. No orders are barked, no coaches spew abuse at foul-ups, no players are at each other's throat. Lines of large young men dance nimbly between rows of orange cones like the ballet elephants in the movie *Fantasia*, the players counting off in unison as the receivers make a string of catches without a miss.

Herman waves at the linemen as they go through their agility drills. "I mean, what is De La Salle going to do about this huge offensive line, 275 pounds average on the front?" He brings up last year's California Southern Section championship game, which Loyola High lost to Poly in overtime. "In the first half, they contained us very well by putting eight men on the line and daring us to throw. Hershel would run on first down and get one or two yards, then on second down Loyola would switch to a 4-3, drop their defensive backs back, and our passes would be incomplete or get intercepted. I kept telling Jaso"—Jerry Jaso, Poly's head coach—"at halftime, pass on first down, run on second. The offense didn't get it going until the last two minutes."

I point out that he'd said his 1964 team had only weighed 167 pounds on the line when it beat El Rancho, the eventual California Southern Section champion. He nods. "That was in the days when you maybe had one player who weighed 250, 260—and he was a freak. Now you have guys lining up to take their turn who weigh 280."

By now there is a circle of players around Herman, listening intently. Herman returns to his story: "But we still had Loyola beat, until they pulled the fumble-rooski. Those Catholic schools have come to the conclusion that the only way to beat us is to trick us. You know what they say about us?" he challenges.

The kids, almost all of them black or Samoan or Hispanic, stare up at him, utterly attentive.

"The only way to beat Poly is to make them think."

Several kids' faces flinch at the slap Herman has just delivered. I'm surprised, too; Herman has just spoken the Poly curse, broken the taboo out loud. After the head coach my senior year did the same thing, we lost every Moore League game but one.

Offensive line coach Tim Moncure, also wearing a VC hat, joins the conversation: "Loyola's coach ran that play at the perfect time, too. Waited until right after a TV time-out."

Herman nods. "That is what I admire about them." The kids' jaws drop at the thought of admiring a Catholic school team. "They're smart. They find a weakness in your game and they exploit it. All night long they showed us a two-tight-end formation and either ran out of it or threw a deep out. Then, third quarter, two tight ends, out pattern—and then the wide receiver turns it up. Quarterback drops the dime on him, and that leads to their first field goal."

One of the players, a 6'7" black kid, interrupts quietly, "Are you saying they're smarter than us?"

"They were patient. They didn't go for it right away," says Moncure. "They set it up."

"The Catholic schools, see, they look for something that puts the focus on you and takes it off them," Herman says. "They get you thinking, 'Oh, we're a public school, we make mistakes.' And they do things, like the Monarch March, the whole Mater Dei team marching in front of your bench, to get you mad. Then when we're focusing on getting even, they focus on getting one over on us."

"But are they smarter? Is De La Salle smarter?" asks the kid. I get the sense that this is not the first time he's challenged a coach.

Herman looks at the young giant. "That's what they want *you* to think. Whether you are or not, Winston, is up to you."

Herman notices how the sidelines are caught up in the discussion and frowns. "Let's pay attention now." He thrusts out his barrel chest, roars, "*Every*thing is game!"

One

RUMORS

On December 7, 1991—nine years and 299 days before the first high-school national championship game—the Concord (California) De La Salle Spartans suffered what they still refer to as their own "day of infamy": they lost a football game. With two minutes and nineteen seconds to play, Percy McGee snatched an interception and returned it for a touchdown, giving the Pirates of Pittsburg High School a 35–27 lead and putting them in reach of an upset over the Spartans, who hadn't lost for thirty-five games.

The Pittsburg Pirates were the underdogs. Pittsburg is a gritty, blue-collar, racially mixed port town on the windswept outlet where the Sacramento Delta empties into Suisun Bay, a distant and distinctly unglamorous backwater of the San Francisco Bay. De La Salle—private, suburban, Christian Brothers–founded—was going for its fourth consecutive California North Coast Section championship and had future New York Giants star Amani Toomer among its standouts on the field.

More than any single player, though, De La Salle had Robert Ladouceur, then thirty-seven years old and completing his twelfth year as Spartan head coach. Before taking the job, only the second coaching position he'd ever held, Ladouceur had been a juvenile probation officer at age twenty-five, moonlighting as a high school football assistant. As De La Salle's coach, he became a legend. Not right away, of course; but soon enough his reputation as a perfectionist started to precede his team onto the field. Seeing him on the sidelines—intense, unsmiling, deep-set eyes—opposing coaches and players found it easy to ascribe a sort of supernaturalism to Ladouceur to explain away their losses to what had been a doormat of a team.

And handing out losses was becoming automatic; Ladouceur's Spartans showed a knack for putting together winning streaks. Five in a row, six in a row, an entire season. Then a twenty-four-game winning streak—interrupted by one loss—followed finally by a thirty-five-game run, which was on the line tonight.

But if De La Salle had a legend coaching that night, Pittsburg had a windfall of talent, including future Oakland Raiders lineman Regan Upshaw, who pounced on a De La Salle fumble in the last minute to secure the victory. For Terry Eidson, who had taken over as the De La Salle defensive coach just three games before the championship when an assistant abruptly left, the memory is indelible—if coded in football jargon. "They came out with a five wideout set and surprised us," he says, self-recrimination straining his voice. To be a Spartan is to be prepared. "I vowed to myself to never get beat that way again."

Upshaw went on to become, after college at the University of California at Berkeley, a first-round draft pick of the Tampa Bay Buccaneers. For the last three seasons as a Raider he has played on the same Oakland (now Network Associates) Coliseum turf where the Pirates had won. But for him, a pro lineman, nothing compares to that night: "Playing the game with all the buddies you grew up with," he rhapsodized in a newspaper interview nine years later, "playing for the glory of football."

While Upshaw's memory is of glories past, De La Salle and

Ladouceur have continued to gather new glories every year: since Upshaw and Pittsburg's big night nine years ago, the Spartans have not lost another game. In late August, when the 2001 season opens, their streak will stand at 113 consecutive victories—and counting.

Ever since the December evening in 2000 when the Long Beach (California) Polytechnic High School Jackrabbits had won one of the most thrilling Southern Section championships anyone could remember, they had been sitting on top of the world; there was no other way to put it. It was more than just a game—it was a vindication, a celebration of community, and a kind of exorcism as well. One man in particular had good reason to be floating. Long Beach Poly coach Jerry Jaso had heard the doubters for an entire year following the outcome of the 1999 championship game, against perennial nemesis Mater Dei of Santa Ana.

The rivalry between the two teams mirrored the social divisions in California education. Poly represented a return to public school glory from the days preceding Proposition 13, which had devastated the state's tax base in 1976 and led to plummeting test scores and the limitation, or in some cases, the elimination, of most extracurricular programs. Private parochial powers like Mater Dei benefited from Proposition 13, able to pick and choose their students, feeling no responsibility to the unprepared, the unparented, the unruly, the physically or mentally challenged, the migrant or the poor. Furthermore, as a private institution Mater Dei could also skim the cream of the crop of local athletes, and *local* was a pretty fluid term in the sprawling five-county Los Angeles Basin, home to almost 20 million.

By the late 1990s the Mater Dei Monarchs would crow over being the undisputed kings of Southern California football, voted number one in the U.S. twice in national year-end polls. The Poly

Jackrabbits had vowed to topple Mater Dei, but for an entire decade had always fallen just short. Yet there can be lessons in losing, and even inspiration, too. Under coach Jerry Jaso, the Jackrabbits would finally learn that winning on the field means becoming a winner off it.

In the 1997 California Southern Section title game, Poly had surprised a favored Mater Dei. Then it was Mater Dei's turn, stealing the 1998 final from Poly and what some are *still* calling the most talented high school team in history. In 1999, it was Mater Dei again, invoking that old Catholic school hoodoo and keeping the Jackrabbits off balance—and off the scoreboard. It came down to a last-minute drill; Poly scored a touchdown with zero seconds left on the clock and trailed by one point. There was no provision for overtime in the California Interscholastic Federation (CIF) rules, so everyone expected Jaso and the Jackrabbits to go for a two-point conversion and victory. Who plays for a tie, anyway? "A tie is like kissing your sister," as Alabama coach Bear Bryant once said.

Coach Jaso sent the kicking team out: stunned silence and even some boos. The kick was good, but the cheers were muted; neither school could really celebrate. And Poly caught the flack afterward. People said that Jaso's going for the tie had tarnished the championship; that he didn't dare go for the win because Poly's public school kids just weren't disciplined enough—that is, white enough—to pull it off. Those Poly Jackrabbits were chokers.

But Jaso stuck by his decision; at least that's what he said. He knew the Poly haters would find something to say no matter what, especially if he had gambled on the two-point conversion after the touchdown and then lost. At least Poly had come away with its second championship in three tries over three straight years, and they'd thwarted Mater Dei. Give it time, and that's all anybody would remember: a historic run in the 161-team CIF Southern Section, whose Division I is the largest and strongest football division in California, and arguably in all of America.

But then came last December's game—against Loyola High School of Los Angeles, another Catholic school, another old foe of Poly's (as what Catholic school wasn't?). For Poly the rivalry wasn't individual so much as Inquisitional: if it wasn't Mater Dei torturing the Jackrabbits, then it was Loyola. Or Bishop Amat, or Servite or Saint Paul.

And the game had indeed been torture for the green and gold of Long Beach. At halftime the underdog Cubs had made 15 yards and no first downs compared to 152 yards for Poly, yet the score was 0–0. A field goal put Loyola up 3–0 before Poly linebacker Marvin Simmons blocked a punt into the end zone, which junior Darnell Bing fell on for a 7–3 lead. With less than two minutes left in the game Loyola got the ball on their twenty. All Poly had to do was hold for four plays. Everybody in the stadium with any sense of history knew to expect a surprise, so there was no way the Poly defense was going to fall for any Catholic schoolyard tricks. Right?

Wrong. Here comes the fumble-rooski, a play so old the Four Horsemen of the Apocalypse might have chuckled over it. The quarterback calls the signals, the center snaps the ball but holds on to it. Then he falls over, hiding the ball between his legs, while the rest of the Loyola team fakes a sweep right—except for this one player who dawdles, then trots over to the center, picks up the ball—which has technically been fumbled—and dashes left for 60 yards, down to the goal line.

The fumble-rooski hadn't been tried in CIF football for fifteen years, which is probably why it works. Loyola scores to take a 10–7 lead with 1:12 left. The anguish on the Poly side is existential. Here it is again, the nightmare from last year's championship—Poly has to try to put something together and score with time running out.

What does Jaso do? He pulls the starting quarterback, a senior, and puts in the junior, Brandon Brooks. The senior has the experience, he started last year, he's 6'4"; Brandon is a shade over 5'9". He's played in tandem with the taller quarterback all season, but still, you don't pull a senior with a minute twelve to go and the championship on the line. Not when Brandon came in at the end of the first half and, after taking the team down to the Loyola goal line, threw an interception.

Jaso has long had a feeling about Brandon. He's looked past the 5'9" body and sees, as he puts it, "a six-foot-six heart." He knows this kid's story: no biological father in the picture; Brandon's mother dying when he was eight; how he's moved from his grandfather's house to his stepfather's apartment depending on his ailing grandmother's condition. He's consoled Brandon after he's made him ride the bench, letting a senior have his shot at starting. And Brandon has responded to the years of Jaso's coaching—coaching about leadership and life as much as about football. "I'm better as a person, better as a leader, on and off the field, because of Coach Jaso," he says. "I've maintained a 3.2 average because of Coach Jaso. Quarterback is a lonely position: on top one minute, next minute you're down. I needed someone to believe in me."

Into the game he goes. After Loyola kicks off, fifty-six seconds are left. On the first play, dropping back to pass, Brandon is sacked for a ten-yard loss. Forty-eight seconds. He throws a quick dart for a thirteen-yard gain, hitting the receiver, Mike Willis, just as he goes out of bounds to stop the clock. On the next play, Brandon tries to hit Willis again; a Loyola player tips the ball, but Willis grabs it anyway and runs for thirty yards. Brandon quickly lines the team up on the new line of scrimmage and spikes the ball to stop the clock. Next Brandon hits Joshua Hawkins across the middle: first and goal from the ten. Poly has four chances left. The first pass is too long. The second goes to 6'7" Marcedes Lewis, leaping over a 5'9" cornerback.

Touchdown!

No, the ref calls: Marcedes had gone out of bounds. The third misses, too.

Fourth down. Here it is, pretty much an exact replay of last year's final play. Four seconds are left and a field goal will tie the game.

But one thing is different this year: overtime. Because of the outcry following last year's tie game, the CIF has changed its rules to allow for an overtime period. Now that a field goal for a tie won't look like such a cop-out, Poly should just kick it, right?

Not so fast. Jaso has a problem. His kicker, Javier Torres, hasn't attempted a field goal all year. Can the coach turn over the fate of this game, the legacy of this team, to a walk-on soccer player?

Everybody is second-guessing Jaso—something of a pastime in Long Beach. Nobody can stand the suspense. *What if he misses? Go for broke, go for the touchdown. Get it over with.*

In comes Javier. He kicks the field goal.

In overtime, the teams get to start on the opponent's 25-yard line; Loyola wins the coin toss, goes first, and after three tries can't get anywhere against the monstrous Poly defense, led by linebacker Ray Tago, Darnell Bing, and 6'6", 290-pound junior defensive tackle Manuel Wright. Loyola kicks a field goal. It's Poly's turn, and Brandon gets the call again. The coaches select the play "right open pass waggle," and Brandon elects to skip the safe short pass to the fullback and instead throws down a deep seam to Mike Willis, open again.

Now Poly is on the 11-yard line and Brandon remembers what

Jaso told him last year: "You're the quarterback. It's your call, your team. If we get there, I promise you we'll win the championship for you." They've been using their star junior halfback, Hershel Dennis, as a decoy in the passing attack. Now Brandon makes the call: 50-BYU, straight out of the pass-happy Brigham Young University playbook. It's designed to spread the wide receivers out and isolate the halfback on a linebacker.

Brandon drops back, pumps, then throws short to Hershel, who dances in for the touchdown, the 16–13 victory, and the exorcism. The stands erupt in celebration; the party afterward in the parking lot of Edison Field—home of the Major League Baseball Anaheim Angels—is wild. A whole corner of the lot echoes with the Poly sound track, Snoop Doggy Dogg and Nate Dogg and Warren G, the kings of the Long Beach sound. Lowrider Jackrabbits are making their cars dance; classic Jackrabbits in their minivans and RVs are handing out popcorn; and everywhere you look are all the many nations of Jackrabbit students—African-American, Cambodian, white, Hispanic, Thai, South Asian, and the Pacific Islanders, Samoans and Hawaiians and Tongans—draping candy leis on the players until their heads are almost disappearing.

That was December 9, 2000, a night to remember. Over Christmas break the national end-of-season polls came out: *USA Today* ranked Poly number two in the country, Fox Sports Fab 50 put Poly second, and the Dick Butkus Football Network ranked Poly number one in America.

National champions!

"It sure feels better than it did a year ago," Jaso said to local reporters.

The warm and fuzzy feeling lasted a month. Around New Year's Day, rumors came down about a possible new preseason opponent for the upcoming season: De La Salle, up in the Bay

Area, town of Concord. Everybody had heard of De La Salle, of course; the Spartans were the other number one national championship team in the polls. Nobody knew much else about them, except for the obvious: another Catholic school. Here we go again.

But not just yet. For the moment, Long Beach Poly is sitting on top of the world.

Two

OUT WHERE THE WEST BEGINS

Meanwhile, the next generation of Spartan standard-bearers isn't spending much time basking in the reflected glory of The Streak—they're burdened by it. Oh, the coaches all *say* it doesn't matter if it's broken; coach Lad has even said he doesn't care. Anyway, it's not the coaches the players worry about so much as the others who take this seriously: the 350 or so former varsity players going back to 1991, about 400 more going back to 1979, all of them *out there,* demanding that these kids take this seriously, too. Some of the older guys get a little weird about it. You've seen them hanging around the games, and you've heard about them, about the players who started this cult, the Scrappers & Lancers . . . You've heard rumors: about the business of painting faces, dressing in rags, rituals that bordered on the bizarre. Doing other stuff that was genuinely *sick,* like picking out a player who was maybe getting a big head or had dogged it in practice and the whole mob grabbing him right out of the shower buck naked and carrying him to the couch in the coaches' office and rolling him in Saran Wrap and giving him a thumping . . . Oh, the coaches put a stop to it, all right. Years ago. But you know those old Scrappers & Lancers are still out there. And do you really think you want to spend the rest of your life never knowing when somebody at a supermarket or a restaurant or an office is going to stop and freeze you with a stare and—you know what's coming next—say, in a slightly too loud tone of voice, "Hey, aren't you from the team that *lost?*" Psychologically wrapping you in Saran Wrap.

Imagine showing up at school the day after. How it would feel at graduation. As for attending any reunions . . . well, what do *you* think?

That's why, if you are a De La Salle football player, the three weeks of Christmas break will be the only time off you take all year. The Streak is present every single hour, as the prologue and, most alarmingly, as the potential epilogue, to your school days.

De La Salle High School opened in 1965 to serve Concord and the surrounding region, a cluster of small towns cut off from the San Francisco Bay Area by the Oakland Hills—hamlets such as Antioch, Danville, Lafayette, Martinez, Pittsburg, Vallejo, and Walnut Creek. It is a wedge of rolling hills and yellow plains that faces the vast wetlands and river channels of the Sacramento Delta to the east, giving it a semirural ambience. To the south is 3,849-foot Mount Diablo, overlooking the practice field of De La Salle, a magnificent reminder of what poet Gerard Manley Hopkins called "God's Grandeur."

Concord was a Spanish land-grant rancho, Todos Santos, whose titleholders, the Salvio Pachechos, were one of the few Mexican families to hold on to their land after the 1849 gold rush. Like most of the neighboring towns, Todos Santos served as a jumping-off and provisioning point for the Forty-Niners.

This really was a corner of the Old West. Mexican vaqueros rode after cattle; John Muir rested up among the orchards of Martinez from his mountain treks; and a teacher at the local school in the 1870s, J. H. Bowles, later became better known as stagecoach holdup man Black Bart.

In January of 2001, the next-generation De La Salle team had history on its mind, too. Matt Gutierrez, the star 6'4", 205-pound quarterback who would be a senior in the fall, savors football and likes to think of himself as playing in a tradition. Without prompting he can cite the characters and crucial scenes of several football books: *When Pride Still Mattered,* about coach Vince Lombardi of the Green Bay Packers; *Junction Boys,* about Alabama's coach Bear Bryant; and *Friday Night Lights*, the classic of Texas high school football. The coaches admiringly call him a "throwback."

The moniker suits Matt just fine, but there's more to it than football. He also likes to see something of himself in an ancestor from Juárez, Mexico. Just after the turn of the century, according to family lore, says Matt, this ancestor "rode with Pancho Villa. At some point Villa made him keeper of the keys to a mine's dynamite store. The army showed up and demanded the keys. He refused to hand 'em over. They lined him up in front of a firing squad and asked him again. Still no. And that's how he died—in front of a firing squad." Matt grins at the thought of this brave and obstinate revolutionary; you get the feeling that he believes the two of them might have seen things eye to eye.

Matt has been the starting quarterback ever since he was a fifteen-year-old sophomore, quite an accomplishment considering that the De La Salle veer offense is complex and requires a decisive leader. "Matt is everything you want in a student-athlete," says Bob Ladouceur. "What Matt says has more clout with the rest of the boys than anything we say as coaches."

But no quarterback—no offensive player—gets too far without the five down linemen blocking in front of him, and Matt is no exception. He is, however, blessed to have two pillars already in place before the season begins: Derek Landri and Andy Briner.

For someone who seems to have been carved by a chain saw out of an oak tree, Derek is calm and self-effacing. He doesn't say much, and when he does speak, it's in an undertone—probably for the best, given that Derek doesn't suffer fools kindly. Intense workouts helped him grow from a 6'1", 226-pound sophomore to a 6'3", 260-pound junior, and he'll add another twenty pounds for this season. He says with a shrug, "If you don't work in the off-season, you're wasting seven months."

Derek is from Huntington Beach, "Surf City" in Southern California, where Poly coach Jerry Jaso now lives. When Derek's parents divorced a few years ago, he came with his mother up north. He admits the move was hard, and not only because it cramped his longboarding style. "If only Concord had a beach," he sighs. Landing in nearby Clayton, a horsey town adjacent to Concord that hangs on to an upscale Old West heritage, he soon found an outlet in the area's fringe of wilderness, becoming an avid bass fisherman, camper, and duck hunter. School and foot-ball took a little sorting out. "If I'd stayed down south, I would probably have ended up at Mater Dei," which had just signed a four-year contract, home and away, to play De La Salle, "so I decided I didn't want to go to De La Salle. I thought it would be cool to beat The Streak. But my mom wanted me to come here—we're Catholic."

If Derek has his way, his next decision won't be difficult at all. Although he has been "offered," in the parlance of college football recruiting, a full scholarship at every PAC 10 school, as well as at perennial national champion challengers Nebraska and Miami, Derek is set on going to Notre Dame. The Fighting Irish have the sort of tradition he admires, it's a Catholic school, and the challenge of resuscitating the currently troubled program appeals to him.

"Plus we have the same fight song," he adds. "That's one less adjustment I'll have to make." His dreams go beyond college. "A pro career is one of my goals. I've always wanted to be a professional athlete." For Derek Landri, this year's goals are laid like flagstones to one end. Winning, yes; perfection, yes; but for him, personally, this is his turn to be the man on whom the Spartans can always depend; he wants to dominate so that opposing teams quiver at the mere thought of setting foot on the same field as De La Salle.

Derek's size is atypical for a Spartan. Andy Briner is closer to the kind of player De La Salle seems to find and develop, year in and year out: the "tweener." When the 2000 season began, junior Andy stood 5'9"—quite short to play the line on a big-time varsity program. Major colleges were excited to "offer" Derek, even as a junior; about Andy they seemed disinterested. Maybe they were afraid of what they'd see—someone who could make plays, outperform bigger players, but a kid who just wasn't physically the right type for a Division I-A scholarship.

Andy had come to Concord as a sophomore to rejoin his family after spending a year living with an uncle in Spokane, Washington. "My parents and I decided I should go straighten myself out," he says, refusing to elaborate. Concord has its rural touches, but Spokane is a true cowtown, where rodeo is as big as football. Andy admits he didn't exactly fit the mold. "I kept my style, I didn't go cowboy," he says, a Bay Area boy at heart. "It's more accepting of new ideas down here. Up there, it's real redneck in Spokane." He wears an ear stud to go with his bristly blond spike cut, and behind his brilliant flash of a grin his blue eyes are wary, measuring. He'd played organized football for the first time in Spokane, making the varsity team as a freshman and playing both ways, offense and defense. He starred at fullback, scoring sixteen touchdowns in eight games, winning his team's offensive player of the year award.

Arriving at De La Salle as a sophomore, Andy found out he wouldn't be playing varsity. "I joined too late, in terms of conditioning, weight lifting, and the mind-set. In Spokane there was no conditioning program. Here, it's Spartan life. When school starts, you work out at six-thirty, go to school, practice, eat, do your homework, and sleep." Even so, as a junior varsity player Andy was dominating: thirty-three sacks in a season, eight in one game.

Andy would have to fit in, both as a Spartan and a transfer. During his junior year on varsity, he was moved to end on defense, even though it would further lower his profile in the eyes of college recruiters; defensive ends just don't come at 5'9". The trade-off, the upside, was becoming a starter. The downside was getting chewed up and worn down from going up against larger kids on every single play.

The third game of Andy's junior season pitted De La Salle against Mater Dei, who were still smarting from their season-ending 1999 championship game tie with Poly. If the Monarchs had won, this showdown with De La Salle would likely have been the first ever national championship game. Mater Dei ground down the smaller and outmanned Spartans in the fourth quarter. During a last-minute drive that showed every sign of ending The Streak, Andy and the Spartans put on a desperate defensive stand. On the next-to-last play, De La Salle's star defensive tackle, 6'5", 305-pound senior Rob Meadows, accidentally drove his knee into Andy's helmet. Andy got a concussion; Meadows blew out an anterior cruciate ligament in his knee. But they stopped the Monarch drive, and the ensuing field goal attempt missed. The following game, De La Salle's top offensive guard, senior Rob Sandie, tore the medial cruciate ligament in his knee—and Andy was asked to learn Sandie's position in a week. A guard is like a fullback without the glory of carrying the ball: starting from inside the line, he is often called for blocking assignments requiring quick movement, fakery, and especially "pulling"—leaving his spot on the line and sprinting out to one side or the other to deliver a block on a defensive end or linebacker, springing the runner into the open field.

Undersized, a tweener, and a junior, Andy would now be playing on nearly every down, offense as well as defense. He could abandon any idea of running the ball and scoring touchdowns—the hero stuff. However, playing at defensive end next to tackle Derek Landri, Andy continued to show his knack for getting to the other team's quarterback. He ended up leading the Spartans in sacks. But he also fell sick with bronchitis in the second half of the season. Unable to rest, taking anti-inflammatories and using three inhalers, he lost twelve pounds before Sandie returned to spell him toward year's end.

By January, the season over, Andy was getting healthy again, looking forward to starting next September at full strength. The coaches promised him a season at linebacker, a position where he might actually attract recruiter interest—if he grows a couple of inches, that is.

Three

"WHAT A PLACE FOR CHILDREN!"

Long Beach was an idea before it was a place. In 1888, when newly built railroads opened Southern California's vast maritime desert to real estate speculation, it had nothing but a beach to offer. But it was quite a beach, and so a resort was born. Since the railroad ran east to the heartland, summering Midwesterners were targeted by developers. The result: a "prohibitionist, camp-meeting town, dotted with modest hotels and rental tents for vacationers."

By the 1890s, Midwesterners who were buying lots all over Los Angeles found Long Beach to be an easy pick. In a 1907 Long Beach High yearbook (*Polytechnic* was added later), a full-page advertisement for the city appeared:

THE GREAT SUMMER AND WINTER RESORT
$100,000 PLEASURE PIER
SURF AND PLUNGE BATHING
THE LONGEST BEACH ON THE PACIFIC COAST
"The climate is perfect, unless you prefer the equator or the poles; the same all the year, warm by day, cool by night, dry and with a delicious sea breeze blowing in from the blue sea every afternoon."

"What a place for children!—and what schools for them!—and $75,000 voted for additional school construction. Southern California is the paradise of children and Long Beach is the nucleus of that paradise."

As real estate advertisements go, this one was fairly accurate—the breeze really does come in most afternoons—but what catches the eye is the emphasis on schools. Today it is a given that education is a major factor in luring new residents to neighborhoods. In the early 1900s, this was an innovative strategy pitched to America's self-improving, upwardly mobile psyche. For the first time, every American adolescent was expected to graduate from high school, a major shift in national consciousness from the 1890s, when less than 5 percent continued on after sixth grade. Long Beach, founded as a summer Chautauqua Town, a place to hear daily lectures and take a bracing salty plunge, billed itself as a new kind of city, one based on educational and recreational opportunities.

The high school that opened its doors in 1896 is still following through on that inspiration, but the city has long moved on to an entirely different—and much more vexing—identity. According to the 2000 U.S. Census, Long Beach is now the most diverse city in the United States. And at the center of the most diverse district in this most diverse city is perhaps the most diverse high school, Long Beach Polytechnic.

In a little over a century the city's population has grown from a handful to over four hundred thousand while adding layer upon layer of race, ethnicity, and subculture upon the initial base of Midwesterners. Once known as "the capital of Iowa," Long Beach is now the capital of rap music; where Poly's most famous students of the era before World War II were composer and bandleader Spike Jones and actor Marion Morrison (known better by his stage name, John Wayne), today the names to conjure with are Snoop Doggy Dogg and Cameron Diaz. One thing that has remained constant throughout the city's tumultuous history: football.

Football has been a Long Beach tradition for decades. As a 1908 Poly yearbook puts it: "The program is part of Long Beach High now, football has come to stay. For three successive years we have tried to make football an interest and now we have succeeded. There can be no doubt that from now on, football will be the game of the High School. Three cheers for the team that broke the Hoodoo!"

By 1914 Long Beach High was a powerhouse, often playing small-college teams and winning its first state championship in 1919. In the Western North America championship of 1920 (Canada also fielded teams), the Jackrabbits beat a team from Phoenix, Arizona, by the gaudy score of 102–0, in front of twelve thousand fans. Graduate Morley Drury went on to become the University of Southern California's first star, "The Noblest Trojan of Them All."

Unlike Concord, which enjoyed the quiet of a rural backwater and remains country at its fringes, Long Beach was quickly ushered into the modern age by a series of accidents of geology. First, of course, was the long beach itself; then the quirk that aeons ago twisted the course of the Los Angeles River so that it emptied into the ocean and formed a natural harbor in this sleepy resort village twenty miles south of swaggering L.A. Soon a race was on to develop Southern California's first major seaport, which the two cities resolved, after many years of rivalry, by joining forces. Oil speculation came next, all over the L.A. Basin, then, fatefully, in Long Beach with a shaft sunk into the city's lone parcel of real estate higher than a royal palm tree: Signal Hill, elevation 391 feet. Drilling into an anticline layer from the

Pliocene era at the intersection of Hill and Temple Streets, the crew hit a tremendous gusher in 1921. The Signal Hill field was so concentrated, with an average production per acre of five hundred thousand barrels, that anyone owning even a sliver of property had an excellent chance of becoming wealthy. Indeed, it has gone into the books as the world's richest oil patch.

Concord has lofty Mount Diablo, serene and unspoiled. Long Beach got lowly Signal Hill, which sprouted tens of thousands of oil derricks and drew thousands of Texas and Oklahoma oil drillers and their families. Shipping tonnage increased 500 percent just two years after the oil strike. Then the U.S. navy established a base, in 1927. Population soared. Even a setback, the 1933 earthquake that caused the deaths of 115 people and damaged or destroyed over thirty-five thousand dwellings, businesses, and schools, proved a boon. The city had to rebuild itself in the midst of the Depression—and Poly's Jackrabbits had to attend class in sixty-three army tents in a field of jackrabbits—but the resulting construction boom helped the city weather hard times.

This was a city that could take a punch, and a good thing, too. With the outbreak of World War II, the navy and its shipyard drew over fifty thousand new residents, the Douglas Aircraft Company (later McDonnell Douglas; more recently merged with Boeing) lured many thousands more; and the area became a transshipment point for war matériel and a torrent of soldiers, sailors, airmen, and support personnel. For a couple of million American servicemen, Long Beach became synonymous with a last night out on the town before crossing the Pacific, possibly never to return. Willingly or not, the Downtown and Central Districts went on a five-year bender—dishing up prostitution, gambling, honky-tonks, and jazz clubs. By accident of its central location, Poly found itself in the middle of the red-light district;

this didn't seem to hurt its considerable reputation as a show-biz high school, a reputation that has never waned.

The social and cultural effects were enormous and sometimes painful to a town whose self-image was grounded in Protestant high-mindedness and prohibition. But the public education system coped heroically with waves of migrants, building new schools that evolved into bastions of the white aviation- and petroleum-engineering middle class. Poly inherited the lower-class children of roustabouts and shipyard workers, as a consequence of the school's location in the shadow of Signal Hill. To the poor, the black, the Hispanic, and the Asian, this oil-based wasteland formed a veritable Hadrian's Wall, quite literally dangerous to cross because of its uncharted tangle of pipes, holes, lakes of crude, and work gangs of rough, often racist oilmen, including card-carrying Ku Klux Klansmen.

Somehow, despite this unvarnished reminder of de facto segregation, the many races and classes and ethnicities all congregated peaceably at Poly High, along with the children of the founding fathers of the city, who came because Poly was still *the* Long Beach high school. Under the resourceful leadership of a single principal, David Burcham, who steered the school from 1904 to 1941, Poly thrived academically and athletically. A story has it that when Burcham was offered the position of superintendent of Long Beach schools, he replied, "Why would I want to take a step down?" From the late fifties to 1966 was to many Poly's apotheosis and is still called the Golden Era, a time of athletic championships of all kinds, stellar graduates going to top colleges, and close familiarity with the entertainment world.

After 1965, the social earthquakes began. In that year the Watts riots ripped the region apart. Long Beach had started out mostly white, with Spanish and Mexican roots; it had also been home to the largest number of Japanese-Americans in the continental United States, at least until their internment in1942. During the war and afterward, the city attracted African-Americans, resettled Pacific Islanders uprooted by the military advance toward Japan, and the Japanese-Americans after they were released from confinement.

But the rising economic tide that had kept life peaceable was now ebbing. Deindustrialization took away the jobs, with minorities losing theirs first; housing covenants restricted black and Asian ownership; increased crime led to tighter policing, and ultimately overreaction, in the minority neighborhoods. The educational system, once the main unifying force in Long Beach, teetered from exhaustion.

The shock waves from Watts, just a few miles up Atlantic Avenue from Poly High, set off local disturbances, both black and white. Stores burned by the score, suburban streets were patrolled by armed white militias. Swiftly, angrily, the social fabric frayed. Residents of largely white communities on the border between Watts and Long Beach, including Compton and South-Central, sold in a panic. This "white flight" became a theme in Long Beach, and the question of who would go to Poly, the only high school out of five with a black and minority population, obsessed everyone from the old elite to the anxious white lower class to the vulnerable and put-upon black community. By 1969 the school was in the heart of a ghetto; violent riots in 1970 and 1972 shattered the campus. Federal authorities who arrived in the aftermath of the riots publicly weighed taking over Poly—and the Long Beach Unified School District (LBUSD). A proud city was left reeling. As the local band War would sing in 1970, in their psychedelic soul lament written in a Long Beach warehouse, "The world is a ghetto."

The following decade was even worse. The end of the Vietnam War brought an influx of refugees, including a large proportion of the 125,000 who arrived in that year, 1975. In succeeding years, an additional 470,000 Vietnamese would find their way to the United States, many of them using Long Beach as a launching pad for resettlement after an initial two-to-five-year period of initiation and partial assimilation. With them came thousands of Hmong, a tribe barely a generation removed from a Stone Age way of life. The Khmer Rouge's killing spree in Cambodia launched another wave of immigration: fifty thousand Cambodians congregated in Long Beach, remaking the Poly district as their own.

The cumulative result was an immigrant population rich in cultural diversity but rife with health issues, economically destitute, suffering from post-traumatic disorders and culture shock, and stranded in an inner city whose other, longer-established minorities were worried about losing their share of scarce jobs, government assistance, and services. The immigrant children adapted in ways their parents could hardly understand, many forming gangs for comradeship, protection, and income—primarily through violent extortion and home invasion.

Meanwhile, the city's Hispanic population, swelled by refugees from Central America's wars and right-wing killings, spawned disaffected youth gangs of its own. The arrival of crack cocaine set off a truly appalling decade. The old-fashioned black, white, and Hispanic gangs had fought with knives, handguns, and shotguns; these new gangs, raised to the standards of genocide, armed themselves with AK-47 assault rifles and Uzis and MAC-10 machine pistols.

By the early 1980s, gangbangers and bystanders alike were dying in droves. This being America, their exploits became grist for song. Directly across from Poly's football field, in fact, was where a great number of early rappers got their start singing about the mean streets of Long Beach: VIP Records, the record-store-cum-recording-studio founded by Kelvin Anderson where Snoop Doggy Dogg, Dr. Dre, Nate Dogg, Warren G, and others cut their first hits. Long Beach and Poly High have a long-established and long-honored place in the rap world's pantheon. So does Poly football: in many a Snoop Dogg music video the rapper wears a Poly football jersey; he also sponsors one of Poly's eight Pop Warner teams.

If we stop here, this story of the "paradise of children" would seem to leave no irony unmined: the original high school of Long Beach had became a national symbol of democratic dystopia. But one further twist was yet to come—because, in the midst of so much going terribly wrong in Long Beach and at Poly High, in the early eighties something began to go terribly *right*. Indeed, Long Beach Poly would begin the 2001 season as the most honored high school in California—and for far more than just its football team. Its 2000 college acceptance record was one any school might envy: three students each to MIT, Cal Tech, and Yale; six to Stanford, fifty to UC Berkeley; and others to Harvard, Princeton, Dartmouth, and Swarthmore; its two hundred University of California acceptances were the most of any school. Poly was in the top twenty nationally for students qualifying to take A.P. exams and led the state in exams passed. In 2000 Poly was also voted the "best athletic high school of the century" in California: the 2001 school brochure for new students could point to seven state championships and twelve CIF–Southern Section titles in the past four years, in basketball, cross-country, football, soccer, track, and volleyball, for girls as well as boys.

The school from which parents and students once fled now selected from thousands of applicants, kids drawn there for the academics. In fact, in 1998 Long Beach Poly was cited by the *Los Angeles Times* as the best overall high school, public or private, in the state of California, based on college acceptances, athletic performance, and the distinction of its extracurricular activities. The *Times* article quoted parents of all races and economic backgrounds who were moving to Long Beach so their children could attend what was still, on the face of it, a ghetto school. And the Long Beach Unified School District had emerged as a national leader of public education, its innovations and processes emulated and acclaimed, right up to the U.S. Department of Education.

As much as quarterback Brandon Brooks is the heart of the Jackrabbits, Hershel Dennis is the soul. When he speaks on the practice field, which isn't that often, he sounds like a coach, correcting mechanics, offering quiet and precise feedback one-on-one. He knows his attitude will affect how others act; he may have silent-screen matinee-idol looks—think Rudolph Valentino in *The Sheik*—but no swagger. When he scores a touchdown, as he did thirty-two times his junior year, there is no dance, no celebration, just a flip of the ball back to an official.

Hershel's mother, Rose, is one of the Poly Moms: wearing the number 34 jersey at every game, selling raffle tickets to benefit the team, strands of red tickets hanging in long loops around her neck like a hibiscus lei. She is Samoan, born Rose Teofilo in American Samoa, raised in 'Ewa Beach on Oahu in Hawaii, along with twenty-one brothers and sisters. She left the islands in 1965 to attend Washington State University.

Hershel's father is named Hershel, too, as was his father. "Call me Dino," he says as he introduces the Teofilo-Dennis *ohana*—Hawaiian for "extended family." Hershel has nine siblings: four brothers and a sister by his father and Rose, and four sisters by Rose and her second husband. All five brothers are named Hershel: the eldest, Hershel Pettiford, is thirty-nine; then, in order of age, there is Hershel Zaire, Hershel Dupree, Hershel Dino, and current Poly Jackrabbit Hershel "Patch" Henry.

Dino—Hershel's dad—grew up in Charleston, South Carolina, and played football himself at North Carolina A&T College with his friend Jesse Jackson, with whom he also pledged the Omega Psi Phi fraternity. After moving to L.A. in 1969, he taught middle-school social studies, went into law enforcement; he has worked for the L.A. Superior Court, Probation Department, and currently as an assistant principal of juvenile halls, working with the County Board of Education.

With so many siblings about, it was decided that Hershel would live in the home of his sister "Little Rose," and her husband, Jim, who raised him as their own child, a form of kinship parenting practiced all over Polynesia. "It was Jim who nicknamed Hershel 'Patch,' " Dino says, "because at the hospital his hair stuck up like a Cabbage Patch doll. Jim was a real nice guy and I really respected him for taking care of Patch as a baby. Jim was white—there was no color barrier there. And Little Rose was like Patch's second mother."

When Jim died of cancer in 1995, Hershel went to live with Mama Rose while Little Rose was in mourning. During middle school in Long Beach he was leaning toward attending Banning or Carson High, schools located in adjacent communities with large Samoan populations. But Rose was good friends with Poly assistant coach Kirk Jones, the school record-holder for yards gained rushing, and he sold her on Poly. "She really wanted me to go to Poly for the academics," says Hershel.

In addition to playing high school and college football, Dino spent several seasons with L.A.'s old semipro team, the Mustangs, and he made sure all his sons played, too. When Dino worked a weekend shift at the L.A. County juvenile hall, he would take the boys with him. "They'd go down to the hall and play football with the guys—the kids who were being detained," Dino says. "Patch would be nine or ten years old, playing ball with older teenagers. I think it made him tougher."

Hershel smiles at hearing this, but says the jailed boys—some of whom were in for violent crimes—never mistreated or hurt him. But the hall did leave an impression. "My brothers and I could see the environment, how those kids live," Hershel recalls. "They're taking orders all day, when to get up, when to eat, when to move. You could see how you didn't want to be there, too."

In the 2000 season, his junior year, Hershel joined the list of great Poly players, breaking Kirk Jones's single-season rushing record. In January he was named a "Dream Team" selection and offensive player of the year by the *Long Beach Independent Press-Telegram*. In Long Beach, where sports traditions are nourished and honored with ceremonies both formal and informal, Hershel had, as a high school junior, all but assured himself of a lifetime of banquet invitations and meals on the house. And he still had his senior year ahead of him, not to mention college, and possibly a career "playing on Sunday," as the folks at Poly tend to call the NFL.

Winston Justice's family is from Barbados; his father, Gary, is an engineer at Sextant, an aircraft electronics company, and his mother, Winifred, works as an office manager at Mitsubishi. They are Jehovah's Witnesses and live in Bixby Knolls, a once exclusively white neighborhood. As a youngster, Winston didn't play football at all, growing so quickly, from 5'4" in seventh grade to a 6'1", 190-pound eighth-grader, that he exceeded the Pop Warner weight limits. He liked basketball more, anyway. When it was time to choose a high school, he was leaning toward Wilson or Jordan, but his dad was firm: " 'Your sister went to Poly, you're going to Poly,'" Winston remembers him saying.

Winston wanted to go out for basketball as a freshman, but his father objected to the sport's rapper image: "The Snoop Dogg world," notes Winston. The elders at Kingdom Hall concurred, even though Poly has one of the top high school basketball programs in the country, a High School Hall of Fame coach in Ron Palmer, and a proud reputation untainted by the play-for-pay scandals that periodically rock nearby Compton and Dominguez. One night before tenth grade started, Winston, his mother, and his sister were watching TV and hatched a plan: Winston would go to basketball tryouts and practices on the sly. "My mom said it was a family decision, not a religious decision," Winston recalls.

Even though Winston stood 6'5" as a tenth-grader, the year off had hurt his progress; he was cut from the junior varsity squad. "I thought to myself, maybe basketball isn't your sport—try football," Winston says. An unexpected advantage: his father decided he liked the sport, even though he knew nothing about it. "Dad and I always watched war movies together, and football was like a war movie, except nobody got killed."

His first season was rocky: "I was getting knocked around in practice. I was easy meat. After the season I said, 'You can't let that happen again.' I started lifting and training." He came into his junior year 6'7", 290 pounds. "But you can't just be big. You have to be fast, and I run a 4.9," he says, referring to the forty-yard dash, football's standard measurement of speed.

Intelligent and analytical, Winston soaked up techniques from Poly line coach Tim Moncure. In his junior year he started the first game and never looked back. By the end of the season he had been offered scholarships from Florida, Florida State, Nebraska, Oklahoma, Texas A&M, UCLA and UC Berkeley, USC, and Washington. In football, a big, fast, smart offensive lineman is highly desirable because he protects your most important and fragile player, the quarterback. This is true in high school, truer in college, and especially true in the NFL, where having a Winston Justice to guard the back of your $30-million star is better than any insurance policy. For this reason, as well as for their tendency to have long and productive careers, offensive tackles are paid like CEOs. A $15-million, four-year contract isn't unheard of for a first-round draft pick.

Winston knows it's an odd situation to be in. "The thing is," he confesses, "I still don't know how to throw a football." Winston's face rarely lets on what he's thinking, but with that one admission, he allows himself a brief, flashing smile that says, "Can you believe this?"

Junior Lemauu is learning to believe it, too. When he arrives at Poly High, the 6'5" Samoan with long, braided hair is never made to feel out of place, even while wearing rubber flip-flops and the cylindrical skirt called a lavalava. In fact, he fits right in. Sometimes there will be Pago Togafau in his lavalava, or Patrick Taliauli in his, leaning against the pitted beige walls of the gymnasium, chatting—or just hanging—with the other Polynesian Polys, such as Nathan or Julai or the two Jonathans or Hercules or Zephyr or Paul or Joshua or Jeremiah. Coach Moncure's wife is Samoan, too.

"When I came here," says Junior, "I was surprised to see so much Samoan tradition at the school. Now I get to lead it. The football team is especially based on a lot of our traditions. We sing on the bus, a Samoan song. When we get off the bus, we sing it in the end zone. Then, before coming out of the locker room, some of us will do a dance. When we are in the tunnel waiting to come out onto the field, we do a certain chant:

Mu-a-ina Mu-a-o
Mu-a-o! Mu-a-o!
Ta-ta-le-ina

Ta-ta-le-ina
Cho-cho-cho!

"This year we changed it a little. We add this at the end of our practices, our games:

Every day and every way
We get better hey!

Four

THE AMBUSH

More than any other field sport, football is about turf. That's the point of the game: conquering ground. Points give the score, but what tells the story is land—land that is marched upon, gained, captured, lost, defended, seized, surrendered. Football, like war, is territorial. Teams play to establish bragging rights to their town, league, section, and, if they're both lucky and good, their state.

But high school football has never had a national championship game. In high school football, there is no interstate play-off system, no Sweet 16, no ladder to the Sugar Bowl, Orange Bowl, or Super Bowl. More than twenty-two thousand high schools in America now offer some form of the game, so the logistics of arranging a national tournament would seem to be mathematically impossible.

That doesn't mean it hasn't been tried. Poly's game against Phoenix in 1920 was an attempt to create a unified title for the Western states and provinces and at least had a claim to credibility because there simply weren't that many teams to include. East of the Rockies, there were too many schools. A game played in 1902 between Midwestern titan Hyde Park High of Chicago and

East Coast champ Brooklyn Poly Prep was an attempt to settle the question, but while Hyde Park's 105–0 victory made a convincing argument for the prairie leaguers (especially after they won a rematch the following year, 75–0), it said nothing about how teams from the South and West might have fared.

Moreover, football had started out in the 1860s and 1870s as a college sport, and college teams supplied the craving for national rivalries and showdowns. The professionals got into the act in the 1920s, though on a much smaller scale; the various professional leagues didn't really challenge the popularity of the college game until the advent of television in the 1960s. High schools had to be content with hometown audiences and, for the successful teams, winning at the sectional and state levels. That was just fine with the schools and their fans, especially with big games in Ohio, Texas, Pennsylvania, and California drawing crowds of thirty and forty thousand people from the twenties onward. In 1937, the largest crowd ever to see a high school game—120,000—gathered at Chicago's Soldier Field to watch two city schools, Austin and Leo, go at it. To accommodate the enthusiasm for legendary coach Paul Brown's teams at Massillon High School of Ohio, considered the spiritual home of the high school game, in 1939 a stadium was built that seats eighteen thousand. Other classic shrines include The Pit in Cincinnati's Elder High, built by parent and student volunteers in the 1930s; Duchon Field in Glen Ellyn, Illinois, which since 1923 has offered fans a view of a lake and fall's foliage along with the game; and Valdosta, Georgia's twelve-thousand-seat stadium, built in 1922, ringed by pines and magnolias. In Texas, juggernaut school teams in communities such as Midland and Odessa were likewise rewarded, usually when oil prices were robust. All over America, Friday night meant one thing: the high school game.

But the big game eluded them all. Sportswriters periodically concocted national rankings, but they tended to be haphazard and flavored by a strong regional bias. While the schools ranked number one naturally agreed with the polls, those ranked lower, or not at all, were understandably much less agreeable, and since top teams rarely played each other due to geographic considerations, there was always a lot to complain about.

It took the establishment of a national newspaper, *USA Today*, in 1982, to give the polls an air of credibility and accountability; its first Super 25 came out that same year. *USA Today* succeeded because of perception and application. First it won over sports-page readers, who accepted the implicit argument that it could be trusted since a national paper theoretically wouldn't have hometown loyalties. Then, by giving at least lip service to previously overlooked states and regions, it legitimized the teams and programs it ultimately anointed.

The *USA Today* polls were soon joined by a number of others, including ESPN; the Fox Sports Network's Fab 50; a half dozen specialty sports services that catered to the high school athletic recruitment process, including StudentSports.com, a magazine and a Web site; and opinionated individuals such as former NFL linebacker Dick Butkus and "superfan" Tony LoBianco, both of whom created eponymous polls. In the early eighties the national championship hunt began in earnest, as ambitious coaches and passionately loyal fans sought recognition and supremacy. The polls became a rite of high school football, the year-end December lists crowning a winner (or two), while the late-August release of the first *USA Today* ranking kicked off each new season.

Although the polls do disagree with each other in particulars, most of the time they seem to be in sync. The same few teams start in the Top 25 every year and spend the season jousting with each other—virtually, that is, since they hardly ever meet face-to-face. In Ohio, the usual suspects are Massillon and Solon and

Archbishop Moeller and Canton McKinley; in Oklahoma, Jenks and Union City; in Texas, Katy, Midland Lee, and Odessa Permian; in the Deep South, Evangel Christian, Moss Point, and West Monroe; in Indiana, Ben Davis; in Florida, Belle Glades, Pine Forest, and Venice; in Pennsylvania, Cathedral Prep and Central Bucks West; in Illinois, Joliet Catholic and Mount Carmel; in California, Los Alamitos, Loyola, Mater Dei, Poly, and more—the consensus is that California is home to more good football teams than any other state. De La Salle joined the rankings in 1985, when, in the midst of its twenty-four-game winning streak, it entered at No. 24.

The conformity of the polls creates and feeds a suspicion that the sports media collaborate to groom their Top 10 lists, from which the national champion inevitably arises. There is most likely some truth to this. But there is a method to the process, based on the vagaries of such a widespread and ultimately unverifiable ranking system.

First, pollsters consider the record: they like undefeated teams, obviously. But they also consider the schedule; does a given team play strong opponents, ones that end up in the playoffs and win championships? Does a team play in a strong league, conference, or state? Has a team played well in a televised game (local cable TV stations now broadcast big matchups)? Has the team made efforts to meet strong teams in its preseason games?

In fact, due to the absence of postseason bowl games, the preseason has become one of the fastest ways for a team to gain in the polls. To arrange preseason games, teams sign contracts with each other, usually for two or four years, taking turns playing in each other's stadium and splitting the gate receipts (which for the better teams can be considerable). If you schedule and beat one or more of the perennial top teams, you're positioned to make a run for a top ranking yourself—if you go on to win your league, that is, and from there win your sectional and/or state championship. Thus, in contrast to the NFL's play-off tournament, contenders for the number one high school ranking have to play at their best from the opening game to the end of the season; this bears a passing resemblance to the college Bowl Championship Series format—except there are no bowls in high school. In fact, the best high schools compete in a nebulous, rarefied, and, what might seem to some, upside-down universe. It's also highly political, as athletic directors assess the relative superiority of each other's program, and try to schedule each year's four or five pre-season games in order from weakest to strongest, in the manner of a learning curve. Since games are locked in from two to four years in advance, there's a definite chess-match aspect to the scheduling.

Pollsters study these chesslike moves, to give weight to a school's football program. To be ranked, a program must never rest; its task is to win in perpetuity, year after year, burnishing the myth each season so that the next year's team can polish it even more. This is a big job even for a legendary coach, so it often becomes the work of an entire school, of players and nonplayers, teachers, administrators, family, alumni, community members, and, yes, the local media who can be counted on to bang the drum and spread the word.

Once a program is successful, however, a school can't just sit back and enjoy winning—to remain a contender in the polls, a team must still seek out and beat other teams that have good programs. This is more difficult than it might seem. High school teams play in regionally defined leagues, governed by state athletic commissions; they're required to play league opponents, whether weak or strong. Inevitably, the best start to drive down the good. Schools accept their losses in football and focus their energies on putting together a winning team in another sport:

baseball, basketball, soccer, track and field, water polo. The parents of football players ambitious to play in college wrangle transfers for them to the strong school, which only makes it stronger. The crowning irony occurs when the local school with The Program becomes so dominant that it effectively eviscerates an entire region—eliminating any suspense as to the outcome of each season. The only thing other schools can look forward to is to see who comes in second.

Now the school with a successful program has a problem: a lack of competitive games to keep its players sharp, and a lack of opponents who will please the pollsters and the state athletic commissioners who seed play-offs. The former means it can more easily lose a tight game; the latter, that its wins will be discounted. When this happens, state athletic commissions and school districts may step in to reshuffle teams into leagues composed only of strong football programs, restrict the ability of athletes to transfer from weaker schools, and sometimes even dilute a program—one that has offended too many sensibilities or warped the school's educational mission—by creating incentives for students to "hive" away from the old school to a new one.

This is why so few high schools have remained powerhouses over a decade, let alone over thirty or forty years—or, in the case of Poly, ninety years. And programs can also be brought low by economic or demographic shifts. For example, from the twenties onward, steel towns have always produced a steady stream of football players, but as America's automobile industry went into decline in the seventies, and the Steel Belt became the Rust Belt, high school football fortunes in steel towns from Pennsylvania to Ohio to Michigan likewise waned. It even happened in Massillon, home of Paul Brown and his storied stadium, where every boy child born in the county is still reminded of his future gridiron duty with the gift of a baby blue football in his crib.

Race relations affect programs as well, particularly in the South. During segregation in the 1940s and 1950s, white teams were weakened by their schools' refusal to accept black students, and black teams were all but invisible outside their own community (although a certain team's "Black Streak" in the forties and fifties remains legendary in the Deep South). By the 1960s, when the civil rights movement desegregated public school systems, all-black and all-white schools alike were thrown into chaos: white students fled to private academies and white taxpayers no longer turned out to support bond issues for the now minority-dominant public school systems. A few of the white and black schools that merged in the South had success with integrated teams; the story of one school that did, T. C. Williams of Alexandria, Virginia, would become the basis of the movie *Remember the Titans*. But after winning the state championship in 1971, the fortunes of Williams declined, both on the football field and as an emblem of social progress. Today the once integrated school has all but resegregated.

One of the worst things that can happen to a program is the dreaded change of coaches; often this is all it takes for a football power to lose momentum. Even a handpicked successor may prove unequal to the job; jealousies among passed-over candidates can undermine all the hard work; the changeover can rattle the players.

It is all very tenuous, football success. That is why the polls tend to return and reward the programs. They are doing something right, have found anchoring structures to stabilize them through demographic, economic, and cultural changes.

There are few ways to keep a program going. It helps if the community feels invested in the school's success. The lack of a local professional sports franchise or college team is a positive thing because it means there will be no competition for the fan base. Local traditions can entice even the children of the upper class—those who might otherwise prefer to work on their tans poolside with a SAT prep book close at hand—to take part in football's initiations and ordeals. And religion is a factor: since they are private, Catholic, Mormon, or evangelical Christian schools can choose and groom blue-chip athletes, yet are absolved from so many of the problems facing public school programs.

All of these various elements that were part of the convoluted rankings equation contributed to the momentum for an actual game. Reaching the upper limits of the polls had become such a dance of hype and marketing that sportswriters, coaches, and fans began yearning to see the issue decided the old-fashioned way: on the field.

The first forays were scattershot. Coach Bruce Rollinson of Mater Dei remembers taking his share of calls when the Monarchs were the team to beat in the mid-1990s: "Some television guy approached us about a televised national championship game. Student Sports approached us, FOX Fab 50 approached us. St. Louis School of Hawaii has been talking to us for years about us going over there. There were football guys from Texas who wanted to pull in powerhouses, but then the old guard said we don't want to get involved with other states, that Texans should play Texans and that was enough."

So how could a game be put together? There was literally no way to match up the thousands of potentially good teams out there. Unfortunately, it was still a job for the polls, however much people quarreled with them, but all the machinery's humming away in the media didn't mean there wasn't a degree of underlying truth to the rankings. The men behind them—particularly *USA Today*'s Dave Kreider and Christopher Lawlor—had had twenty years to iron out the wrinkles, acknowledge and compensate for regional bias, and gather information from coaches. They had developed a national database of high school programs.

The pollsters had a pretty good idea of what a blockbuster game might look like. They'd watched, over decades, the rise of the Jackrabbits, the Spartans, the Monarchs, the Tigers, and the other top programs. In an effort to level the field, the polls practiced a little revisionist history, taking a long look at past teams, and they took note not just of a program's record but of its alumni: the number of players who had gone on to college and professional careers.

But the pollsters still faced one major problem: the De La Salle Streak.

De La Salle stopped losing games in 1992. In 1997, De La Salle tied the twenty-two-year-old national high school record held by Hudson High of Michigan: seventy-two victories in a row (the Division I college record is forty-seven, held by the University of Oklahoma). On the occasion of the seventy-third victory, President Bill Clinton sent a congratulatory letter, and *Sports Illustrated* did a story.

Having dispensed with high school and college marks, two years later the Spartans tied the NCAA's overall winning record in any sport—eighty-eight victories, set by UCLA coach John Wooden's 1971 and 1972 basketball teams. The Spartans broke that record, too, with dozens of TV crews and media members on hand to capture the moment, and Wooden himself offered congratulations to Bob Ladouceur—who in numerous interviews had expressed his admiration for Wooden's coaching philosophy.

With a winning percentage that kept rising—from .923 to .943 and upward—it's no wonder that awards started to come Ladouceur's way: National High School Coach of the Year (1995,

USA Today); first ever recipient of the NFL's National High School Coach of the Year (also in1995); induction into the High School Coaching Hall of Fame (2001) at the ripe old age of forty-seven.

But even all the awards, and the numbers, do not do justice to Ladouceur's achievement. In the reeling off of Streak highlights, it is easy to forget that each undefeated season is the work of an entirely new team. Every year stars and veteran senior players have graduated, leading to off-season rumors of impending decline and the snapping of The Streak. It hasn't happened.

The nature of a football season also heightens the aura surrounding the De La Salle program. Teams play once a week, allowing time for thorough, if compressed, preparation. Yet in nine years no one has come up with a strategy that has worked against De La Salle. This has made rival coaches a little crazy; some, it's said, to the point of getting out of football altogether.

Ladouceur has also managed to drive the pollsters crazy. Every year that De La Salle didn't end the season ranked number one, The Streak mocked the anointed winner. When De La Salle was crowned number one, every other rival for the mythical honor would grit its teeth and dismiss The Streak as a put-up job, complaining that the competition in Northern California simply wasn't on a par with that in Oklahoma, Texas, Florida, Pennsylvania, Illinois, or Southern California.

Indeed, for a number of years this resentment seemed to affect De La Salle's rankings. Part of the problem was the level of competition they faced in the Bay Valley Athletic League—with the exception of Pittsburg, none of the other teams ever gave the Spartans much of a game. Meanwhile their monotonous habit of winning the BVAL every single year, almost always in a blowout, often a shutout, angered some BVAL opponents so much they accused De La Salle of cheating—and yet, when the school offered to appear before league committees and answer any questions about recruitment and under-the-table payoffs, no accuser would come forth. This did little to quiet the whispering, which often attends parochial school football success. (Southern California's San Clemente School District at one time forbade its teams to play Mater Dei, Loyola, and any other Catholic League opponents, in the belief that they were recruiting and even subsidizing players.)

It seemed a no-win situation; the Spartan opponents were indeed too weak, but with so many BVAL teams to play they couldn't fill out their preseason dance card with stronger teams. Although they received a No. 3 ranking from *USA Today* in 1992, an undefeated season, the following year, paradoxically, it dropped them from the top ranks.

In 1994, ESPN, at that time in the poll business, gave the undefeated Spartans their number one year-end ranking—a thumb in the eye of rival *USA Today*. The following year, in 1995, De La Salle opened the season unranked by *USA Today*, but got the satisfaction of demolishing thirteenth-ranked Pittsburg, 27–7, in the fifth game of the season. The Spartans also scheduled and defeated their first Southern California team, Rancho Buena Vista, which went on to the semifinals of the CIF Southern Section. Yet there was no compensatory reward in the polls at the end of another perfect year—one that broke California's forty-seven-game record for consecutive high school football victories. Even after the Spartans weathered incredible national publicity to close in on and break Hudson High's seventy-two-game winning streak, the result was another undefeated season, another CIF Northern Section championship—and still no number one ranking from *USA Today*.

By now everybody had had enough. De La Salle and the BVAL parted ways. As Spartan athletic director and defensive coordinator Terry Eidson wrote in the commemorative issue program for the 1997 season:

> Geographical boundaries, unfair advantages, competitive equity. These terms have become the battle cry of many public schools throughout California as frustrated principals, coaches and athletic directors try to find a solution for Catholic School dominance in high school football. Of course hard work, dedication, and commitment by our young people could never be the reason for our school's success. So the time has come for De La Salle to take these matters into their own hands.

Nineteen ninety-eight, then, was the watershed year: The Streak had to be tested against all comers or else risk recriminations by the polls.

The first test would be against Santa Ana's Mater Dei, signed to a four-year contract the moment the Spartans got out of the BVAL. Coach Rollinson had been head of the football program for twelve years; when the 1967 Monarch grad took over, the school had been "in the doldrums since the 1970s," he says. "For twenty-six years there, Mater Dei wasn't even in the play-offs." Under Rollinson they received two year-end number one rankings and five CIF Southern Section championships in the 1990s.

"How did we get back?" he asks. "I have a great coaching staff. The players have come." Strong competition made the Monarchs stronger. "In the early nineties we started to play Poly and we had some wars. Great memories. Phenomenal wins."

Yet when Mater Dei lost to De La Salle 28–21 in the 1998 preseason, it dealt a severe blow to the whole theory of poll ratings. It also upset Long Beach Poly's secret plan: "We had the team of the ages, so-called," recalls Poly athletic director Joe Carlson.

Coach Jaso's Jackrabbits were loaded with Division I prospects, including future Stanford quarterback Chris Lewis and USC wide receiver Kareem Kelly. "We wanted Mater Dei to beat De La Salle," Carlson explains, "so if we met Mater Dei come championship time, we could take it"—the number one ranking, which would be Poly's first.

Instead, the Jackrabbits fumbled away their Southern Section title, to the Monarchs. The Spartans went on to win the 1998 CIF-NCS championships, as usual. At the end of the year the Spartans not only tied the John Wooden–coached UCLA basketball team's eighty-eight-game streak, they broke through *USA Today*'s resistance and won the year-end number one ranking.

After that eighty-eighth game, winning seemed to actually get easier, and the rankings followed. The Northern California vs. Southern California argument was again upended by a 42–0 Spartan blowout victory in 1999, Matt Gutierrez's debut, over then top-ranked Mater Dei. Another national showdown didn't come off as planned when highly ranked Evangel Christian of Monroe, Louisiana, abruptly pulled out of a preseason game without explanation. Evangel, home of the five greatest passing quarterbacks in high school history, evidently didn't want to risk its own potential number one ranking in an actual game.

Since 1998, De La Salle has been put in the odd if admirable position of cooperating with its potential assassins to remain on top. In 2000, two teams came close: Buchanan High of Clovis, California, came to Concord with a dream of stealing The Streak and missed by seven points; then Mater Dei hosted the Spartans in Santa Ana and came within a chip-shot field goal of sending the game into overtime. Suddenly it was as if everybody had the same idea at once. Two close calls in one season suggested that De La Salle might be vulnerable. Somebody was going to end The Streak, and that somebody would almost assuredly win the number one year-end ranking if they finished their own season undefeated. Like relatives showing up at the bedside of a wealthy elderly maiden aunt, the powerhouse programs came around to pay their respects.

Talk of a one-off game kept resurfacing. When Fox Sports had sent around its routine television contracts to schools in the late 1990s, a clause had been added allowing for a mid-December game, one week after the high school play-offs had concluded, between two teams chosen by Fox as national championship contenders. Most state high school athletic associations, however, dismissed the idea out of hand, putting an end to the whole notion.

Allan Trimble, head coach at Jenks (Oklahoma) High School, whose team had just missed grabbing the gold ring on several occasions, pushed to break the stalemate: "It would be wonderful, even if it's mythical, to have a national championship game. Yes, it's going to be difficult to get permissions, but here's my idea: Let's get De La Salle and us together and play in Tempe, Arizona, the week after state play-offs. It'd be a great bowl. It'd be great for the kids, great for Oklahoma football. It would be expensive, but we could get a lot of it underwritten." If you build it, and you win it, the top ranking will come, the thinking seemed to go.

Over at Long Beach Poly, coprincipal Mel Collins had his doubts. "Fox and StudentSports.com's Andy Bark talked to me about something they were proposing—a national championship game. We just knew nothing would come of it because we were so constrained by our CIF rules. The bottom line is we're just not interested in a play-off. We've got a full plate of things going on at Poly, not just football."

Mater Dei's Rollinson also had reservations. "The problem is, these are high school kids. There are already fourteen weeks of games, plus three weeks of practice, and now all of a sudden they want to keep going? That's too much." He paused, then shifted to a lower, more gravelly register: "Yet, to be honest, if I was asked if I could do it, I'd say yes. *Hell* yes! I'd *cherish* the opportunity."

If a post-play-off bowl still seemed far off in the future, if not an impossible dream, that left the preseason. There was one basic, mind-bending complication: How could the number one and number two teams actually meet when all teams were already locked into their schedules? Two top teams would have to gamble on playing each other, then hope they would get the blessing of as many of the polls—*USA Today*, Fox Fab 50, Student Sports, DickButkus.com, the Tony Poll—as possible.

The closest any game had ever come to achieving this alignment of stars had been the 2000 Mater Dei–De La Salle contest. If Mater Dei had only been ranked a couple notches higher . . . Rollinson still sighs over what might have been.

The turning point came in mid-October of 2000, a talk-show ambush sprung on De La Salle by denizens of one of the more football-mad states in the union: Hawaii.

When it comes to football, Hawaii is a throwback to the days of Red Grange, Grantland Rice, Jim Thorpe and his Carlisle Indians—a world of colorful characters, overheated rhetoric, shameless ethnic stereotyping, innuendo and imbroglio, and thousands of highly knowledgeable fans, not a few of whom gamble heavily. Like Massillon, Ohio or Odessa, Texas, Hawaii is one of the warrior city-states of football: a place where football is an obsession, where local teams are asked to carry their community's reputation against the outside world.

Hawaii's obsession lies in the realities of postcolonial economics and oil prices; strange as it may seem to those who view it as a tropical tourist paradise, the Islands have more in common with Rust-Belt-wrecked Massillon and oil-boom-busted Odessa. Hawaii is too far away, too expensive to get to, for college teams and pro franchises, and it's been mired in a two-decade-long recession, desperate to stimulate a nontourist and nonplantation economic base to give its children a reason to stay home. Despite yearly efforts to attract major league sporting events, the state has barely managed to hold on to the NFL's Pro Bowl, and that is mainly because the pro players and their families love going there for a week.

All this has only amplified the love Hawaii feels for its high school teams. It is proud of them, convinced they are the equal of any, and wants the rest of the United States to take notice of them, but the mainland, twenty-five hundred miles away, does not appear to be listening.

Now, convinced that a rare opportunity to make its case was within its grasp, Hawaii prepared to throw down a gauntlet. It, too, had a dominant Catholic team, St. Louis of Honolulu; it, too, had a twenty-one-year veteran coach, Cal Lee; his record of 231-31-4 was the closest to Bob Ladouceur's 249-14-1 of any coach in America; his sixteen consecutive section championships stacked up well, too.

The problem was—once again—the polls, where Hawaii, like De La Salle in the old days, got less respect than it felt it deserved. In addition to the usual problems of the unranked, Hawaii has to overcome the perception of it as nothing more than a place for mai-tai-slurping tourists. "St. Louis can't win a national title," Rollinson says flatly. "They don't play anybody who's good enough." This was exactly the image Hawaii wanted to shed, and it had partially succeeded by scheduling opponents from California and Utah.

In past years, Hawaii's coaches and state athletic officials had made repeated overtures to Mater Dei, Loyola, and De La Salle, but perhaps a bit naively. "I've talked to Hawaii people before," Rollinson says. "They called about wanting us to come over, maybe with De La Salle, and play a couple of their teams. Well, why would I pay my own way to come to Hawaii and get hit in the mouth? Why would I give up our game with De La Salle, which gives us a chance to play in front of twenty-eight thousand fans in Anaheim Stadium, all that gate money, plus a shot at a national title? *No way.*"

By 2000, though, Hawaii's overtures began to sound sweeter. "I have to admit, they are now starting to get real," Rollinson says. "They're talking about paying our plane fares, hotels, et cetera. I know they've talked to De La Salle about it. Hey, if they were to play De La Salle before we get them, that would be great for us." He laughs. "Go ahead, beat 'em up a little before we meet them."

And Honolulu's St. Louis was now ranked number eight in the Fox Fab 50, and De La Salle number one. Sportswriters, state athletic officials, and hotel owners floated the notion of a late-December showdown, a game that would follow the California state play-offs. Eventually, a persistent radio talk show host from Honolulu managed to get the elusive De La Salle coach himself on the phone and ask him to join a live call-in show on prep football later that night.

Bob Ladouceur recalls that the 11 P.M. starting time alone was enough to make him say no, so athletic director and defensive co-ordinator Terry Eidson agreed to take his place. The way Ladouceur tells it, when the subject of a post-play-off game came up, Eidson, not wanting to appear rude, didn't immediately rule it out. "All Terry said was that we'd be interested one day in being in a game with them," says Ladouceur. "Well, it got blown up huge—made the *San Francisco Chronicle* here, made the front page in all the Hawaii papers. We were going to be in a big game with St Louis on December twenty-third."

Ladouceur laughs at the memory. "It was tabloid journalism at its finest. The next day when Terry came in, he gave me this hangdog look and"—Ladouceur spreads his hands and shrugs—"he goes, 'But I never said a thing!' "

As athletic director, Eidson had reason to be chagrined. He'd commented, politely, that a St. Louis–De La Salle game would require both teams to walk away from their respective play-offs. This was interpreted as a statement of intent. Hawaii talk radio burned up the airwaves, Internet sports sites carried the news instantaneously, chat rooms filled up, and the phones started ringing.

St. Louis immediately attempted to exploit the misunderstanding by obtaining a play-off exemption from the Hawaii athletic association. The assistant athletic director of St. Louis, Georges Gilbert, heard Eidson's protest over being hustled into a game and accused De La Salle of ducking Hawaii. "It seems like there's an excuse being created every time we try to get the game going," he said in an interview with FOXSports.com. "If they want, we can call it an exhibition game. I mean, we're willing to give 'em everything: they can keep their ranking, their streak, and play in their backyard. When they want us to play, let us know."

Eidson's exasperated reply was used by the media to exacerbate Hawaii's resentment. Respect is always part of big-game intrigues, but for many Hawaiian locals there was a racial subtext to De La Salle's perceived snub. This was about respect for Polynesian players, particularly Samoans.

The rise of Samoans in football has been one of the game's more fascinating quirks: a case of an entire people adopting a foreign sport as a medium for defining manhood. In football circles today, Samoans are sometimes referred to as "vitamin S" for what they can do for a program. Today, there are more Samoans in college and pro football, relative to their numbers in the general population, than any other ethnic group in the United States. And yet, comparing their plight to that of the black football players of the postwar college era—whose numbers were limited by unwritten quotas and who were left off traveling squads on visits to the South—Samoans have felt slighted and marginalized for reasons unrelated to their athletic abilities.

Polynesians started playing football in the early days of the sport (Melville's Queequeg would have made a great linebacker). But it was a single Samoan star, Mosie Tatupu, who would have a dramatic effect on the role of this robust Pacific people in the game. Mosie came to Hawaii in 1972 from Samoa to attend the prestigious and exclusive Punahou School. The school had been founded by blue-blooded Yankee missionaries to educate their children alongside the children of Hawaiian royalty, then expanded to foster an Islands elite. It would be quietly hinted that as a freshman Mosie was not just a fourteen-year-old who happened to be large and mature for his age, but that he was possibly as old as eighteen. Mosie had been brought to Punahou—recruited, it has been alleged, his tuition and lodging paid for—to play football, which he did rather well. In fact, he is remembered fondly for his battering-ram offense, and his one-man-wrecking-crew abilities on defense. By his senior year, when he may well have been twenty-one years old, Punahou was virtually unbeatable.

Mosie went on to star at USC and then for the NFL New England Patriots, his name beloved by broadcasters, who loved to linger over its pronunciation after a big play: *Mo-zee-Ta-Too-Poo!* His example spurred hundreds of young men of Samoan heritage, on the mainland as well as on American Samoa, to apply themselves to the sport. Football meshed well with the warrior traditions of Samoan culture, and with Samoan genes, which produced NFL-sized bodies. As one chat room visitor to the Polynesian Café Website says, "Football is Samoa, and Samoa is football."

Many Islanders contend that mainland high schools fear this single-minded focus and ferocity. There is undoubtedly some truth to this. But there is also well-founded concern over Hawaii's slippery standards over players' ages and graduation classes. While Punahou has long since become a model for its sparkling-clean program—and, perhaps as a result, no longer is a powerhouse—every year in Hawaii some school is penalized for having played fifth-year seniors or academically ineligible players.

It is a coach's right, indeed is his duty, not to schedule an opponent if he believes they may hurt his players—by, for example, putting men into a boy's game. Whatever was going through Eidson's mind, the issue became moot when the Hawaii athletic association shot down the alternative play-off scenario. But this wasn't the end of it: FOXSports.com, alertly picking up the fumble and running with it, came up with a new accusation: "Perhaps the bigger issue here is why De La Salle hasn't faced a team outside California during its record streak, and why it hasn't faced Poly, number six in the country."

The Hawaii papers and talk shows took up the tune—the honor of the state was at stake. "If De La Salle is afraid to play us, why don't they at least play Poly?" There is no question that Poly is well regarded in Hawaii for its Polynesian pipeline; the famous tie with Mater Dei in the '99 finals was quarterbacked by St. Louis transfer Brandon Fasavalu, a Samoan kid whose younger brothers, Jonathan and Junior, were on the current Jackrabbit team. But Hawaii's programs don't like the Jackrabbits all *that* much; as Jerry Jaso says, "How come they never talk about inviting us, huh? How come it's always Mater Dei or De La Salle?"

Throwing Poly's name into the ring, then, had a touch of public relations bullying to it—scheduling as a game of chicken. Poly's athletic director, Joe Carlson, was diplomatic: "We're talking to De La Salle. We'll see what comes up. . . . I don't think they're dodging anyone. I think they're open to it. Next year would be a good year for us to play them. But they're booked."

Again the ambush failed: this time, the California Interscholastic Federation ruled that no school could play in any other games during the play-off part of the season.

But Coach Lee had one last ace up his sleeve. St. Louis and its community boosters would offer De La Salle a *pre*-preseason game, what they call a game zero, in Hawaii the following season. *An all-expenses-paid trip to paradise!* No excuses, right?

For the plan to work, and for the St. Louis Crusaders to be in position to take over the number one poll spot should they beat De La Salle, Coach Lee's team had to take care of business in the state championship game, against country cousin Kahuku, a public school on Oahu's rural north shore. This didn't seem like too much of a problem, seeing that St. Louis had won sixteen championships. But Kahuku broke the private parochial grip on Hawaiian football, defeating St. Louis in the season-ending game.

In late December, Coach Lee and St. Louis made the offer to De La Salle anyway. Eidson was flabbergasted by the details: He had to agree to fly his boys to Hawaii to play their first game of the season, in the middle of the week, against a non-jet-lagged St. Louis squad that would already have played three games (Hawaii's season opens earlier than on the mainland). The Spartans would have to arrive in Hawaii on Tuesday, play on Wednesday, fly home on Thursday, and play again, twice jet-lagged, on Friday, 150 miles down south in broiling Clovis—against Buchanan, their first regular preseason opponent, who had nearly beaten them last year. All this when the kids are supposedly in their first week of school?

"Thanks but no thanks," said a sardonic Eidson. Sympathy for a winner like De La Salle can sometimes be hard to find, and of course the Spartans were blamed for not having their priorities straight.

Not too long after the latest exchange seemed to burn itself out, the end-of-season polls came out. De La Salle received its Christmas present: from *USA Today,* a number one ranking, its second national championship.

The same poll put Poly at number two. This was widely taken to be a nudge to both teams to find a way to play a championship game. It was, in fact, the first time the top two spots had gone to schools in the same state—making a game geographically possible.

Days later, Dave Smith, editor in chief of the Dick Butkus Football Network, rated Poly number one and De La Salle number two. Now there were dueling national champions. The consolidated Fox Fab 50/StudentSports.com ranked DLS number one and Poly number six, after Jenks, West Monroe, Katy, and Cathedral Prep—but everyone knew these polls were about De La Salle and Poly.

Etiquette required Poly athletic director Joe Carlson to make a courtesy call to Eidson. Poly had open dates for the third and fifth games. De La Salle's third game was against Mater Dei, so that was out. The fifth date was held by Bishop Amat, a Southern California Catholic power the Spartans had pummeled 56–7 last year. Eidson felt he couldn't initiate talks with Bishop Amat, but gave the go-ahead to Carlson to do so. "Just don't mention me or any suggestion that we're behind this," he said.

Carlson phoned Bishop Amat's athletic director. When Carlson identified himself, the reply was to the point: "I hope you're calling to take the De La Salle game off my hands. My boys are tired of getting whipped."

On January 10, 2001, the game was finally on.

Five

THE CLASH

With De La Salle vs. Poly, separated by four hundred miles of California freeway, the outlines of a national championship matchup could now be glimpsed, through a fog of rumor and hearsay. Not everything was in place—the late-August *USA Today* and StudentSports.com polls still had to cooperate by ranking the two teams in some combination of number one and number two—but it wasn't too early to speculate about the identities of the participants. What sort of rivalry awaited us? Whom should we root for?

On one hand we had the rich, white (except, it seemed, for key athletes), private, Catholic (Christian Brothers), suburban, Northern Californian De La Salle Spartans, reigning number one in the nation, and currently riding that nine-year winning streak. Nestled in its high-tech exurb, De La Salle clearly represented the new America of the gated community, the school voucher movement, the SUV-driving teenager, and our winner-take-all culture of success. That the Spartans were coached by a religion teacher, variously described as a perfectionist and a mystic, whose very name, Robert Ladouceur, suggested a black robe out saving souls in the wilderness, was almost too perfect.

On the other hand, we had the Poly High Jackrabbits, poor, public-schooled, ghetto-based, and diverse—African-American, Cambodian, Caucasian, Chinese, Hispanic, Japanese, Korean, Laotian, Pacific Islander, South Asian, Thai, Vietnamese, and more. In contrast to suave Concord we had gritty Long Beach, with its roller-coaster history, as eventful and hypercondensed as a Monty Python routine, and Poly, its pride and joy, which had taken every bounce and bump along the way. Factor in Poly's 54-1-1 record (they hadn't lost since 1996) and all those famous faces, musicians, rappers, and actors who've passed through its gates: Cameron Diaz, Snoop Doggy Dogg, John Wayne, Billie Jean King, Spike Jones, Marilyn Horne, Van Heflin. And don't forget the football players: Poly has sent more (thirty-nine) to the National Football League than any other school in the country, including such all-pros as Gene Washington, Willie McGinest, Mark Carrier, Earl McCullough, Tony Hill, Leonard Russell, and Morley Drury. Then there was the coach, Jerry Jaso, who'd spent twenty-one years coaching at Poly and was revered for providing the push that sent a storied program to the very top.

These two towns and schools couldn't be less alike. Concord's median household income was $42,000; Long Beach's, $32,000. Concord had a 3.1 unemployment rate; Poly, 6.1. Concord was ranked the number two "best place to raise a family" in California, whereas Long Beach had 78 percent of its families on federal assistance. Nine percent of Concord's crime was classified as violent as compared to 19 percent of Long Beach's. The statistics about race were, of course, telling: Concord was 70 percent white, 9 percent Asian, and 9 percent Hispanic/other and three percent African-American; Long Beach was 36 percent Hispanic, 33 percent white, 15 percent black, and 12 percent Asian.

It was just the sort of clear-cut story that appeals to the media. This would be a clash of civilizations, a virtual blueprint for a contest between the American Dream and the American Reality. Down on the field, it wasn't hard to imagine how the game would be hyped: snotty college-bound white kids vs. brash-rapping street players. Baby-blond Terminators vs. Gangstas With Attitude.

Or, as my brother-in-law, Brian, a Loyola High School and Notre Dame graduate now living in Northern California, said when I told him about the game: "Catholics vs. Convicts, baby. *Bring it on.*"

Six

GOD'S TEAM

Surely, given The Streak's march into the history books, Concord must be busting its buttons with pride: massed student sections waving pom-poms, football-mad boosters, a packed stadium, shops and businesses closed and "gone to the game."

But to hear De La Salle athletic director and defensive coordinator Terry Eidson tell it, the picture isn't so predictable: "We have no relationship to the community. None whatsoever. Oh, they gave us a plaque at the end of last season, something about The Streak. But they don't care about us. And we know that at every home game there will be a contingent of Concord folk who come to get drunk and root against us. It's a big thing for them—they want to be here when we lose."

Eidson unbends—a little—to explain: "We are a school founded by and run for the Christian Brothers. Our relationship isn't with Concord. It's with God and the Roman Catholic Church, as exemplified by the teachings of Saint John Baptist De La Salle."

So De La Salle isn't Concord's team, but a team that happens to play for God in Concord. Since this seems to be more than a semantic distinction, what has estranged the rather pleasant-seeming town and the miraculous little high school in its midst?

Through the 1930s the area had remained a pleasant rural backwater. As in Long Beach, oil had been discovered, but the strike wasn't big or dramatic: only a scattering of rigs sprang up. Due to good ship anchorages and rail lines along Suisun Bay and the Sacramento Delta outlet, there was a large and continual military presence during World War II. Two million troops passed through nearby Pittsburg on their way to the Pacific Theater, but most without debarking—again, quite unlike Long Beach. Even so, supporting the war effort led to population and business growth. Fortunately for Concord, the booming—and seedier— waterfront action was confined to the port towns, such as Antioch, Martinez, Pittsburg, and Vallejo.

The major event in the area during the war took place at the munitions transport Naval Weapons Station at Port Chicago on Suisun Bay, hastily built between Pittsburg, Martinez, and Concord. A 1944 explosion equal to the size of the Hiroshima atomic bomb obliterated the site and killed 320 people, 202 of them black sailors. Though only seven miles away, Concord escaped unscathed thanks to the protection of its low, rolling hills. What followed was the largest mass mutiny in U.S. navy history by the remaining 300 black sailors, who had, even before the disaster, protested unsafe ammunition-handling procedures, round-the-clock work shifts, and their bigoted white Southern officers. Although they were represented by future Supreme Court justice Thurgood Marshall, 250 men were convicted, 50 of them sentenced to fifteen years' hard labor. Today the Port Chicago mutiny is largely forgotten in Concord and beyond, though the fight to clear the sailors' records continued. (A single symbolic pardon was eventually granted to survivor Freddie Meeks in 1999 by President Clinton.) Instead, the mutiny has taken its place in the alternative history of black Americans, alongside other tragedies removed from or slighted by the mainstream record, such as the 1921 Tulsa riots, the 1943 Detroit riots, and the New York draft riots of the Civil War, in which blacks lost lives and property without much widespread notice, let alone recourse to justice.

Concord's rural atmosphere enjoyed a brief revival after World War II. According to the *Contra County Gazette,* a 1946 Pow Wow festival boasted of "a whiskerino contest, 'calaboose,' and typical Wild West trimmings . . . famous square dance teams, trained dog acts, vaudeville." But everything was about to change. Concord's open spaces began to be squeezed by its urban neighbors, Oakland and San Francisco to the west, Sacramento to the east, and San Jose to the south. Soon the hills and plains began to vanish under the tracks of yellow Caterpillar graders.

De La Salle opened in 1965, conceived not to educate the children of these suburbs, but to train priests. The Lasallian mission, started in Reims, France, in 1679 to provide for poor children who would otherwise be lost to the Church, stresses love and education for students and asks that followers live this heritage. The school came about as part of a decision to break the Archdiocese of San Francisco, extending from inland Stockton to the Oregon border, into regions to accommodate the postwar demographic changes.

Within a decade the entire area became a sea of housing developments—Western-style ranchettes, split-level A-frames, and tract houses that looked as if they'd been snapped together from LEGO blocks. Communities such as Walnut Creek, which was zoned to control sprawl and commercial development, ended up on the more exclusive end of the suburban scale. Concord's leaders scorned protective zoning. "Concord is sort of like an unattractive girl," Byron Campbell, a local wealthy investor and conservative Republican, liked to remark for the San Francisco newspapers. "Nobody calls. But then a few years go by, and she starts filling out a little, and the phone starts ringing. But she has so little self-esteem that she'll say yes to anybody."

In the 1980s, the town's leaders said yes to the Bank of America. The historic downtown gave way to a sinister-looking black-glass corporate fortress and a couple of forty-story mirror-glass condominium towers that sat half-empty, town life having promptly departed for the strip malls and shopping centers that popped up at primary intersections: the typical Tinkertoy joints of a LEGO community.

Yet almost as soon as they'd plowed under downtown's central park, with its eight-hundred-foot pergola and hundred-year-old wisteria vines, Concord's leaders began casting about for an identity. They scrambled to make up for the hollowness of the new plaza—and town—by commissioning postmodern, "shamanistic" sculptures and site-specific art. The town planners succeeded in bringing the suburban citizenry together—in angry reaction to a particularly vapid (and expensive) downtown art installation: a clattering bunch of fiberglass rods called Spirit Poles. People hated it. Soon the culture wars were in full swing. A series of conservative city initiatives—antigay, antiaffirmative action, antiart— caused the dramatic resignation of the six top city officials, including the only African-American, leading to headlines in the San Francisco papers such as "How a Good Town Gets a Bad Name" and "East Bay Hotbed of Homophobia and Bigotry." *Parents* magazine dropped Concord from its annual list of "Ten Better Burgs for Bringing Up Children." According to the *San Francisco Bay Times,* in a burst of hyperbole, Concord was "dangerous and inhospitable to just about anyone who isn't white, male, and heterosexually identified."

It's undeniable that the town is hardly a bastion of diversity. A

1989 census reported that Concord was 91 percent white, 5 percent Asian, and 2 percent black. Today the "browning" of California has only barely affected Concord; it is still 70 percent white, 9 percent Asian, 3 percent black, and 9 percent "some other race," including Hispanic and/or multiracial. Several of its neighboring towns are indeed more diverse, probably because housing is more affordable: Antioch (65 percent white, 22 percent Hispanic, 10 percent black, 7 percent Asian), Pittsburg (43 percent white, 32 percent Hispanic, 19 percent black, 12 percent Asian), and Vallejo (36 percent white, 23 percent black, 24 percent Asian, 16 percent Hispanic), with percentages adding up to more than 100 percent because individuals may report more than one race. All the same, calling Concord "dangerous" would seem to be an exaggeration in light of its low crime rate, including bias crimes. Although the Port Chicago mutiny, as well as the internment of local Japanese-American citizens during World War II, may have left a lingering undercurrent of minority resentment, the greater source of Concord's anomie would seem an outgrowth of its sprawling, automobile-centered, commuter culture.

When the De La Salle streak came along, one might reasonably assume that it was a welcome distraction for all, perhaps even an impetus to rally around something positive for a change. But this wasn't the case. Rather than pride, Concord and its ring of outlying towns resented how De La Salle could so easily appropriate the East Bay's population, skimming off a portion of its elite students and athletes. Those looking for a symbol of the divide need look no farther than over the back fence of De La Salle's practice field: on the other side is Ygnacio Valley High, a public school struggling with overcrowded classes, gangs, the need to raise standardized-test scores, chronic underfunding, and a perennially mediocre football team. Here, every morning as they enter Ygnacio Valley's front gate, students need only glance to their right to be reminded of the same private parochial vs. public school tensions that hang over Poly High and Long Beach's rivalry in the Southern Section with Mater Dei, Loyola, and the other Catholic powers. The chill starts here, at the fence, but it deepens into something resembling enmity in the outlier communities—because, unlike in the Southern Section, where a dozen or so Catholic schools compete for the same talent pool, De La Salle has the entire East Bay region to itself.

Thus the strong get stronger. The price De La Salle pays is isolation. Like true Spartans, they embrace the role.

Among his peers, Bob Ladouceur's success has been garlanded with superlatives. But this same coaching fraternity has at other times raised questions of fairness in recruiting and seemed reluctant to give Ladouceur his due. Part of this is because he doesn't fit the football coach stereotype of a bluff, blustering jock—a man's man, happiest drawing up plays on a napkin over a pitcher of beer. In fact, Ladouceur doesn't drink, he's not a glad-hander, and he avoids talking football—although not conversing about current events, politics, books, or the moral issues facing educators and their students. This disconnect between The Streak and The Man frustrates those who only want to know the answer to one question:

How does he do it?

Ladouceur tried to explain, once, in 1998, when he set down his philosophy in a speech. "What Is a Spartan?" was written to satisfy all the requests for speaking engagements that he was starting to receive. It also answered his critics, and Ladouceur still gives the speech today:

The public's perception of what we do or what we stand for is drastically different than what actually takes place. I can imagine that this is probably true for many organizations. This is especially true for our football team. People are constantly writing the local papers questioning the integrity of our program. They say we cheat by recruiting the best athletes, give out athletic scholarships, actually pay money to players and occasionally buy a car for a superstar. My opinion about this is usually, "Someone's got too much time on their hands—or they need to get a life." It's upsetting insomuch that it questions the integrity of school officials and coaches sworn to uphold the ideals of our founder St. La Salle. What's worse, it completely nullifies the hard work, sheer grit, and determination of our student athletes at De La Salle.

Society has its share of pessimists and skeptics. Many believe that success cannot be achieved without dishonesty. It's hard for them to see our success and not assume that it was achieved by cheating, stealing, or just blind luck. But I don't care what society believes. I know the truth and I sleep every night with a clear conscience.

You see, success is in the eyes of the beholder and is most certainly relative. Many measure success in wins accumulated and titles won—we don't. Don't get me wrong, we are very proud of breaking the national record for consecutive wins and being ranked in *USA Today*. But wins and titles are just an outcome generated from the true meaning of success. It's what got us those titles that we are most proud of. Winning is just a by-product of many, many short-range goals that must be accomplished along the way.

To explain the experience of a team sport and pinpoint its success is very hard to articulate. This is true for most experiences where people are involved in interpersonal relations. The reason is, the knowledge gained or lessons learned are very hard to measure. We are far from a scientific environment and there are too many variables that contaminate the project. This is why some educators see little value in interscholastic sport. The knowledge gained cannot be measured by GPAs or an aptitude test. It's difficult to measure what we call intangibles. That would be like trying to measure one's faith or someone's capacity for love. What is learned is written on the hearts and minds of every member who participates and experiences.

We measure our success by how well we have embraced the spirit and essence of those intangibles. And I'll share a few of them with you.

First off there are many student athletes who have fought, sacrificed, achieved, and won at De La Salle the past twenty years. They have set the groundwork or foundation for a tradition. The first thought of tradition, or the word *tradition*, seems to have a negative connotation in today's rapidly changing world. The word itself conjures up the thought of being old-fashioned, backward, and even stubborn in the face of truth; and for some traditions I would suppose that's true. Thomas Eliot once wrote: "Tradition by itself is not enough; it must be perpetually criticized and brought up to date under the supervision of orthodoxy."

Please don't be misled, our tradition is not the color of—or how we wear—our uniforms. It is not what we eat at a pregame meal. It is not the plays we run, and to a large degree it is not how many wins we have accumulated. The wins are just a by-product of what our tradition actually consists of. These are just the trappings of a tradition; shallow, hollow; in fact they have nothing to do with tradition at all. Those who believe that this is tradition will eventually realize that they didn't belong to, or experience, tradition.

Our tradition begins with a commitment. There is a qualitative value we place on that word—*commitment.* If I had to choose just one lesson a student would learn from participating, it would be learning how to make a commitment. If they say yes to participating, then they must understand that they have said yes to entering into a relationship with me and everyone involved with the program. With that comes enormous responsibility. Essentially it means that I am going to expect the best from you and you can expect the best from me. It isn't enough to say, "I'll show up." We may say we are committed to many things in life; but to what degree?

Commitment is a precursor to many adjectives used to describe our tradition. It is the title of this speech: "What Is a Spartan?" The key is to infuse commitment into everything we stand for and what we do.

Is it enough to say we work? No. What makes our work ethic special is that we are committed to work. We don't just go through the motions. We know the pain and dedication necessary to ready our bodies for topflight athletic competition galvanizes us into a team; and through this process we are already heavily invested before the season begins.

Success to us is understanding that where preparation meets opportunity, greatness can be achieved. Preparation for us is long, tedious, and difficult, and the windows of opportunity are brief, short, and intense. I know for a fact that nobody—at least among our opponents—outworks us. We prepare well, and when ready, we welcome, not fear, our opportunities. This is the cornerstone upon which all achievement emanates—that boring, monotonous, nose-to-the-grindstone, hard work.

We are committed to the achievement of short, long-term, individual, and team goals. These goals are carefully planned and diligently monitored. They are not just wish lists. Our goals serve as the blueprints for our success. What makes our goal setting different is we don't just state our goals or write them down; we figure out actions, behavior, and attitudes necessary in order to accomplish those goals. Every goal must be accompanied with a plan of action, and if it's not, it really isn't a goal at all.

Our tradition calls for a commitment to accountability. This is not an assumption—this is a promise that I will be there for you; and I can count on you being there for me: from the way you spot my barbell, to the effort you give on a double line team block, to the lift you give me home after practice. In the end, to be able to claim "I was there for you" is not only the most difficult one could make for himself, but one of the most rewarding when it comes to assessing the quality of our humanity.

Our tradition is built on trust and honesty. Having the courage to say, "This is who I am; can you help me—or can I help you?" It begins sometimes with a painful evolution of our strengths and weaknesses. Laying our self open to be vulnerable. But it is only through this process that real growth and change can occur.

I don't know if any of you have figured life out. When I was younger I used to place value on the tangible. Wins, outcomes, statistics, anything that was finite—an end point. I always felt that someday I would arrive at some place and time with a fantastic conclusion. In so doing I lied to myself; believing life would be complete. But to fool ourselves into believing we have arrived is just closing the door on life itself. Wins came, championships were won, recognition was received— but I felt no different. What I discovered is we never arrive, and we never will. The journey we are on is that "Never Ending Story." It is the endless pursuit of truth. The best we can do is come as close to the truth as we possibly can.

That journey is no walk in the park, it is littered with setbacks, disappointment, and broken hearts. It is only through the pain of significant self-examination that we can hope to right ourselves and remain on the straight and narrow path that will lead to true fulfillment and inner peace.

To be a part of Spartan tradition means one must be courageous. This does not mean just being brave in the face of a tough opponent—rather it's having the courage to conquer our own cowardly spirit. That little voice inside of us that says, "I can't," "It's too hard," or "I am not good enough." The biggest reason why we don't achieve is because we don't believe we can. We place roadblocks in our own way, sabotaging our own efforts. It takes courage and determination to crash down those roadblocks and push the limits we have placed upon ourselves; what others have placed upon our ability.

The famous Jesuit scientist and philosopher Teilhard de Chardin claimed that "the meaning to existence is the passing on to something greater than our own immediate selves." It was his belief that everything living is in a constant state of striving for perfection. Isn't this the essence of fulfilling human potential? The reason why we achieve is because we believe we can.

The most important component of Spartan tradition is our commitment to create a brotherhood among ourselves. This task is bigger, tougher, and more elusive than any opponent we ever face. It's understanding that I must lose some of myself in order to find others. Individual egos must die in order for a team to live. It's learning how to be a team player. To claim I am a good teammate or team player simply means I know how to sacrifice for a just cause, cooperate with my fellow human, respect the dignity of others, and can respond when called upon. This is what I call harmony, the key to understanding.

Which one of us at this very moment is not a member of a team? Everyone here today is on a team. Parents work as a team raising and caring for their children. When involved in clubs, city government, and community projects we are members of a team. My classrooms are teams. The question we all must ask ourselves is "What kind of team player are we?" We must understand that sometimes our needs and wants are secondary to the greater good of the whole.

Now this may sound odd to you; but the reason we win and what beats at the heart of our neighborhood is love. Yes, we win because our players love each other. They are not afraid to say it or embrace each other as a sign of that affection. This is just an outward sign. To love someone; words are nice but insufficient—actions speak volumes. And that's not too easy.

Put simply, love means I can count on you and you can count on me. This translates into being responsible. Responsibility is learned and not inherited. Being responsible to forty-five teammates is not so simple. It means following team rules and knowing that my attitudes and actions have a profound effect on the success of the whole. We pride ourselves on that exact accountability. We recommit to each other on a weekly basis before games. We commit that my contributions to the team will be my best self.

This commitment extends to all facets of my life. It's how I conduct myself as a person—from the classroom to the field, to the outside community. Wherever I go or whatever I do, I carry my team with me knowing full well that I am connected to a group that loves, accepts, and respects me.

We try to make our football team a safe place to be. Safe to be our self. There is nowhere to hide on a football field. Teammates know each other, coaches know the players, and the players know the coaches. All attempts at not being yourself fail miserably. The key is to be the best self you were created to be. We work hard at breaking down the walls that separate us called race, status, religion, jealousy, hate, and culture—and truly experience each other on a purely human level.

Now, what does that all translate into? Well, our founder, Saint John the Baptist De La Salle, says that the spirit of our Lasallian family is a spirit of faith and ardent zeal. And that the motivation force of zeal is love. I have witnessed this zeal. Another word for which I call passion. You should see the passion with which our students play. I stand on our sideline sometimes in utter amazement. I watch them fight, compete, and push themselves far beyond what they thought was previously possible, all because they felt connected to others who care.

Every year I teach a religious studies class for seniors called Senior Synthesis. The class design is to help the seniors make sense out of four years of religious education and how they will apply it to their futures. In it I pose a question: "What is your passion?" When I pose this question to the seniors they usually get this blank look on their faces as if they've never heard the word before. And, regrettably, more often than not the answer comes back: "I don't know." I think: how unfortunate. How in the world could we do a good job of anything—unless we have faith in it and have passion for it?

Please don't misunderstand me; I am not a football nut. I have often heard it said that football builds character. I disagree; I believe it reveals character. There are many different people, events, and experiences that contribute to character formation. Every single person at this gathering has a special talent. Mine, I think, happens to be coaching—many times I wish that I had certain talents my students possess, but that's what God gave me.

This point could not be better illustrated than in Jesus' parable of the Three Servants in Matthew's gospel. In it, a wealthy landowner gave three of his servants a certain sum of money to see what each would do with it. The first two returned the money with profit. They used their courage and ingenuity to parlay their sum into something more. The third hid the money and just returned what he originally received. The landowner didn't expect much—he just wanted the servants to have the courage to use what talent they had and do something. The key point to the story is, and I quote, "The landowner gave to each servant according to his ability." The assumption here is that each of us has some sort of ability: talent. Now it's our responsibility to discover what that is and, what's more, have the courage to use it.

Again the question "What are you doing in your environment?" Are you sitting still or are you working on discovering and developing your talent? In my mind I say, "I hope so." You see, we are privileged to be here. God not only gave us some sort of ability, but also by fate or will placed us in an environment to develop those talents. And for what purpose? Is it to allow us to make a fortune? I don't think it is.

Let me share with you some words from one of my childhood heroes, Bobby Kennedy. He said, "For the fortunate among us, there is the temptation to follow the easy and familiar paths of personal ambition and financial success so grandly spread before those who enjoy the privilege of education. But that is not the road history has marked out for us. Like it or not we live in times of danger and uncertainty. But they are also more open to the creative energy of humankind than any other time in history."

Those words were spoken thirty years ago; however, I believe they are more applicable today than they have ever been. Ignorance is not an option for us; we are the fortunate that Kennedy spoke of. We now have a choice and that choice is a moral decision. Either we accept and serve or we don't.

We open the paper every day, breathe a collective sigh, and cry out, "Why?" Why is there hate, prejudice, war, crime, pollution? We see ourselves as victims, powerless to control what happens to us. We too often want to relieve ourselves of all responsibilities and believe that things are beyond our control. The sad or good news is there is very little beyond our control, and what is, we should offer up to God's will.

As for now, my faith remains with us assembled today. That we will put on the armor and join the fight in this wonderful, beautiful, yet fragile world. That we use our talents and abilities to be agents of change, knowing full well that many of us have the solutions to our collective problems.

Seven

MINOR MIRACLES

During the first week of January the past seven years, one man greets the New Year by unlocking a windowless cinder-block shed on the north side of the De La Salle campus. The House of Pain is open for business; its proprietor is Mike Blasquez, head athletic trainer and strength and conditioning coach of the De La Salle Spartans.

This year he carried a box of forty-five computer printouts, each a dozen pages long, individually tailored for each team member. Their first game was still over six months off, and their final game—should the Spartans go on to the North Coast Section championship contest, as they had for each of the past twelve seasons—was eleven months from now. But the kinesiological blueprint of the 2001 varsity football team was ready.

A Spartan can expect to spend at least ninety minutes a day in the two-room shed, as well as taking part in drills and running out on the field. Blasquez choreographs workouts that dramatically increase strength, endurance, agility, and explosiveness—the latter particularly important in football—while adding pounds of muscle to an athlete's frame. Every pound added to the bar, every medicine ball tossed, every flurry of light repetitions versus heavy, is in the plan, a precision that allows Ladouceur and his coaches to schedule exactly when the boys will reach their peak—actually, two peaks: Week 5 of the preseason, and Week 13, the NCS final.

Blasquez, who joined the staff in 1993, was named National High School Strength and Conditioning Coach of the Year in 1998. His presence allows Ladouceur to do other things during the off-season, including his teaching and administrative duties and, of course, tinkering with his offense and defense.

"Training kids in the off-season is a burden," Ladouceur says. "It's not something football coaches want to do. Their thing is putting eleven on eleven. The off-season does not excite football coaches. That's the beauty of having Mike. He gets the kids excited. Motivation is not what you think. A lot of people think it's the charismatic personality, but it's not. It's about establishing goals and meeting them. In the off-season our kids are motivated, but not about football. It's about another ten pounds on the squat, a gain of ten pounds of muscle. I was real fortunate to get him."

De La Salle athletic director and defensive coordinator Terry Eidson concurs: "Mike does a lot of the off-season work—all of it, really."

Every good high school football team has a strength and conditioning program, but the Spartans are almost certainly the only players who deliberately work at the Division I-A college level, and it shows. Pound for pound, they are the strongest teenagers in America.

Derek Landri and Matt Gutierrez are big. Andy Briner is solid, incredibly strong, and has a *motor*. And then there are the smaller players, each one a miniature football miracle, forged in Blasquez's House of Pain, turned on the lathe of Bob Ladouceur's teachings, and buffed by the pressure of The Streak.

Alijah Bradley and Maurice Drew, for instance, are definitely on the small side. Alijah, who will be a senior in the fall, is 5'7", and Maurice, who will be a junior, is 5'6"—Smurfs, as football folk like to say. But Alijah and Maurice have moves—they are nimble, hyperactive runners who can cut, stop on a dime, reverse direction, jitterbug, and bounce out of a tackler's grasp. Each gained about five hundred yards in the 2000 season, mostly in relief action (most of De La Salle's games are blowouts by halftime). But the basic question about their size lingers: Can they take the beating of a thirteen-game season without their bodies breaking down? Can they survive the impact of a hit from a truly monstrous lineman, such as Poly's 6'6" tackle Manuel Wright, who, despite his 305-pound bulk, has the speed of a running back? This is especially critical because both Alijah and Maurice are, rather incredibly, penciled in to play both offense and defense. Football teams on every level, from high school to the NFL, tend to split up offensive and defensive squads; only a couple of players do double duty. At De La Salle the opposite is the rule. Lots of key players go both ways—Nate Kenion, Derek, Andy, Javier Carlos, John Chan, Nick Barbero, and Brendan Ottoboni. Still, for Alijah and Maurice to do it is asking a lot. Their performance, particularly their freedom from injury, will be a result of the hours they put in with Mike Blasquez in the House of Pain.

Alijah, the senior, has his heart set on going to the University of Michigan, and he has the A average and study habits to get him there. But he freely admits an immediate concern drives him: expunging a bad memory—something he feels is a blot on his honor—last year's opening preseason game against Buchanan High, which De La Salle came perilously close to losing.

Buchanan was an unknown quantity, a relatively new school from Clovis, a wealthy suburban enclave in an agricultural area in the Central Valley, 150 miles south, near Fresno, which in Bay Area terms is the outer limits of civilization. The Central Valley is California's equivalent to the Mississippi Delta: hot, flat, endless, agricultural.

The Buchanan Bears had begged for a game, readily agreed to come into De La Salle's own backyard for the slaughter. Only it hadn't been a slaughter. After going up 30–12, the Spartans ran into trouble against a relentless and quick-firing attack that sent as many as five receivers out in intricate, layered, weaving pass routes. High school teams tend to a run-first offensive philosophy to minimize fumbles and interceptions, but the Bears executed perfectly while the Spartans turned the ball over twice. Alijah struggled offensively and, like all of the defenders, ended up with tire tracks on his back as Buchanan drove for two touchdowns, the second making the score 30–24 with 3:13 to play (it would have been 30–28 if all four Buchanan extra points hadn't failed). The Spartans took the ensuing kickoff and squeezed every last second off the clock for victory No. 101. The Streak had survived.

"I let the team down, and I let myself down," says Alijah. "I have something to prove; I want to clear my name."

This year's rematch would be played down in Clovis, in late August, when the thermometer hits one hundred degrees by noon. The visit promised to be a barn burner, and Alijah made himself a promise that this time he would be the one to strike the match.

Maurice Drew had similar feelings—in truth, probably every player who'd been there still experienced a burst of shame at the thought of almost losing on their very own Owen Owens Field on the first game of the season. Although only a sophomore, Maurice had felt that a lot had been expected from him on both offense and defense. "I didn't produce," he says, and the feeling persisted the whole season, even if his statistics were respectable.

Maurice is from Pinole, a small town thirteen miles from Concord, where his dad owns a car-detailing business and his mom works at Pacific Bell. The family game is supposed to be basketball—his mother's father had played for the University of the Pacific when it was a national power—but Maurice gravitated to gymnastics as a four-to-six-year-old, eventually becoming a football player with decidedly gymnastic abilities.

Maurice's mother made the decision to apply to De La Salle. "She wanted me to go here for the education," he says. "I didn't want to leave my friends, but most of them were troublemakers. Still, going to an all-boys school . . ." He grimaces. "I thought I'd never see girls. I'd heard you'd turn gay if you went there. I'd heard the education was hard. I worried about getting to Concord, because I didn't have my driver's license."

Once Maurice arrived, his worries waned. He found that De La Salle had a structured approach to ensure that incoming freshmen aren't overwhelmed by their studies. His confidence grew as his focus narrowed. "Not having girls makes it less distracting," he says. He got his license, and a car coolly detailed by Dad. And he discovered that he didn't have to give up his hometown friendships, either. In the second semester he was pleased to be joined by a friend, Eric Love, who had been on De La Salle's waiting list. Not only that, but "it turns out I play against my friends in football," he says. "Some of my best friends are on Antioch, Deer Valley, San Leandro—we'll be in the middle of a game, hitting each other, and at the end of the play we'll say hello."

A three-year membership in the House of Pain can assure a Spartan a well-muscled suit of armor. Quickness and cleverness, which Alijah and Maurice both have, can do a lot to keep you out of harm's way. But, depending on the position you play, some physical disadvantages can't be overcome.

That is Scott Regalia's problem. Scott plays center, perhaps the most curious position in the game: the person who crouches in the middle of the offensive line and is responsible for starting each play by flipping the ball between his legs to a back, usually the quarterback. No one else will touch the ball as many times in a game; nobody else has the fate of the game in his hands every single play; nobody else starts every single play. Nobody else begins a play bent over looking backward between his legs, completely at the mercy of some 240-pound gorilla on the other side of the line, who is going to have the jump on him every single play and is going to try to take his head off every single play, too.

In the hierarchy of high school football and life, centers don't get Most Valuable Player awards or the girl. Still, they are respected in the fraternity of the line and by the offense. A measure of their importance in the eyes of the coaches is that the center is often the only other position besides quarterback in which the starter is withheld from playing defense—he's too valuable to risk losing, or even to get hit. He gets hit enough as it is.

This year it was Scott's turn to step into the center of the line. He'd been a tight end as a freshman, switching to center as a sophomore. It looked like a sacrifice to many, but not to Scott: he wanted to play, and if center was the ticket, then center it would be. As a junior on varsity, he didn't get into many games, but he learned his new position. Now he had seven months to prepare himself, to get stronger in anticipation of what those massive defensive linemen would do to him. And he needed those seven months, because Scott really was too small: 5'10", 180 pounds. He'd be going head-to-head with the likes of Poly's 6'6", 305-pound Manuel Wright, 6'5", 300-pound Maurice Murray, and 6'1", 300-pound Ernesto Villasenor. When the other teams looked at him, on paper and on film, they had to be licking their chops.

Eight

SOMETHING IN THE WATER

The weight room at Poly is no House of Pain. When Winston Justice wants to lift, he goes to Gold's Gym, where he has a membership, but he's lucky. Most Poly kids don't have the resources to become gym hardbodies, says trainer and tight end coach Rob Shock.

What Poly does have to make its children strong is a World of Pain. Darnell Bing, for instance, was born in Compton, its name synonymous with gang violence; when he moved to Long Beach at age six, however, Poly's extensive Pop Warner program gave him and his friends a healthy, structured, and instructive way to fill the very rich hours between childhood and adolescence. It was here Darnell formed a tight bond with many future members of the Poly squad: Brandon Brooks, Randy Estes, Marcedes Lewis, Rod Williams, Derrick Jones.

Pop Warner, America's largest and oldest (since 1929) youth football program, offers both boys and girls a chance to play the tackle game starting at the age of five. Eight teams are sponsored by Poly, and they practice and play on the school's fields, which for years bore so little grass they resembled landfill. Still, all year long you see players in Poly green and gold, some seemingly no larger than Smurfs or Cabbage Patch dolls, girls as well as boys, all in pads and high black socks, going through drills and running plays. Players from Poly practices drift over to watch, talk with friends and relatives. Local heroes from decades past stroke their chin whiskers and discuss the hot new seventh-grader at tailback: Is he as good as Hershel at that age? Mothers and grandmothers pull up lawn chairs. Uncles and brothers ambitious for their kin to do well *at the next level* demonstrate swim moves, jerk and pull moves, spin moves, separation moves. As the golden light fades on bulbous Signal Hill looming in the background, football comes to resemble a county fair, a town commons, Poly's playing fields of Eton.

Having a commons can help soften life's rough edges. Darnell's father has been away in Folsom prison for a while, and Darnell misses him. "He's in for something he didn't do, he was with somebody," he says. "He'll be up for parole in two to three years." His father writes and they talk on the phone. "He asks me questions to make sure I'm not hanging with the wrong crowd and tells me to watch the people I'm hanging with"—typical parental advice, albeit from a more informed perspective than most.

Darnell is unequivocal in his praise of the job his family and, in particular, his two older brothers, now aged twenty-one and twenty-three, did in raising him. "My brothers made sure I wasn't in trouble," he says, "made sure I got my schoolwork done. We did lots of fun things together, too. We liked to bowl, go to movies, go in-line skating." An eyebrow lifts a fraction. "I picked up some moves from skating."

Brandon Brooks recalls Darnell as just another 5'4" Pop Warner Smurf in seventh grade. Then the hormones kicked in, and he was 6" then 6'2", and now 6'3", carrying a trim 215 pounds at sprinter's speed. He started as a running back and free safety in Pop Warner when he was nine, but in his fourth year actually got a shot at quarterback. The team went 13-1. Freshmen aren't allowed to play varsity in California, which turned out to be a good thing for Darnell; he came down with a growth-related degenerative condition in both knees, Osgood-Schlatter syndrome, forcing him to become inactive for the first time in his life. By his sophomore year the growth plates in his leg bones had stabilized, the condition had gone away, and he was a starting safety—playing one of the most demanding positions in one of the most demanding programs in the country.

In addition to the physical package—recruiter's shorthand for size, straight-line and lateral speed, vertical leap, core strength, and growth potential—Darnell has a relaxed, Zen kind of calm in the midst of the maelstrom of a typical football play. And he can hit. After a solid hit, Darnell always bounces up to his feet, clapping his hands enthusiastically, leaving a stunned runner peering up and, perhaps, wondering, "Didn't I see him rollerblading down at Belmont Shore last weekend?"

So the recruiters are all over Darnell, wanting an oral commitment now, in his junior year. He takes their calls, listens politely, and says he'll let them know when he makes up his mind. He opens their letters, reads carefully, and puts them in the top drawer of his dresser. So many colleges—all across the country, the biggest names—want Darnell Bing! It feels good, of course. What feels even better is the thought of his dad being able to see him play when he gets out.

"At Poly, there is something in the water," insists a school administrator, watching Marcedes Lewis make a graceful catch of an orange tossed into a crowd of clamoring students. "And there's the proof."

Of all the striking and self-possessed young men on the Poly team, Marcedes Lewis arguably possesses the highest of what

Hollywood would call a Q rating. His frequent smile ranges from charming to megawatt-level charismatic, his eyes are intelligent and inquiring. His 6'7" body is proportioned like a dancer's—long, graceful legs and arms that move sinuously. He is rarely self-regarding or boastful, but often witty, even kind—he's a hit with young children.

Marcedes was raised by his mother, Yvonne, who had him when she was just fifteen. "He was very muscular at a very early age," she says. As a child, "he was a daredevil," she recalls. "He'd try anything once. And when we would go to the mall, I'd look away for one minute and he would be gone. But I always knew where to find him—at the pet store, looking at some puppy."

Yvonne and Marcedes moved around a lot. "I was real young, just a girl," she says. After attending various Long Beach schools, Marcedes transferred in junior high to Mayfair in the adjacent suburb of Lakewood, mostly to get out of wearing the uniforms that Long Beach had made mandatory in the lower grades. "I just couldn't face buying five pairs of navy blue pants," Yvonne deadpans.

A single mother of two (Ashley was born three years after Marcedes), Yvonne worked three jobs to support her boys. Two of her jobs were in home security, where she met Mike Withers, and they began dating. It was Yvonne's first romantic relationship since Marcedes and his brother were babies.

Mike is white, Yvonne black, and Marcedes at eight years was old enough to be troubled by the racial issues. "He wasn't getting any peer pressure, but he was concerned he would," Yvonne said in an interview in the local paper. "I told him he was more worried about Mike being white than anyone else." In the end, "[Marcedes] loved Mike. Nothing else mattered." Mike and Yvonne soon had two children of their own.

Still, the attention that came with being from a mixed-race

family added to that which Marcedes was already receiving for his athletic skills, especially when he shot up to 6'1" in seventh grade. Football came first, and although he didn't start playing basketball until ninth grade, he showed a flair for that, too.

Yvonne, worried that Marcedes's education had slipped through the cracks while she was working, decided to reverse the trend. "My husband has been the one who has given him the advice regarding sports," she says. "I've given him the stuff regarding character and everyday life. And I stayed on him with his grammar. At the age I had him, I didn't get on him the way I should've. So I've stayed on him ever since, right through high school."

Once he arrived at Poly, Marcedes did his growing up in public. He wasn't just someone who was good at one sport and contributed in another—Marcedes was a football and a basketball star at a school whose teams were always ranked near the top in the state. And Marcedes kept growing, to 6'4", then 6'5"—which forced the football coaches to make a practical, and for Marcedes, confining, decision. Forget about being quarterback, line up at tight end, block for Hershel, and catch the occasional pass as the quarterback's third or fourth option. "He didn't fight it, and eventually he grew to like it," says Yvonne. "Of course, this is his mom talking here—who knows what Mar really felt inside. But he did tell me once that because of the people in front of him, he knew he wouldn't be getting a shot at quarterback."

Marcedes, going into his junior year, had to wait his turn behind the senior wide receivers. That was the Poly way, and the starters, Mike Willis and Joshua Hawkins, were bona fide Division I-A scholarship recruits. But Marcedes was every bit as good, even if at tight end. He could be the "go-to guy," flying downfield, making acrobatic catches, and soaring into the end zone. Why should he be condemned to blocking oblivion just because he was seven inches taller than the average wide receiver? If anything, that should be considered an advantage.

But, for the good of the team, Marcedes buckled down for his junior season, blocking for Hershel and Brandon. It wasn't all bad—he did manage to catch a few balls, score some touchdowns, and after the season was over, the main college recruiting services rated him among the top five tight end prospects in the country.

Suddenly every big-time college program in America was calling Marcedes at home. But his heart was already set on UCLA—on basketball—to wear the powder blue on the hallowed court of John Wooden. He would play tight end on the grass in the fall and play forward on the parquet court in the spring.

There was just one glitch. When it came to basketball, UCLA sounded like every other school. *Come and play tight end for us, and we'll see about getting you some minutes in basketball.* Marcedes, though, wanted to try for it all.

Nine

CALM BEFORE THE STORM

From January until May all was quiet on the football front, at least on the surface. The only real news came in the second week of February, as it does every year, when the top athletes must announce their decisions regarding college.

Intercollegiate sports in America is governed by the NCAA, which has evolved a three-and-a-half-division format—Division I-A and I-AA, Division II, and Division III—based on the size and scope of each school's athletic program. In sports, Division I-A is king of the hill; its 117 members include such juggernauts as Florida, Ohio State, Michigan, and USC, and its athletic scholarships set the gold standard. Neither need- nor academic-based, these four-year "rides" can be worth at least $100,000, not including meals, lodging, transport, and the per diem players receive on road trips. The scholarships mean a lot to financially strapped parents, and even more to families who have never had a child attend a four-year college. Their ultimate worth in the eyes of many players, however, is that they are the only realistic ticket to the next level, the National Football League.

Many high school football teams never send a single player to a "D1" school, as the Division I-A programs are called. Most count themselves lucky if a single player lands a ride at one of the I-AA schools, which do offer full scholarships but cannot meet the Division I-A requirement of a fifteen-thousand-person attendance average at home football games; I-AA teams play in less glamorous conferences and attract fewer NFL scouts.

A ballpark estimate is that for every 330 high school seniors playing football, one will receive a full four-year scholarship. In 2000, a school-record-tying six seniors from the 2000 De La Salle team received scholarships, four from D1-A programs; from Poly, nine would be getting scholarships, seven from D1-A programs, once again the most of any school in California, and tied for the most in the country with Belle Glades, Florida, and Midland Lee, Texas. (Poly also had the most graduates—five—playing in the NFL in 2000, tied with Ely of Pompano Beach, Florida; St. Augustine, in New Orleans; and Willowridge of Houston.)

For coaches at both schools, the off-season months gave them their turn to make up for lost time. "I always hate it when the season ends," says Poly assistant Herman Davis. "My wife has all those 'honey-dos' lined up for me the moment I come in the door." Painting, landscaping, fixer-up projects, and the list goes on; coaches' wives are a long-suffering lot.

The long hours of the coaching profession may well be hazardous to relationships. There is probably at least one strained or estranged marriage, sometimes several, on every staff in America. Moreover, the financial rewards don't do much to make up for time apart. A twenty-year veteran head coach in a public school district with regulated wages, such as Jerry Jaso, may top out at $55,000. Even if he continues to teach and coach for another ten or twenty years, he'll likely get no more than cost-of-living increments. To rub it in, a public school coach's salary is common knowledge around town. This isn't the case at a private school. At some big-city parochial football powers, such as Mater Dei and St. Louis, the head coach is rumored to pull in $100,000, but the majority of Catholic schools pay well below the public school average for teachers and generally offer an extremely modest pension plan. Bob Ladouceur, who teaches as well as coaches, is better compensated than many of his parochial peers, perhaps even making as much as a Rollinson or a Cal Lee. He could also supplement his income with speaking gigs, but has little time or inclination to do so on top of his fund-raising efforts for the school.

A small-college head coach can make six figures with perks thrown in; a Division I-A head coach at an elite football program is another breed entirely, often pulling down seven figures when all the side deals are counted. High school coaches don't, however, make the leap to the Division I big-time.

Pay is a sensitive issue at Poly, most of whose sixteen coaches earn a pittance for their long hours. Only a few Poly assistant coaches are teachers or on staff; most work full-time jobs, as firemen, personal trainers, bus drivers, small businessmen, coaches of other sports at other schools, and probation officers. At De La Salle, the coaching staff numbers around fifteen. The top three are teachers or administrators, one is a trainer, one a stockbroker, and several at the freshman and junior varsity level are still finishing up undergraduate or graduate degrees while drawing a salary.

Somebody up at De La Salle has a secret. Matt Gutierrez isn't telling anybody about his wrist except those who need to know. If somebody asks why he isn't playing on the basketball team anymore, particularly when the Spartans are on such a terrific run, he says it's a sprain.

That's what he thought, originally. Last June, back in 2000, during a crank-it-up session in the House of Pain, Matt felt something pop in his right wrist. From then on it hurt. But it seemed minor, and in football you play with pain, especially if you think of yourself as a team leader. But it kept on hurting, and when the season began, the quarterback coach, Mark Panella, noticed that his throws weren't tight. When a good quarterback throws, the ball rotates in a tight spiral, which allows it to slice through wind and air without fluttering, even for thirty, forty, fifty yards. When a great quarterback like Matt throws a good ball, say a forty-yard bomb to a receiver racing full speed for the far orange cones that mark the end zone, it will describe an arc that lofts it over the defensive backs yet delivers it to the receiver's outstretched hands still locked in that tight spiral, rotating not fluttering. Now Matt's throws were unraveling at the end, starting out tight, then going wobbly for the last few yards; even his formerly crisp, dartlike short passes were hanging out to dry, flapping like laundry on a line.

Everybody assumed the sore wrist had affected Matt's mechanics. He was setting up wrong or throwing from a too open stance. But although they looked at film to correct any flaws and the trainers worked on the hand and the wrist, the zip just wasn't there, and the season was upon them. Though Matt's injury was kept secret the entire year, its effect was noticeable. It was one reason the Buchanan game was so tight, and the almost fatal interception that gave Mater Dei the ball in the fourth quarter was definitely a result of weakness and pain. Matt saw the receiver making his cut—it was a risky, across-the-gain throw, but in his mind he knew exactly how much to put on the ball, how fast to throw it, and when—but then his wrist had spasmed in the act and failed him. Afterward, The Streak still alive by the grace of a missed field goal, Matt had fallen to the ground, sobbing, blaming himself for what had almost happened.

When the 2000 season ended, Matt jumped straight into basketball as in every other year. The wrist kept bothering him, but not that badly. He played with the team in Christmas tournaments in Hawaii and San Diego. When they came home in January, the first day in basketball practice he jammed the wrist hard. He tried taping it, but this time the pain was too great to pretend to himself that he could gut this one out.

X rays and tests revealed the wrist's history: "It turns out I broke it that June lifting weights," Matt says. "The doctor said the body formed a false joint, so it didn't hurt all that bad." Surgery would be necessary. When Matt came out of the operating room, he says, "They told me it had broken and never healed." Then they told him the bad news. Necrosis was a possibility.

There are not too many places in the world where *necrosis* is a household word, but the San Francisco Bay Area is one of them. Followers of the Oakland Raiders had seen the career of the only bona fide two-sport professional athlete of modern times, baseball and football star Bo Jackson, cut short by avascular necrosis. A degenerative condition that occurs when blood circulation is for some reason reduced to a damaged area, necrosis had also crippled San Francisco 49er running back Garrison Hearst after he broke an ankle. Hearst had nearly lost his foot to gangrene, which set in due to the necrosis. Although he held out hopes of playing again, at the time of Matt's injury Hearst's once-promising career seemed over.

Apparently Matt's wrist break wasn't getting enough blood. It wasn't necrosis yet—but they'd have to watch closely and maybe say a little prayer or two. For now, the prescription was no throwing. For the first time in Matt's memory, he didn't have a football in his hand, couldn't work out with his receivers on the timing routes, couldn't even lift or otherwise keep his right arm in shape.

If the bones didn't heal, if the blood didn't start flowing, Matt could kiss off his dreams of being a scholarship quarterback at a

Division I university. If it was necrosis, he'd be lucky if he could hold a bag of buttered popcorn at the cineplex.

For Matt, one of the country's elite players on the threshold of the biggest game of his life, the worst agony was not being able to prepare. Everyone in the De La Salle program knows by heart the John Wooden quote "Failure to prepare is preparing to fail." Matt dreaded catching sight of himself in the bathroom mirror. "I was atrophying," he says. "And I couldn't do anything about it."

For the coaches, it meant considering the unthinkable: breaking in a new quarterback when everything in the current offense was tailored to Matt's talents and relied on Matt's instincts to run. They were fortunate to have a senior backup, Brian Callahan, who was as much a student of the game as Matt—not so surprising, given that his father was offensive coordinator of the Oakland Raiders. But if Matt was lost for any amount of time, there was no doubt that the balance of power would shift to Poly.

Football success does not always ensure happiness. This is a truth all too rarely acknowledged in America.

Cal Lee was finding that out in spades, over in Hawaii. Lee was the winningest coach in Island history, charismatic and darkly handsome, a mind as well as a motivator, the man who had brought a sophisticated passing game to a place where brute force had been the norm, and who was, if you were a football coach, the opponent you most dreaded.

But as the media frenzy—only let's call it a *media tsunami* for the touch of local color that football scribes so adore—over the De La Salle game subsided, as the sea pulled away to reveal the bare bottom of the ocean floor, Lee was left flopping and vulnerable. And his critics moved in.

Why would a man with twenty-one years of coaching, a winning record like Lee's, have critics? Well, you'd have to ask someone at Damien Memorial about that. Damien is a fellow Catholic school, named after the famous "leper priest" of Molokai. It's not a football power, but it has a long history of playing the sport.

Since 1982, Damien hasn't had much luck against St. Louis; hasn't, in fact, won a single game. In its last two games before entering the 2000 season, St. Louis had beaten Damien by scores of 83–0 and 82–0. There was criticism of Lee for these pastings, including some by his fellow coaches. The majority of football coaches do not enjoy putting up numbers like these, but it cannot be denied that a minority of implacable souls from the life-is-tough school scorn taking it easy (needless to say, these are the coaches of winning teams).

Blowouts are something of a St. Louis specialty, but it's not all Lee's fault. He certainly wasn't taking an easy path when he put in an ambitious, pass-driven offense; most high school coaches *hate* passing, seeing it as an invitation for kids to turn the ball over. High school offense starts with the run—it tends to calm those shaky adolescent nerves and keeps bad things from happening that demoralize you and keep you from competing. Lee's airborne strategy is actually gutsy and much, much harder to teach. It requires repetition, and it requires success for the kids to believe in the system and to execute it. Unfortunately for the Damiens of this world, repeated success for a pass-first offense often leads to blowouts.

It does seem unfair to get on Lee for simply letting his offense do its thing. But one other aspect to the blowouts cannot be avoided: they get the attention of pollsters. Blowouts are part of marketing a top ten football team, especially to sleepy-eyed sports editors on the mainland. So maybe this wasn't just a case of the offense simply doing its thing, after all.

The 2000 Damien game seemed to push public opinion over the edge. Perhaps Lee felt he needed another blowout to put the pressure on De La Salle to pony up to the bar. There was a strange symmetry to the final score, 84–0, the highest margin yet by a single point. It may be that this one point is what caused the tsunami, because after the shellacking, in which the Crusaders were up 77–0 at halftime, the Damien principal excoriated Lee in the press. He also announced that henceforth Damien would rather forfeit than play St. Louis in their conference.

This being Hawaii, there was considerable discussion of Damien's outrage in the press. It was hard to deny that St. Louis had run up the score, and harder to justify it, but some people tried: Wasn't this a case of sour grapes? What did people want to do, tell the St. Louis boys not to try? What kind of lesson was that? Wasn't it rather un-American to penalize success? In a free-market world, what prevented Damien from going out and getting a coach and the players to compete against St. Louis?

Actually, football's inversion of Gresham's law that the good drives out the best answered the last question. When St. Louis took the field, its varsity numbered 113 players—far in excess of even Mater Dei's "Monarch Marchers," 99 strong. While schools such as Damien and Wailua struggled to find enough players to field one team, St. Louis could field five teams. This, ironically, explained away the charge of running up the score: when you have 113 players on varsity, the only way to keep them happy is to let them have their fun. And scoring is definitely fun.

As it happened, during the 2000 season poetic justice was at hand. Time and demographics caught up to the Crusaders, in the form of North Shore country cousin Kahuku. The Red Raiders had themselves a sharp young coach in Siuaki Levai, who had finally harnessed the power and, yes, finesse of its pan-Polynesian population. Kahuku had come close in several championship games, but never beaten St. Louis and Lee; it was sort of like the rivalry between Poly and the Mater Deis and Loyolas, before Jaso took charge.

On December 1, 2000, that all changed when Kahuku snapped St. Louis's streak of fourteen consecutive state championships, 26–20. The one game reversed the two teams' fortunes, just as Lee was scheming and scrambling to lure De La Salle into his sights. Suddenly, when the season-ending polls came out, Kahuku was ranked number sixteen and former number eight St. Louis was near the bottom of Student Sports Fab 50. After twenty years of building St. Louis up, Lee essentially saw his reputation and ranking cherry-picked by this newcomer from the plantation. So much for the thanks of a grateful country!

If the De La Salle deal had gone down before the loss to Kahuku, it's entirely possible all would have been forgiven. Hawaii is very much a go-along, get-along state, its bureaucracies informed by the consensus-building philosophy of its majority Japanese-American population. If the De La Salle contract had been signed, a wave of excitement and enthusiasm for The Game would almost certainly have swept aside, even if only for another year, the complaints about St. Louis. But the deal did not go down. Instead, Poly signed with De La Salle. The sea withdrew. And the sanctions began.

The first rule to emerge from the Hawaii High School Athletic Association was to limit varsity football squad size to sixty-five players. Within a month, thirty-five sophomore and junior players at St. Louis transferred to a public school in the neighborhood where they lived.

The second decision, a month later, was intended to cut down on blowouts, by implementing a running clock when a team was ahead by thirty-five points in the second half.

The third rule wasn't approved until summer, but everybody knew it was in the works. It would break up the existing league structure of Hawaii's most populous island, Oahu, home of St. Louis and Kahuku. It, too, could be taken as a measure restraining Lee and St. Louis's dominance.

Pundits referred to the changes collectively as "the St. Louis Rules." The effect, of course, was to ensure that St. Louis would *not* rule, at least as before. In fact, even if The Game was still six months in the future, it wouldn't be wrong to say that the first loser had emerged: a coach and a school twenty-five hundred miles away, across a deep blue sea. In mid-July, Cal Lee would resign as coach to become St. Louis's athletic director.

In mid-February, Jerry Jaso reflected on the upcoming game with De La Salle: "I think the story of De La Salle is that, initially, they won a lot of games with a really disciplined group of kids who were not necessarily great players. They won with a tremendous coaching staff and tremendous organizational ability. But lately, in the last four years, they've gotten very athletic, too. They've added great athletes to the roster.

"Now they have great players, extremely well coached by Bob Ladouceur, and they execute very well. That's the key. People say that Northern California football is weak, that it's stronger down here. I won't even argue that. But if you win one hundred thirteen games in a row, I don't care where you're from, you're a great team. De La Salle has beaten Mater Dei two times down here and once up there. They've answered the bell."

He laughed when asked about the polls. "Get this: I just heard that when the polls come out in June, we could be number one and they could be number two."

When Student Sports, Super Prep, and other recruiting services came out with their lists of top recruits, five Poly players had made it into the top five nationally in their position, the most ever of any high school in history: Darnell Bing, Hershel Dennis, Winston Justice, Marcedes Lewis, and Manuel Wright. (Marcedes was actually listed as the number one recruit at his position.) Quickly dubbed the Poly Five and the Big Five, their photos popped up on the pages of the *Long Beach Independent Press-Telegram* and on the Internet.

For De La Salle, Derek Landri and Matt Gutierrez were given respectable ratings, although not in the top five. Andy Briner and his other teammates were not ranked.

On May 16, 2001, the *Press-Telegram* ran an article that reverberated across the country. Sportswriter Ted Kian had a scoop, and he played it with the cool of a veteran poker player drawing for a royal flush:

"At this juncture, it is only speculation to discuss the Poly football coaching situation."

That was all it took, of course. The piece put a collective lump in throats all over Long Beach. Jerry Jaso was . . . interviewing. Kian took pains to note that Jaso was in fact one of three candidates for linebacker coach at Long Beach City College. But nobody doubted that Jaso would be hired. A week later, on May 24, it was official: Jaso goes. Long Beach heaved a collective sigh of disbelief.

Everyone wanted to know why, but Jaso remained unflustered. There seemed to be no compelling reason. "I'm happy at Poly, but the Long Beach City job is a good opportunity for me to move into college coaching," he said to Kian. "I could essentially coach many of the same players I've coached or faced at Poly."

But why choose "the eternal obscurity that is being linebacker coach at Long Beach City College," as the *Press-Telegram's* Doug Krikorian would write? A coach of Jaso's connections and reputation could surely catch on with a big-time college program. Jaso's response was that he didn't want the gypsy life of the college assistant. "I have friends coaching at major colleges," Jaso said. "In the last five years, one of them has lived in Idaho, Portland, Montana, and Utah. He loves it, but it would be hard for me to tell my kids we're moving every year, and I couldn't even imagine telling that to my wife. I want to stay in this area."

Everyone wanted to know how could he do this to Poly, to Long Beach, on the verge of the biggest high school game ever? Didn't he want to take his shot at The Streak and a national championship?

"As far as I'm concerned, we won a national title when Dick-Butkus.com ranked us number one in the nation," Jaso replied.

The ruckus lasted a solid week. "*ESPN Magazine* just reported that Poly has more potential first-round [NFL draft] players on its 2001 roster than either USC or UCLA," wrote *Press-Telegram* columnist Dave Keisser. "Friends of Jaso have told him he made a mistake leaving Poly." That was putting it mildly. Actually, it was as if an entire city had told Jaso he'd blown it, walking away from the most talented team in Poly—if not high school—history.

Yet there was no anger, no dumping of garbage on Jaso's lawn or effigies hung from lampposts. Up north, Bob Ladouceur's reaction was to ask if Jaso had any children (three boys) and if so, their ages (seventeen, fifteen, thirteen). The father of three himself, Ladouceur then said his chief regret was not spending more time with his daughter, now nineteen: "If I could have one thing back in my life, it would be those years," he says.

Wheels were already turning. The day after Jaso's resignation, defensive coordinator Raul Lara was appointed interim coach for spring practice. A young (thirty-five) and ambitious 1984 Poly graduate, Lara was a natural candidate for the head coach spot. Yet the decision set off a tense discussion in the program and the community.

Along with Lara, Poly had four longtime assistants, all dedicated Poly grads, including Don Norford (Poly '64, twenty-three years at Poly, NFL High School Coach of the Year); Merle Cole II ('68, twenty-one years); and Herman Davis ('64, eighteen years), all of whom could have been head coaches somewhere else at various times in their careers. Each quietly took himself out of the running.

That left Kirk Jones. Two years older than Lara, Kirk Jones was the running backs coach and a Poly legend. The school's and the city's all-time single-season record holder for yards gained rushing, Jones had gone on to star at the University of Nevada–Las Vegas and had played professionally two years in brief stints with the Saints, the Patriots, and the Browns. Kirk was in his seventh year of coaching.

Lara had the longer and more impressive résumé: twelve years' coaching experience, defensive coordinator and linebacker coach. Jones had sentiment in his favor; he was a record holder and former team star, and his father, Ike, had been a Poly assistant in football and track. Lara wasn't a teacher at Poly, but a Los Angeles County parole officer who supervised forty-six student parolees from a campus office; Jones taught in Poly's Intensive Studies Program, working with students who were learning disabled. Finally, and for some most importantly, Lara was Hispanic, Jones was black.

For those with a memory that stretched back to the 1980s, an unpleasant but unavoidable whiff of déjà vu hung in the air. The situation had all the earmarks of another unspoken racial episode, as had happened with Jaso and Thomas Whiting. In 1984, Jim Barnett, the coach who had brought Poly out of the bad years and back to its accustomed prominence, announced that he was moving on. The assumption had been that Jaso would get the job, but nothing is ever simple at Poly. All it took was a little communications snafu, some hints of community turmoil, and the people upstairs decided to avoid making a decision between Jaso, who was white, and Whiting, who was black. The right colors to see in this, the school board and administration decided, would be green and gold, Poly colors—because that's what Jaso and Whiting, working together, would symbolize. And it couldn't have started out better. In 1985 the Jackrabbits won it all, thanks to the presence of three future NFL Rookies of the Year: Mark Carrier, Willie McGinest, and Leonard Russell.

Then eight years of almost great football followed, in which Poly never got past the semifinals. When Whiting announced he was taking a coaching job up north, at a school named Pittsburg, everybody wished him well, though some breathed a sigh of relief. The first year after Whiting left, Jaso reinstalled the Barnett Wing-T offense, which Whiting had junked, and took the Jackrabbits past the semifinals. Every year for the last five years Poly has made the finals. As for Whiting, he'd done okay at Pittsburg, but could never get past this one team . . . De La Salle. So when his son Brandon, a Poly grad, was drafted out of Cal Berkeley by the Eagles, Whiting got out of coaching and followed him to Philadelphia.

One thing was for sure: the question of who would coach the Jackrabbits in the national championship game wasn't going to be settled without intense debate. If any good news was to come out of the situation, it was that Poly people have become much more practiced at dealing with racial issues since the 1970s. In fact, working through racial problems is the school's special mission; that's why they send the tenth-graders to Poly North, the camp in the mountains, to get to know each other and to learn how not to give in to anger, stereotyping, paranoia, disrespect. Still, although Poly's coprincipal experiment—Shawn Ashley is white, Mel Collins black—had been wildly successful, it's safe to say nobody was looking forward to another cocoach situation.

Perhaps being a parole officer made Raul Lara more organized, more formal. His defense crushed opponents in the regular season and carried the Jackrabbits in the play-offs. Jones was "a little rough, yet gentle when you got to know him," as one coach put it. He was dedicated to teaching and coaching. His expertise in working with the running backs, in a program known for its great ones, put him at the center of Poly's identity.

Yet although some people hinted that Lara was more qualified, nobody was saying it out loud. In American sports the words *qualified* and *unqualified* have an unfortunate legacy: they are the code words black head-coach candidates hear as they're shown the door, in colleges, in the pros, the NFL, the NBA, and most notoriously in baseball. Ever since Dodger executive Al Campanis was quoted that black people "may not have some of the necessities to be, let's say, a field manager, or perhaps a general manager," there has been an excruciating behind-the-scenes struggle in American sports to give black coaches their place at the table. The tension has filtered down to the high schools and even to Pop Warner.

For the black community in Long Beach the issues of "qualities"or "necessities" had such a long and infuriating history that it was a wonder things stayed as cool as they did at Poly. Latent racism persisted for years, down at the shipyard, over at the McDonnell Douglas aircraft plant, in the longshoremen's union at the port, in the big city oil leases—as if someone had hung up a sign that read: No Blacks Need Apply.

In athletics the debate centered on who would play quarterback. At Poly every year, three or four quarterbacks would arrive from the feeder junior high schools. Almost every time, the black Stephens, Hoover, or Roosevelt Junior High quarterback would end up behind the white Bixby Knolls quarterback from Hughes Junior High. Then the coach would take you aside, if you were black, and tell you to play wide receiver or defensive back.

Nationally, the controversy came to a bitter head in the sixties and seventies, at all levels of play. *Sports Illustrated* was good for at least an article a year on the subject. The early arguments were nothing more than dressed-up racism: whites stand taller in the pocket, blacks get happy feet; whites keep their cool, blacks get excited.

The same canards were repeated, in college, to Gene Washington, the best quarterback to come out of Poly and Long Beach—at least, until Chris Lewis. Washington was the first black star QB at Poly, set all the records, and nobody doubted his "qualifications." Yet as soon as he went to Stanford in 1965, they put him at wide receiver. It was poetic justice that Lewis ended up quarterbacking Stanford for much of 2000.

Nonetheless, progress came to Poly a decade earlier than it came to the rest of the country. Starting in 1969, Poly had a string of black quarterbacks; nowadays it's a nonissue. However, that doesn't mean that parents and players aren't still suspicious when the suggestion is made, Why don't you switch to wide receiver? To defensive back?

It happened to Marcedes Lewis, in ninth grade. Merle Cole III, Poly's receiver coach and son of Merle II, took Marcedes aside and said, "Mar, you may have a chance to play quarterback on Saturday, but if you switch to tight end, I guarantee you have a chance to play on Sunday." Translation: Marcedes might make it to the college level, where the games are on Saturday, as a quarterback, but if he wanted to play on Sunday, that is, as a professional, he had to make a switch. Not later, but now.

Marcedes didn't like hearing it, but he couldn't complain about the source. Some advice sounds different when it's a black man telling you. At Poly, this is the "taking it to another level" conversation. Poly coaches, alumni, and sideline griots accept that life is layered with challenges that grow progressively more difficult, so it is best to prepare for the next level before you get there. In football, the focus begins in the Pop Warner years, where excellence is expected by seventh and eighth grade, because the coaches are watching for the players they will slot into next year's freshman team. Freshman year itself is an audition for the next level: varsity. Varsity at Poly, it is firmly believed, is one level higher than regular high school. By senior year, players should be working and thinking at college level.

The idea of "the next level" is part of the football philosophy at Poly; it's about staying calm, workmanlike, unflustered, no matter what happens. It's Jaso going for the tie against Mater Dei, Brandon Brooks with forty-eight seconds to go in the Loyola game—and Marcedes swallowing hard and accepting that he will be playing tight end. Making hard decisions calmly takes you to the next level.

Lara and Jones handled their situation in true Poly fashion. When Jaso's resignation was finalized, and Lara's interim appointment announced, Lara went to Jones's office to talk things over. They shook hands, said, "May the best man win, but in the meantime, let's make this season the best we can," and got to work planning spring practices.

Unfortunately it wasn't going to be that simple. Out in the community, Kirk Jones was quickly elevated into a standard-bearer for a cause—to be Poly's first black head coach. Lara looked like the front-runner, but there were rumors of complications. His immediate supervisors at the L.A. County Department of Probation seemed to think he couldn't be both head coach and Poly's in-house parole officer.

Spring practice got under way, and the players didn't know what to make of it all. Jaso had left them on the eve of the greatest game; they had a temporary head coach and an assistant coach some said would be the new head coach. But they didn't give in to distraction, they kept their cool; as usual, they took it to the next level. It was pointed out that it was something of a Poly tradition for the departing coach to leave his successor a fully stacked deck, that Barnett had done the same thing for Jaso and Whiting. It made the kids feel better; maybe these adults had some kind of plan, after all.

Not so the community. The suspense, and the rumors, mounted. But there's always gossip about Poly, no matter what the subject, so it wasn't such a big deal. It didn't seem divisive—yet.

Kirk Jones had begun having weight problems while a player at UNLV. A foot injury had healed slowly, and off his feet he'd ballooned to more than two hundred pounds, and not enough of it muscle. The extra weight made him slower, so he dieted and worked himself down again, then went on to success at UNLV and a brief NFL career.

Later, married and a father of three sons, teaching and coaching at Poly, Jones learned he had acute pericarditis, an inflammation of the heart lining. Though friends knew of his condition, Jones was so lively it was hard to believe that this strong, big, hearty athlete lived with constant insecurity. As the years went by, Jones appeared to most people as healthy as ever, except for an occasional flu. A few of the older coaches, who were dealing with health issues themselves, did caution him about monitoring his illness and watching his diet, particularly after his weight soared to 240 pounds.

The news hit Poly on Monday, two days before school let out for summer vacation. At 5:15 P.M. on Saturday, June 9, Jones had suffered a massive heart attack and died at his home. As word swept the campus, the coprincipals, administrators and teachers went to groups and classes offering counseling. "Kirk was a role model, a big brother to many of these kids," said Mel Collins. "He taught special ed, and he coached the stars. He had an eighty-year-old heart in a thirty-six-year-old body, and that's what killed him."

The shock devastated the team, the school itself went into a schizoid state of mourning as, while preparing to celebrate graduation, grief washed over the community.

Players, friends, and coaches filled the early Friday afternoon service. All talk of a game evaporated, but football was present, as the theme of Kirk Jones's life, and his legacy. Chuckie Miller, Jones's lifelong friend and former teammate, said to a reporter, "Kirk was the perfect guy for the job because of his Poly roots and because he's such a respected figure in the community. And now he's gone, and we'll never know what would have happened."

Ten

SOUR RHUBARB

There are four players whose height and size make them stand out, even amidst Poly's herd of young giants. One, with the craggy face of a black Caesar, is 6'7", 300-pound offensive tackle Winston Justice. A second is Marcedes Lewis, the 6'7" tight end. The third, Junior Lemauu, plays defensive end at 6'5", 245 pounds. He's going shirtless today, hair lashed in a two-foot club that emerges from under his helmet like a stegosaurus tail, torso a funnel of muscles and sinews, fingers flexing in black gloves— looking as if he had just jumped off the cover of a Doc Savage pulp fiction.

The fourth is the largest of them all. "A grizzly," Herman Davis says. "Just be thankful Manuel is ours." Manuel Wright, 6'7", 315 pounds, saunters off the field for a drink.

Manuel has just made headlines across the country. At a recent photo shoot for *Student Sports Magazine*, which was putting a selection of top Jackrabbit athletes on its cover, Manuel announced that he could be turning pro out of high school. His remarks coincided with the NFL draft as well as a contentious debate over the number of high school basketball players who were skipping college in favor of the NBA. As Manuel intended, he drew a lot of attention—no one had imagined that the problem would reach football for another ten years, if ever. For the sports media, Manuel provided a nice week of gee-whiz stories on the death of education and the ill effects of black teen millionaires as role models.

I'd asked Jerry Jaso about the likelihood of Manuel, or any high school player, ever "declaring," as the intention to turn pro is known. After stressing his affection for Manuel and pointing out that he was, after all, still just a big kid, Jaso said, "There's no truth to it. Kids have a lot of growing to do in football. It would be a mistake physically, emotionally, too. A seventeen-year-old who went to training camp in pro football would get pretty beat up.

"Basketball, you can hop into it and just compete. Football, the skill and the physical aspects are dominant. Basketball is more free-flowing; football has a great deal more structure and strategic planning and reading of defenses. Seventeen- and eighteen-year-olds need the four years of college, the four more years of lifting weights, to get ready for the NFL.

"In fact, if you look at it, football is almost the only sport where age is an advantage. NFL quarterbacks come into their prime at twenty-eight, twenty-nine years." At other positions players mature earlier, "but there's still a lot of technique involved."

Leaving the field for the secure parking lot on Jackrabbit Way, I overhear Winston Justice ask a player if he has a car today. I offer Winston a ride, and he accepts. As we walk slowly into the lot, I try to make conversation. Winston is not chatty.

Turns out that he lives in Bixby Knolls, my old neighborhood, and he went to Hughes Junior High, where I went. Winston lives on Thirty-seventh Street, off Bixby, right around the corner from my old best friend Dell. I ask him, "Hey, do the outdoor hoops at

Hughes still have those steel nets on the basketball courts?" For the first time, Winston speaks a complete sentence: "I love the slinky sound those make when you hit a jumper."

As we approach the car, I ask Winston if he wants to grab a bite to eat. "You mean do an interview?" he asks. Sure, I say. "I already did an interview, with the *Press-Telegram*," he says. His deadpan manner, or act, whichever it is, is getting to me and I throw him a curve: "You can do more than one, you know."

Cruising with Winston, I muse on the ironies of place and race, the poetic justice of a black family living in the old neighborhood. I wonder if Winston has any idea that in the early sixties Bixby Knolls and Cal Heights felt like some frontier outpost in which the beleaguered white race was making a last stand. During the '65 Watts riots I'd seen neighbors handing out rifles and shotguns. The panicky, gruesome mood had continued when black students started arriving in greater numbers at Hughes, their parents having found apartments on the borderlines of the district. One day when I was fourteen, it finally happened: a black family, the Terrys, moved in. A few days later, while I was walking to Hughes, the news came gusting like fallen sycamore leaves up the sidewalks, swirling from group to group: somebody had burned a cross on the Terrys' lawn. We all detoured to see.

I take Winston to Jongewaard's Bake n' Broil. The hostess leads us past empty tables in the front section and through the kitchen to an empty back room. In a moment a waiter materializes—not one of the sweet older women or perky young blondes. He's about 6'5", with a *Happy Days* comb-back and ducktail. Of course, I think: they've put their biggest guy on my biggest guy. But it's no contest, because my guy is huge.

Still, I have realized the subliminal reason why I chose Jongewaard's: pie. Long Beach is a pie town; must be those Iowa roots. Fresh strawberry and peach pies, mile-high meringue pies, banana cream pies, pop up in my mind whenever I come home. So I order pie, the whole time telling Winston about Long Beach being the old "capital of Iowa," how my grandparents took me to the city's Iowa Day Picnic once and entered me in a pie-eating contest. Of all the kids, only I was given sour rhubarb: the judges had figured out that we weren't from the old stock.

Winston looks at his menu, up at me. "I've never eaten pie," he says. "I don't like sweet things." He orders a Denver omelet and a glass of water.

We eat and talk—about Hughes, the neighborhood, what his plans are. His manners are formal; the Justices are Jehovah's Witnesses. I wonder if he had the door shut in his face at our house when he was small.

In our conversation I mention the large sums of money available these days for a left or blind-side offensive tackle in the pros. He nods and brings up a recent article in the *Los Angeles Times*, which mentioned a number in the $15-million range. This is one schoolkid who has done his homework.

Later, after dropping Winston at his house, I realize that he may be able to buy the entire street one day, if he should want to.

Eleven

PRECIOUS BLOOD

Steep hills hem in the San Francisco Bay to the east. Outside these natural city walls, Concord and its surrounding towns have always waited—for the gold seekers of 1849, for the railroad, and today for the daily commuter, who, as in some fairy tale, must travel through a long, dark passageway, the Caldecott Tunnel. Cut in 1924, the tunnel has never been equal to the volume of traffic that squeezes through its rock-ribbed neck—today's rush hour expels a dense, concentrated stream of cars in both directions.

My head is still spinning, my heart fluttering, when a Concord exit flashes into view a few miles later. I'm ejected from the freeway's millrace of cars onto an eight-lane surface avenue, where traffic is just as urgent. My eyes scan desperately for some sort of landmark; the center divider planters brim with bright blue-and-white flowers, and precisely spaced trees. No billboards, no stores along the roadside, no signs. The streets solidly residential. Then a corner with two gas stations appears, then more houses for another mile, then the brief cove of a shopping center, and then the street I've been warned about, Winton Drive. I turn into a football-field-sized parking lot.

The school is low and modern, trim red brick faced with beige stucco. With no spires, bell towers, domes, crosses, statues of the Virgin Mary, no logos or stencils of mascots, it's not obviously Catholic, or even educational.

I am met by Brother Christopher Brady, the principal of De La Salle, who is my age, forty-nine, and beginning his second year at the school. "This school was set up originally to train brothers," he mused in our first telephone conversation. "It's what we now do in football, I suppose."

Brother Chris admits that he does like football. His nephew, Tom, was a quarterback at nearby Serra High and has made it to the pros, as a backup for the New England Patriots. But Brother Chris is also frank about the extra burdens The Streak has imposed on the school. "Yes, it's great publicity; yes, it's something we take great pride in. But we are an institution for the education, intellectual and spiritual, of young men. And I do worry that people don't see us as more than a football school—which we most certainly aren't."

Brother Chris tells a story. "The year the high school first opened, 1965, the school anticipated a large enrollment from the area's Catholic elementary school, which was called Most Precious Blood Elementary. So the time came, the eighth-graders took entrance exams, they were marked and sent off and then never arrived. We couldn't find them. And we're worried because no exams, no students. Well, lo and behold, it turns out that someone at the post office saw that 'Most Precious Blood' on the address and put them in the refrigerator. On ice!"

A number of points are to be made with the story, besides the humor. One is that De La Salle is self-sustaining; it receives no financial assistance from the Catholic Church; the 1,050 students are enrolled at a tuition of $7,000 a year—steep for California, indeed for anywhere, but necessary. A second point is that the outside world typically misunderstands or overreacts to the rituals and nomenclature of Catholicism; a post office's innocent misreading of the Most Precious Blood address label, for example. The third point is that De La Salle actually does take the Most Precious part seriously, even if Brother Chris shows he can laugh about it, too. "The children are our ministry," he says.

In 2000 there were 450 applications for 240 places at De La Salle. "Catholic families in this area don't have a lot of options," Brother Chris says. "It's very difficult to say no. But we've reached our limit in terms of space." The school does have some non-Catholic students, both to keep its mission to serve the poor, and also to maintain diversity. Currently about 2 percent of the student body is from below the poverty level in income; the school's goal, according to assistant principal and former dean of admissions Rudy Schulze, is to match the surrounding community, which is about 5 percent. Racially the student population breaks down to 69 percent Caucasian, 10 percent Hispanic, 9 percent Filipino, 6 percent Native American or other, 3 percent other Asian, and 3 percent African-American.

The school offers a full menu of advanced placement and honors courses and involves students in an active campus ministry, with extensive required social service commitments, such as working at a soup kitchen in San Francisco's Tenderloin District. For companionship of the opposite sex, the boys need look no farther than across the street at Carondelet High School.

De La Salle's academic reputation contributes to the admissions pressure. With a mean SAT score of 549 Verbal and 577 Math, compared to a statewide mean of 497 Verbal and 518 Math, the school's seniors do better than all but those in California's wealthiest school districts. Perhaps more importantly, graduates are inspired to move on: "We don't call ourselves a college preparatory school, but ninety-seven to ninety-eight percent of our graduates go off to college," says Brother Chris. In 2000, almost three-quarters of the class enrolled in a four-year college or university, while 26 percent signed up for a junior college. (This record is particularly noteworthy in a time when more women than men take the SAT, attend college, and graduate—123 degrees for every 100 awarded to men.)

Like Catholic schools all over the country, De La Salle is esteemed for the discipline and values it teaches young men. But the school does not boast of doing the job single-handedly. Part of a student's admission hinges on his parents' commitment to the school, which is not shy about requiring parents to take an active role—attending PTA meetings and volunteering. Brother Chris explains that parents are also expected "to be operating from the same core values that we have. Parents have to agree; they have to say yes. That's a big point; that we're all marching to the same drummer."

The school is bright and open, with a sunken inner courtyard set up for summer basketball camp. Behind the gym an Olympic-sized pool shimmers with thrashing and splashing. On the other side of a chain-link fence is a lush green football field with a modest but gleaming set of aluminum bleachers, screened by trees, a hedge, and a fence from the steady drone of eight-lane Treat Boulevard. To the right of the formal football field is the practice field, another well-kept expanse of green, which includes, at the far end, the baseball diamond.

Coming straight from Poly High, I find the contrasts startling. There is no barbed wire at De La Salle, no seventy-year-old scuffed concrete walls, no rutted and torn field, no hovering police helicopter every afternoon when school lets out—as there is at Poly.

The De La Salle team is on the practice field, in shorts and shirts; helmets are generally worn for touch-tackle scrimmages and passing-league games. Within two minutes of the 3:15 P.M. start, players are stretching and putting on shoes.

I am watching alone, which feels a bit awkward. At Poly, the sidelines are crowded with bystanders, parents, uncles and aunts, former teammates, even the media—half of them on a cell phone at any given time. At De La Salle, an unofficial rule keeps everyone off the field except for the occasional visiting graduate or member of the media. The three or four parents and die-hard fans who come to watch do so by climbing to the top of the stands and peering over the back. Today's visiting graduate, Shaun, the athletic director and defensive coordinator Terry Eidson's nephew, has come to work out—and to work out his baby brother, Ryan, aka Flea. All afternoon Shaun, who plays at Brown, exhorts the team both verbally and by example, putting the team through the drills as if The Streak depended on it.

In less than five minutes the team has formed up in ranks and is running, setting, firing out, turning in unison, sprinting to a chalk line and, with one hand on the ground for balance, spinning around, then sprinting back.

Terry Eidson shows up, with his two daughters, six-year-old Kayleigh and Hannah, who is three. The girls begin running the blue plastic rope ladders laid out on the ground, showing signs of having absorbed the proper techniques. A group comes over and cheers them on, then takes to the ladders themselves. Every third trip the order and angle of their foot placement changes, sideways, backward, crossovers.

Across the field, another group is sprinting wearing blue drogue chutes puffed out behind. I ask Mike Blasquez, the strength and conditioning coach, if the mini parachutes are for resistance training. "No, there's a good crosswind today, and I'm having the running backs wear them to get used to being knocked off balance."

Now giant plastic hoops are laid on the ground, end to end, and pairs of players race each other around and around, doing figure eights against a stopwatch held by Eidson or Blasquez, who watch intently. Derek Landri attacks the ovals, hurling his 280-pound frame around them like a Mack truck handling a grand prix course.

For a brief spell I have company, a senior, Pedro Cabrera, sidelined by turf toe, or bruised metatarsal phalangeal joint. He excuses himself—he's going to assist in calling cadences for the drills; nobody is ever idle, not even the injured.

The backs and receivers begin running plays. Matt Gutierrez, who's been at the head of every drill all day, pushing himself as hard as Landri, completes every play with a ten-yard sprint. Watching him take the snap and make a handoff, I do a double take. Instead of using a football, they're handling heavy red-and-white bowling pins. It is explained: we have entered the summer period when, according to CIF rules, no footballs are allowed on school grounds. Only the kicker, who must bring and handle his own ball, is exempted. Nothing, however, forbids bowling pins.

The receivers break up and head for the track oval, where they will run sprints and quarter miles, for their straight-line speed. The backs and linemen will pull sleds. The kicker, James Bloomsburg, introduces himself and asks if I will hold while he kicks field goals. "I can't ask the other guys because of the rules," he explains. "I usually just hope someone from the media shows up." I'm not sure if he's joking.

After a water break the players pull out truck tires and fifty-pound iron disks from weight sets and rig them to harnesses. Strapped in, they sprint from line to line, in thirty-, twenty-, and ten-yard increments; they look like plow horses. Derek Landri drags his plow over to the equipment maven, Chris Rodriguez, and asks him to add another weight. Using an electric drill that hangs from his crowded tool belt, Rodriguez ups Landri's load by half. Soon Landri is charging the lines, knees and fists pumping, shoulders and hips rock-steady, towing his pile.

Then it's back to the House of Pain, where Mike Blasquez puts the team through their paces. Each player carries his chart and knows what to do, swiftly rotating from weight station to weight station. Mike blows a whistle every sixty or ninety seconds. When players are off the machines or weight racks, they step out into the open passageway between the buildings and throw eighteen-pound medicine balls to each other.

I ask one player how they manage to gain weight with all the incessant exercise. "When I go home, all I do is eat until I pass out," he says. "And I'm lucky, my metabolism isn't that fast. Some of the guys, when they go to bed tonight, will set their alarms for two A.M. in order to wake up and drink a protein shake before going back to sleep."

It's twilight when strength and conditioning is over. As I'm leaving, I ask Terry Eidson where Bob Ladouceur is. "Vacationing in Lake Tahoe," he replies. "This is it for him, his one week of the summer to be with his family."

The next day brings word that De La Salle's second preseason opponent, Calvary Baptist, has canceled. The hole in the schedule produces exasperation in the coaching staff. It represents a loss of revenue—"There would have been thousands in the stands," points out Eidson—but even more the opportunity to tune up in a real game, instead of against one's own teammates.

After four hours of field workout and weight workout, the team splits up. Backs and receivers head for a passing-league game at Diablo Valley Junior College, about fifteen minutes away. These are controlled scrimmages with officials and a clock, but the emphasis is on teaching, not winning—at least for De La

Salle. Since an offensive player is down when a defender tugs off one of two nylon flags worn on a Velcro belt, the contact is supposed to be light and bracing—at least for De La Salle. Other teams are known to take full-contact shots at Spartan receivers, going after a measure of preemptive revenge for what will happen to them in the regular season.

At one point after De La Salle completes a pass, Eidson calls it back, much to the official's surprise. "We were in an illegal formation, ref," Eidson says. The official looks miffed, but Eidson implores, "Coach, they've got to learn." It's a great teaching moment, but also a nice bit of gamesmanship: De La Salle is so confident that they call penalties on themselves.

The forty-eight-minute session is about to end, De La Salle behind, when Flea Eidson takes a deep pass from Matt Gutierrez, outruns two men, and scores with seven seconds left.

Everything I saw on the field looked pretty good. Then I sit in on the postgame assessment given by Ladouceur, just back from vacation; Eidson; and their core staff: quarterback and offensive assistant Mark Panella, a mortgage banker and '85 graduate; line assistant (and dean) Joe Aliotti, a Pittsburg graduate; linebacker assistant Nate Geldermann, class of '95 and one of a legendary set of twins who played for the school; and Terrell Ward, first-year defensive backs coach, who had a short NFL career. The kids get what amounts to a full-scale verbal flogging.

"You receivers," Ladouceur says, "you've got to make catches. If you don't make them, you're not going to get these opportunities again."

Terry Eidson says to all the wide receivers, "If you catch a pass against your chest instead of away from your body, with your fingers, you will do ten push-ups. If you drop a pass that you tried to catch against your chest, you will do twenty."

To a defensive back, he says, "You're not taking any chances.

You're getting burned for not taking any chances. At least risk something if you're going to get burned.

"I'm playing starters the rest of the way," Eidson decides. "I've worked a lot of you all summer long, and we've only got two games to play. If you've got any questions about the depth chart, please come and see me. That's the way it is: fifty guys on the team, eleven on the field. I'll tell you right now, I know who's in the secondary. It's extremely unclear who's at linebacker, extremely unclear who's at receiver. The situation for our number three, four, and five receivers is completely muddled. Those spots were there for the taking, but no one stepped up. You guys—I'll say this to your faces—blew your opportunity." Flea sits right in front of his uncle, head stiff, eyes straight ahead.

Eidson softens. "This wasn't a good day, but I know you had a workout before."

"No, no, no," interrupts Ladouceur, his voice rising. "What I saw out on the field was not a difficult workout—short stations, quick whistles. That was like a Week One summer workout to me. Not only that, it was about eighty degrees out there, not hot. Last year at this time it was one hundred and five. We got crappy throws today from the quarterback position. Nobody was hit in stride, everybody had to wait for the ball." Pause. "What a disappointment." Long pause. "Balls were late. Three of them to the wrong guy, too."

Ladouceur excoriates the defensive backs for their coverage: "You were *horrible;* they *murdered* all of you underneath," and then he sums up, to the whole team: "You didn't play like Spartans. If I had known this would have happened here tonight, I wouldn't have brought you. You're not that good, you're not that talented. I saw nothing. Nothing to build on. What was good? Who was good?"

The team's faces are crushed; the diatribe is flattening, yet

Ladouceur is not deaf to how dark he sounds: "I'm not *trying* to be an ass about this. Refresh my memory."

A murmur up front. "I thought you guys did well all summer," Ladouceur says. "It just didn't look like it today. I'm not saying all hope is lost. But you sure didn't do it today.

"Here is what's going to be the battle cry this year: 'If you're going to lose a game, if you're going to lose The Streak—lose it to a team that deserves it.'

"If you don't—" Ladouceur stops himself. He's calm, conversational. "Then you'll really be disappointed in yourselves. You'll want that moment back. You know, you guys that played last year, you know what I'm talking about. If in the Mater Dei game we had come out on the wrong end of that, that would've been okay."

Andy Briner is hurt. He shows up late for drills with one pant leg stuffed full of ice. "Groin pull," someone groans. Out on the green of the practice field a brilliant day turns dark. Andy's bright smile seems a little brittle, but he's not conceding anything yet. Still, this is a blow to the team and to him.

Just last summer Andy was a strong but undersized junior; now the House of Pain's training and Andy's physiological and mental assets have turned him into a wolverine: fast, explosive, unstoppable. He brought down the quarterback, the dreaded "sack," an impressive 17 ½ times. Sacks turn games around, kill drives, turn quarterbacks gun-shy, push back field goal attempts from sure-thing to just-maybe.

Earlier this summer Andy went to the Student Sports MLO All-American Strength combine, one of many sponsored "combines"—in this case, a joint effort by a college recruiting service/magazine/Web site and a nutritional supplement company—where high school players who want their abilities entered into a national database are tested in the forty-yard dash, vertical leap, and bench press, for both weight and repetitions. Hundreds of prospects take part in these combines, which play a large part in the offering of college scholarships. Derek Landri also participated and ranked sixth among linemen nationwide, which advanced his standing as a top prospect.

Andy, however, was the shock of the combine. According to a formula ranking everyone—linebackers, running backs, linemen, defensive backs—according to relative strength, Andy placed fourth. Everyone knew Andy was strong—he had broken the school record for the bench press at 407 pounds—but *fourth strongest in the nation* was over the top. And yet the distinction didn't do all that much for Andy's college prospects. To the size-obsessed recruiters, Andy was still a tweener, in the wrong physical mold for defensive end, the position at which he excelled. Even though he was up to 5'11", 232 pounds, he needed another three to five inches.

The coaches had been willing to try Andy at linebacker, to showcase him to recruiters. But a groin pull prevents lateral motion, and linebackers are constantly shuttling from sideline to sideline, shedding blockers as they go. So Andy will stay a defensive end for now. He goes off for treatment, still smiling, giving a shrug to his teammates' comments. If he's hurting over losing a chance to give recruiters an opportunity to see what he can do, he's not going to show it.

Matt Gutierrez is also missing from practice, but for a positive reason. He's been invited to the Elite 11 Camp, another Student Sports–sponsored summer session, this one for quarterbacks. Located in the sunny Orange County resort community of San Juan Capistrano, the Elite 11 was conceived and is directed by high school coach Bob Johnson, whose son Rob, a QB with the Buffalo Bills and Tampa Bay Buccaneers, is still his camp's top graduate. The Elite 11 is all about instruction, visibility, and contacts: a velvet-rope-encircled oasis for the most exclusive and worshiped position in the game. The players work out with celebrity pro visitors and get a taste of life at the next level. Johnson gets to build his network and, some critics have alleged, advertise his high school team to any would-be Joe Montanas and Jerry Rices who may be inclined to transfer.

It's a nice gig for Matt, and it's there that he has a funny run-in with one of the top receivers brought in to catch passes for the Elite. The guy is huge, with a wide receiver's hands and body control popped into a tight end's frame. Marcedes Lewis comes over and introduces himself. Who knows but they might end up on the same team together at some point in the future? "Hey, see you in October," Matt says.

Besides Concord, some major-program towns are represented at the camp: Massillon, Ohio; West Allegheny, Pennsylvania; Ben Davis of Indianapolis. Seven of the quarterbacks are 6'3" or taller; none is shorter than 6'0".

Poly's Brandon Brooks, listed at 5'11", rumored to be 5'10" or even a tad shorter, is among the many uninvited.

Other players get away on family vacations and visit college campuses. The NCAA allows prospects up to five expenses-paid college visits, and those on the hot list of recruiters, such as Matt and Derek, could create for themselves a fine summer social calendar if they wanted to. Matt and Derek don't. Those with letters of interest but no firm offers often go to camps at the schools of their choice, hoping to get noticed.

The unrecruited, such as kicker James Bloomsburg, are on their own.

Bloomsburg is proactive. Since transferring to De La Salle for his junior year, he's been on a systematic campaign to net himself a four-year ride to a top college. Not a lot of kickers are recruited, a handful at most every year, but Bloomsburg has marketed himself assiduously by going to camps and campuses for three-day kicking clinics. This July week he's at Purdue.

It was James's field goal that gave De La Salle the winning margin against Mater Dei last year, and he also kicked a crucial field goal against Buchanan. His kickoffs often boom out of the opposing team's end zone, frustrating their attempts to get good field position. His punts soar, giving the gunners time to circle under them and tackle the punt returner before he can get started. All in all, James is quite a package, even if he has been a little inconsistent of late.

At Purdue he kicks well, but the head coach is off on a recruiting trip. The assistant is enthusiastic, but James had hoped for an offer on the spot—he might have accepted, too. A lot of players like to gather their offers, enjoy the attention, the evening ritual of phone calls from coaches who want to entice you, and recruiting services and reporters who want to interview you. James isn't that way. For one thing, he could go to a top college without football, given his mid-700 SATs and that his father is a software millionaire, already retired in his early fifties; he's almost the only dad who is a frequent visitor to practices.

But James has crafted a plan to go to the pros, and kicking for a Big 10 program or the equivalent is the next level. The path to the pros at every position is greatly assisted by a scholarship, because once schools have invested the money in you, they're inclined to train you, give you plenty of opportunity, and stick with you should you hit a slump. Without a scholarship, a kicker is particularly vulnerable, at the mercy of every soccer player who gets it into his head to try out.

Ladouceur speaks to the team before they take the field for the next passing-league game. "You guys lost your competitive edge last Tuesday. You're not attacking these guys, there's no confidence. I don't get it. It's very un-De La Salle-like. It's like a morgue." Pause. "A bunch of corpses." Longer pause. "Donkeys."

Matt's at the Elite 11, so Brian Callahan is at quarterback. Brian's job is to be ready, to take part in preparation and film study as if he's going to start, to role-play the opposing team's quarterback in practice to give the defense an idea of what to expect, and to come in once the Spartans have hung twenty-eight to thirty points on the other team. It must be a little frustrating, but you'd never know it from Brian's cheery manner.

The team gives up a touchdown on a long pass, which leaves the De La Salle coaches fuming at the play of the safeties. Eidson berates them: "This is *Monte Vista*. How fast do you think Poly is?" Pedro Cabrera and Flea alternate making some nice catches, and De La Salle scores twice.

After the game, when Ladouceur addresses the team, he says that while the first half was weak, the second half was better. The key lesson is about controlling tempo. "Once a game starts up, it's hard to recapture a feeling. Try to have it all straight in your head what you're going to bring to the game."

The next day at practice, Brown University safety Shaun Eidson is playing defensive back against his brother, Ryan the Flea. The two get off, bump, claw for position and footing; the defensive back trying to squeeze the receiver off his prescribed route. As a quarterback has at most 3.5 seconds in which to make a decision and throw the ball, it doesn't take much to confuse him; he's looking for a receiver either arriving in a prearranged spot or streaking along a seam in the defense. If the receiver is a yard or two off, the quarterback may not see him and abort the play or, worse, may throw to a vacant spot—possibly into the hands of a roving defensive back.

The brothers go at it again, hand-to-hand struggling, much to the delight of the other receivers and coaches. Shaun is bigger and burlier than Flea, but Flea gets free for a catch. But: "That's an eleven-yard route," says Uncle Terry, "and you only ran nine. No first down, ball turned over, Long Beach Poly's ball. *Receivers!* Find your area. You guys are always cutting your routes short. Get the first-down distance."

Next Shaun drives Flea out of bounds, forces him to break off his route. His grin is sunny as the day. "Embarrass the brother," he congratulates himself; he leaves tomorrow for Brown's summer football practices.

Another visitor, Steve Lilly, is greeted with friendly razzing. He was on the team that started The Streak and is now making a documentary about the team. "When does it end?" I ask. Lilly says he believes he wrapped it up last year, but the Poly game is giving him second thoughts. "I might do some this year, just a little," he says.

Ladouceur is following the conversation while directing drills. "It would be good to follow it to the logical conclusion," he says. We wait. Ladouceur lofts an eyebrow. "When the other shoe drops," he says, meaning De La Salle's losing.

Lilly watches him go, then turns. "In a sport that is basically considered barbaric, we've got a coach who basically turned it into an art form."

It's been a hard week, so what are the boys of De La Salle going to do over the weekend? Kick back by the pool, play video games, sleep, cruise the mall checking out the girls?

No. They're going camping together. Forty-some guys, who should by all rights be utterly exhausted, have organized, with little parental and no coaching input, a caravan and campout on the shores of Lake Berryessa. There's no adult supervision, but nobody worries. Beer drinking, dope smoking, getting girls into trouble and worse—these things are not an issue.

What *is* an issue at De La Salle is brotherhood. It is taken seriously, stressed at every stage of the school experience. With the football team, brotherhood comes first, before strength and conditioning, before practicing, even before winning. The team not only hikes and camps together on weekends, they undergo a purification ritual together before games. There is a team dinner, followed by a team meeting that turns into a confessional, and then, the next day, a chapel, its theme and content determined by the players. "That's the key to the whole thing," one De La Salle graduate says. "If you get yourself invited to one of those, by all means don't refuse. We're talking *powerful.*" Those from rival high schools have used other words for the process: cultlike, weird, creepy.

On my way out I stop by the athletic department, which consists of a cramped annex off a cramped foyer with a sprung sofa that adjoins an even more cramped, closet-sized athletic office. Bob Ladouceur is sitting in the annex playing solitaire on the computer. He looks up and smiles wryly.

Someone once asked Ladouceur what the secret was to this program that turns average, journeyman players into an unbeatable unit. His answer was simple: "Pain." Given everything I've seen, I suspect that he means existential pain as much as he does physical.

Twelve

FALL

In July, high schools all over the country take an enforced break from football. This is the dead period, instituted by state athletic commissions to spare the kids from the worst heat of summer—and because, otherwise, coaches would never stop holding practices, players would never rest, and parents might never see their sons.

The three weeks pass swiftly. Although prohibited from any contact with their coaches, many players simply get together and conduct their own workouts, running the same drills and following their strength and conditioning regimens. Even those who do leave town on family vacations spend hours running, doing crunches, and lifting weights if they can find a gym. Such dedication is considered necessary—if not mandatory—at good football programs, and not just because it helps ensure success in games; it also prepares the player for what awaits him on his return: two-a-day practices in mid-August, which at De La Salle is when the heat hits the eighties by midmorning, before climbing up to as high as 105 degrees.

The first week back is called hell week and fully lives up to its universal nickname. Hell week is when most of the freshmen and sophomores quit. It can be dangerous if proper hydration isn't strictly monitored: in this summer of 2001, seven high school players would die of heatstroke, along with an NFL lineman, Korey Stringer, and a college defensive back, Rashidi Wheeler.

Many parents—particularly mothers—are disturbed by hell week, and ask why anybody should submit to its ordeals. It would seem that there is no pat answer, except to note that teenagers have always sought, or accepted, trials of the body and spirit; where none exist, they will make up their own. As Bob Ladouceur has said on numerous occasions, "People underestimate the power of adolescents."

The antecedents of today's rituals are instructive, if not exactly comforting. In ancient Sparta, all boys were taken from their mothers at age seven, their days filled with exercise and athletics, tests of endurance and hardship. At eighteen they began combat training; at twenty, they took up residence in barracks (even if married, they could not live with their wives); only at thirty could they apply to election as full citizens. This harnessing of the male energies of society was exceeded by the Zulu of Shaka, who created age regiments of men who trained and fought together and were not allowed to marry until they were forty. Both Sparta and the Zulu were unequaled at war in their time and place. Compared to them, what these Spartans go through is a week at the beach.

Different teams and coaches around the country have varying attitudes about hell week, but no one would ever get rid of it. It's a crucible. "Football doesn't build character," reads one coach's T-shirt at De La Salle. "It reveals it."

But football also reveals the character of its communities. The program at De La Salle takes up so much time that one player's mother, after talking up the school's academics and Ladouceur's inspiration, wistfully added, "We're proud of the boys, but we never see them." If the boys are as much workaholics as their long-commuting, hardworking parents, then it's part trade-off, part sacrifice—maybe even part baby-sitting. When the four years are up, the football program returns mature, self-reliant, and self-aware young adults to their families (just in time for them to go to college).

Unlike at most other schools, including Poly, where parents lobby openly and loudly (and, more rarely, threateningly) for more playing time for their children, there is no parental input into the De La Salle program. Yet the fathers and mothers have nothing but praise for the result. "He's grown up faster," "He's so disciplined now," "It's just made him more mature," are typical comments from parents.

This apparently unanimous parent and student buy-in leaves the public expression of doubt to an unlikely source, the school's principal. "Part of me does think, well, we've got the record, we've gone so far beyond it that nobody's ever going to catch us," says Brother Christopher Brady, "so maybe it would be a good thing to lose. There are lessons in losing, too." He pauses, then smiles. "But then you can't exactly tell the kids to go out and lose, can you?"

On August 22, 2001, *USA Today* devotes the sports section to its season-opening poll. There's a big color photo of what everybody is calling the Poly Five—top-rated recruits Darnell Bing, Hershel Dennis, Marcedes Lewis, Winston Justice, and Manuel Wright.

Poly is rated number one. There's a separate, smaller story on the number two team, De La Salle. The first ever national championship game is in sight; as long as neither team loses beforehand, that is.

In the De La Salle locker room, the coaches pounce at the paper; they haven't seen it yet. A photo of the Poly Five, torn from a *Los Angeles Times* article of a month ago and prominently posted on the bulletin board outside the locker room, has been taken down. Nate Kenion, the senior running back and safety, studies the sports page thoroughly. "I wasn't really surprised," he says. "Poly has more name players returning, so in a way they deserve it. It does put us in a slightly better position, coming in as underdogs. Either way, no question about it, this is going to be some kind of game."

Over at Poly, the coprincipal Mel Collins has the paper in front of him, too. "It might be the kiss of death," he says of the number one ranking. "In a poll like that, until it's taken away from them, De La Salle should keep it."

Collins has spent the dead period on a horseback trip in the Canadian Rockies with his family. Now he's all business. "I'm negotiating with Fox Sports, and Student Sports wants to go in with Fox. They're talking about five thousand dollars. That's a lot, considering that Fox has never paid to televise any high school game before. I'm trying to talk them into maybe five thousand dollars more if the teams come in undefeated."

Collins is no neophyte in media dealings. Through Poly-graduate connections in Hollywood, the school has become a favored location for movies and TV shows. The outside has a gritty inner-city high school look, perfect for *Boyz N the Hood;* the 1930s art deco campus interior was used for *The Insider* and *American Pie.* Cameron Diaz has yet to play a scene in her old school, but you never know.

One De La Salle staffer confides that the school continually turns down sponsorship deals. "We could cover every inch of the field," with logos, he says, "but it's not who we are." The Spartans do have a shoe deal, which Poly does not; a player pays $45 and gets two pairs of shoes, one for practice, one for games, and a pair of gloves, a savings of perhaps $100 per capita. That's $5,000 right there. In the last few years the money available for sports promotions in high schools has risen sharply. "The money in protein shakes and supplements is huge," he says. "The pressure on high school sports is warping it. High school is the last pure place, but it's eroding fast, except for football."

Similar comments have come from media, administrators, and coaches all over the country. The money and influence of basketball shoe manufacturers, supplement and power-drink companies, and athletic recruitment services, which sell student-athletes a chance to be listed on a college clearinghouse Web site, is pervasive. They sponsor events, games, combines, and all-star games. The corruption in high school is greatest in basketball, where coaches at some championship schools are reportedly paid serious money to steer a top prospect to a college or, now that high school kids are leaping into the draft, to an agent. The basketball shoe money in college, where coaches accept six-figure fees to guarantee their amateur student-athletes are properly shod, is where the real action is, though.

Why is football staying pure? "Nobody walks around in football cleats at the mall," one insider says. "The right basketball shoe might sell one hundred million pairs—and have you seen some of those prices?"

From the looks of their hardened faces, all traces of teen baby fat melted away, arms and calves taut, these Spartans have been burning their candles at both ends.

A pair of receivers wrestles a heavy device on a blue tripod, consisting of two tan wheels set at angles to each other, a black wheel, and an electric motor. It's a ball gun—"JUGS, THE FOOT-BALL MACHINE" is written on its flanks—bought by receiver Chris Wilhemy's father and donated to the team. It starts up with a whirr; Terry Eidson places a ball in a slot, adjusts speed and angle, and fires it. Zoooooommm—ouch! A receiver shakes off the sting. A line forms, and Jugs starts spitting footballs, perfect spirals, right on target, wherever Eidson wants to put them.

Andy Briner sprawls on the grass, slowly putting on his pads. He gets a sour look and says, "Still not getting better." All he can do is rest, he says, though this is a relative term. He was on the exercise bike earlier and is now out on the practice field. "They won't let me play linebacker, only on the line," he says, frustration palpable. "Coach is talking about flying me to Canada for some treatment that's still unapproved in the U.S.—some kind of ultrasound." He smiles faintly. The fourth-strongest player in the country is no doubt thinking of scholarship offers receding in the distance.

For the duration of practice, six to eight stations work out simultaneously around the field, a mini-character-drama unfolding at each one. Football exposes you, Ladouceur likes to say. Flaws in technique, thinking, aggressiveness, are targeted and worked on. After a tightly scripted hour, practice culminates in a full team run-through, offense versus defense, with each side taking turns mimicking the sets they will see against opponents.

Practice is ending; it's time for announcements. "As of today," Ladouceur says, "summer is over." He pauses to let that sink in. "As far as energy goes, you did not look good at all. We'll start over tomorrow, same drills as today. I'm looking for an inside backer, a tight end, a wideout. If you want to play this year, it's time to step up. Summer's over. Don't be going to bed at twelve-thirty, watching movies and all that. Get your clocks set."

As the players leave the field, a passing car roars by on the other side of the foliage-covered fence. A hoarse voice shouts, "Fuck De La Salle!" Ryan the Flea laughs. "They always do that," he says.

Mike Shuman, a former San Francisco 49er turned Channel 7 sportscaster, talks to Bob Ladouceur about the rankings. "You're defending national champion and not even number one in your state," teases Shuman. "How does that feel?"

Ladouceur sighs. "We try to make it as much fun as possible.

We're gonna raise the bar for the kids, see how they respond. Just as you would in history, math, English—you don't want to make it easier."

Shuman tries again to get a rise out of Ladouceur. "They're all trash-talking—Buchanan, Mater Dei, and Poly. They say you're going down."

Ladouceur laughs. "Maybe they're right. I've already prepared the kids about losing. If we lose to one of these teams this year, we'll be losing to one of the best teams in the country. That's all we can ask for."

At the end of the last practice before school begins, Ladouceur makes an announcement: "When school starts, you come to school prepared. With your books, your notebooks, your pens, paper, calculators. Show up with it. Don't say, well, it was the first day of school, I didn't know we'd do anything. That's a horseshit excuse. Make up your mind now, you're going to be a student." He pauses.

"I *know* teachers are going to give you homework tomorrow." A longer pause. "As they used to say in Communist Russia, 'The social life is dead.' That's true here."

The players give disbelieving laughs, shakes of the head: What is it with these coaches?

After practice there's an evening freshman orientation. A group of upperclassmen's parents welcome the newcomers. One of the veteran parents says to another, "I hear we have ninety-eight new kids. At seven thousand eight hundred dollars each, *that's* football."

The next morning, the first day of school, finds Brother Chris, tall and sandy-haired, in the middle of the street, wearing his black rabat, directing streams of traffic into the lot with gallant sweeps of his arms like a toreador, the folds of his black cape swirling about him.

First game is in a week.

Thirteen

MINORITY RULES

Back in Long Beach, Poly has also been sweating out its two-a-days—and with the national championship game in sight, the Jackrabbits, like the Spartans, are worried about the possibility of a letdown beforehand. De La Salle faces a tough opening game against Buchanan, then two weeks off caused by Calvary Baptist's cancellation and a bye week, followed by Mater Dei, and St. Francis, another Northern California parochial school. Poly faces Westchester, a team that always has speedy receivers; Banning, the defending L.A. City champion, which resembles Poly in its size and power; Narbonne, smaller than Banning but a team that runs a tricky option offense; and Fontana, a frequent Southern Section titlist and the number one–ranked team in the 1987 year-end poll.

Coach Raul Lara sits in an upstairs office with a blue-and-gold police emblem on the door. He doesn't wear a uniform or sport a badge, and with his crisp white polo shirt, pale tangerine-tinted Oakley sports glasses, and neatly barbered goatee, he looks both cool and intense. He talks of how he juggles work and coaching and reveals that he almost didn't get the head coaching job after all. Once the interim appointment that followed Jaso's resignation became official after Kirk Jones's death, Lara was told he couldn't take the job. "The Long Beach Unified School District didn't have the problem," he says, "the agency did."

The L.A. County Probation Department had decided Lara had a conflict of interest. "They said I had to resign as head coach" or go back to his former job at a county probation camp— a four-days-on, three-days-off shift that Lara had left to spend more time with his family. "My supervisor gave me two weeks to think about it. I said, 'I've done this [coaching] for twelve years, I've done it your way, but now that I'm a head coach I can't do it anymore? There's no way I'm going to resign, so I might as well go back to camp.'"

Word of the impasse leaked. "To make a long story short, they said there was a way," Lara says. "The way I heard it was, the Board of Supervisors got wind of it and said, 'Why can't you make this work out?'"

The L.A. County Board of Supervisors are the true masters of Los Angeles, their power greater than that of any mayor or council. So for now, Lara could go back to juggling his two jobs.

The phone rings, and he picks it up. "Probation Department, Lara speaking."

On the field, a bright white tent with an orange-and-green Gatorade logo provides shade for the trainers, who dispense water bottles from tubs full of ice. A skyjack—a thirty-foot-high filming platform that rises on a hydraulic scissors lift—is in place, with a cameraman overseeing the practice. Two of coach Lara's children tag along behind their dad, leaping about, then going still to listen to plays being called: "Bronco 8!" The players transition from smash-mouth athletes to baby-talkers in their presence. When it's not Hershel's turn to run a play, he'll step back and gently goof with Jazmin, nine, and Emmanual, seven. (Lara's third child, Camile, is just a baby, too young for practice.)

Jazmin leaps on the back of tight end coach and head trainer Rob Shock, who carries her around while he watches the scrimmage. The message on her T-shirt reads, "Stay out of gangs."

Herman Davis's foghorn voice booms, "*Every*thing is game, *every*thing is game!"

Receivers are running a gauntlet of players holding foam bags who give them hard shots, left and right, as they try to get to a spot and make a catch, knowing that they'll be hit by a defensive back as soon as they do. The object of the drill is to keep receivers from getting too "grooved," too easily upset in game conditions; the problem is it's succeeding too well. Nobody can make a catch. Players are moaning, crying out, batting at passes rather than extending to make the grab.

Enter Marcedes Lewis. He takes all the hits in stride, pivots, stretches out his long arms, and goes to the ball, tucks it in, and wraps up in time for the hit. Then he trots away, leaving the other receivers quiet.

Some favorite sideline regulars are here today. Freddie Parrish III, a barrel-chested former UCLA receiver, affable and sophisticated in well-cut Hollywood-style business attire, works the cell phone for his mortgage banking company. He pauses to comment: "Everybody wants a good game, nobody wants a blowout. This is the best one, this is the big dance."

Parrish and his wife, Sylvia, who is Canadian, are parents of a transfer junior, Freddie IV, and two ninth graders, Cruz and Ashley. The two Freddies and Ashley are black, Sylvia and Cruz white. "We call it a blended family; we don't use the step-word," says Parrish.

Parrish III speaks about straddling the black-white divide, which he does in both work and family life. "Our motivation for taking Freddie to Poly was that the Poly environment was very conducive to learning," says Sylvia. "We knew he would be rub-

bing elbows with other kids who are trying to get to college."
Sylvia holds a SAT class every Sunday from 11:00 A.M. to 1 P.M. at
their office. The participants are six seniors: Winston, Darnell,
Marcedes, Manuel, Brandon, and Daniel Butler. Freddie IV and
another junior transfer, quarterback Leon Jackson, also attend.

The presence of Freddie IV and Leon, who came from Beverly Hills High School, brings up the issue that most roils high
school athletics. Just as the critics of De La Salle whisper about
recruitment, Poly's critics mutter about transfers.

There are reasons for these rumors. Catholic schools can indeed take a student from anywhere, give him financial aid if they
choose, and even find a job for a father who happens to be a
coach. They claim not to recruit, but questions persist when
Mater Dei, or Bishop Amat, or Loyola always seem to have a 6'5"
quarterback and a blue-chip running back to go with a bruising
line.

De La Salle's case differs from the accusations that have
dogged most other Southern California Catholic schools. For one
thing, until the mid-nineties the Spartans were undersized and
not hugely talented. They were also largely white, with no more
than a couple of black players. The Spartans won, as Jaso says,
with superior coaching and superior conditioning. As they up-
graded their level of competition, the number of black players increased: from two to seven in '94, to nine in '95. Nine black
athletes out of a class size of (then, approximately) 225 would, as
a representation of the student body, come out to just over three
percent. This matches Concord's numbers for its black population, which is one mark of a diverse student body, but since it also
matches De La Salle's percentage of black students, it indicates
that a black student is perforce an athlete. Harsher critics of
American athletics, such as UC Berkeley sociologist Harry Ed-
wards and author (*Hoop Roots, Brothers and Keepers*) John

Edgar Wideman, would call this evidence of a plantation system of sports, not a mark of diversity. However, since '95 De La Salle's participation of black football players has hovered around six and lately has actually decreased; this year's team has three black seniors in a three percent black student body, which would seem to indicate that diversity is increasing and that the plantation question is moot. There is also, on the plus side, De La Salle's emphasis on academics and its high number of college-bound seniors.

In the public sector, the plantation accusation was raised in the sixties and seventies, but usually in relation to the numbers within a particular school or system. At the time of Poly's riots, "gifted track" classes were nearly all-white and Asian; white fraternities and sororities dominated student government and extracurricular activities. As a result, some students turned to gangs or burgeoning political organizations, including the Black Panthers and La Raza. Under the threat of a Federal takeover, the school district, led by a black Catholic seminarian turned educator, Carl Cohn, reinvented Poly through the expansion of AP classes, magnet accelerated learning (PACE) and international business (CIC) programs, and the breaking down of the huge student body—which today numbers 4,600—into additional academies. Students who aren't in PACE or CIC belong to one of these four themed units, or else attend an intensive off-campus center called PAAL (Poly Academy of Accelerated Learning), which allows 480 students, about 20 of them football seniors, to make up or complete course requirements via intensive studies. This emphasis on academics for every student was accompanied by the creation of Poly North, the boundary-breaking, trust-building sessions held for sophomores in a rustic mountain setting.

The parochial complaints about the public schools—the things that make Terry Eidson see red—center on open enrollment and transfers. Enrollment used to be tightly bound by geographic boundaries; where you lived determined which of the five Long Beach high schools you attended. To facilitate integration, this changed in the mid-seventies. For a time white students had to stay put, while black students could go to any Long Beach school; it wasn't unusual for an ambitious player to transfer to Jordan or Wilson if it looked as if he wasn't going to start. It was no accident that Poly football didn't do too well in those years.

Frustrated by the dominance of Mater Dei and other Catholic League teams in the eighties, the public schools had talked often of rebelling against their tight zoning rules, but the specter of opening the floodgates to opportunistic stage fathers and hustling coaches kept the lid on. Then politics came into play, with the voucher and charter school movements, which threatened to drain the public schools throughout California of taxpayer and parent support. Shortly before a ballot initiative, the state legislature voted for open enrollment, allowing students to "follow quality," whether in academics, arts, or athletics. Theoretically, it meant that a student could live in San Diego and play football in San Francisco.

The CIF quickly created a web of restraints to prevent chaos, but for the first time public high school athletes could do what Catholic athletes had been doing for generations, which was shop their talents around, see where they had the best chance of starting, and which team had a shot at winning. (Unlike public school applicants, Catholic school athletes could also see what sort of financial aid package might open up—an aspersion which is hotly denied by all, especially De La Salle, but a practice that seems to have occurred all over the country.)

Poly definitely benefited from the change. "Open enrollment exists, and we didn't create it," says Poly athletic director Joe Carlson, who oversees all the paperwork and eligibility of student athletes. "People are upset about it, and sometimes have a right to be upset. If a kid leaves in his junior year to come here, it can become a magnet for his friends in the sport. But, you know, it's more than the wins, it's the placement in college that attracts transfers."

Poly's prominence attracts scrutiny and keeps Carlson busy ensuring all of the school's programs are squeaky clean. One thing Poly is known for, and that counts heavily with parents of potential transfers, is that it doesn't just keep an eye on the high school course-work requirements for students; it also keeps them NCAA-eligible. "We're pretty conscious of what kids need to do in regards to academics in order to get a college scholarship," Carlson says. "That's not something all schools do."

For as many advantages as they bring, transfers bring as many problems. For one thing, they upset the orderly succession from Pop Warner, to freshman team, to junior varsity team to varsity, the way players typically climb the ladder. Since teams have a strong bias toward their homegrown products, transfers, if used unwisely by a coach, wreck team chemistry. They can help a team lose as much as win, and leave a program—particularly one as community-driven as Poly's—in tatters. This is why Poly is very careful about, and indeed can almost be said to discriminate against, transfers.

Today, every coach has his list of transfer woes: the kid who comes in and freaks out because he's not going to start right away; the parent who freaks out for the same reasons; the kid who gets bumped to second string and immediately quits and applies for a transfer; the star quarterback who leaves because his father magically has gotten a job as an assistant coach at a top program known for quarterbacks; the kid who's happy at his losing school but whose parent, devoured by ambition, forces a transfer to a big-time program. *"It's the parents,"* every coach and administrator from Hawaii to Jenks to Concord to Long Beach says. "It's not so much the kids as the parents." (One Southern California football parent had his baby quarterback teethe on frozen raw liver in order to raise the perfect NFL specimen.)

Two of Poly's three most visible football transfers, Leon Jackson and Kevin Brown, wanted to come to Poly for the exposure to recruiters. There was a mild sideline ripple of worry that Leon, a tall junior who is also an excellent punter, might take Brandon's starting job, but it never amounted to anything—particularly after the two boys' fathers visibly bonded and refused to let any rumors take flight. Kevin's mother Linda, who's in the International Hall of Fame as a softball player, recounts that Kevin had said, "Mom, I want to excel," even though he already was an all-CIF defensive lineman in his district. "When I visited and got the story on the school's academics," Linda said, "I felt a lot better."

Freddie Parrish IV transferred for the exposure as well, but made national headlines for another reason. Switching to South Torrance High as a sophomore, he played his way into a starting job over an older kid. After a game, the father and uncle of the usurped player attacked and beat the South Torrance coach and another who came to his assistance, while uttering a racial epithet about Freddie IV. The incident, which resulted in multiple charges of battery against the perpetrators, was cited nationally as an example of a rising tide of parent and fan violence in sports. Freddie IV finished out the year at South Torrance, and played alongside the player whose father and uncle attacked their coach; there was no further trouble. Freddie IV was an all-CIF cornerback choice at Division 10, which is the lowest competitive level, determined by school size and program strength, but he wasn't comfortable returning, not so much because of the incident but because of what somebody had said to him after the season. "Somebody came up to me," says Freddie IV, "and said, 'You're real good, but you play in Division 10. How good would you be at a higher level?' That really made a lot of difference for me."

The Parrishes settled on Poly; as Freddie's father says, "He needed to play in a bigger arena." At the practices over the summer it became obvious Freddie IV could be a starter, but that he wouldn't take anybody's job away. Instead, he practiced at cornerback, wide receiver, running back and rover back—roles he could be called on to fill at various points in a game.

Merle Cole III, known as Little Merle, who is as soft-spoken as his father is raucous, is probably in the saddest position of anyone on the staff—filling his friend Kirk Jones's shoes. "Yeah, I walked with Kirk," he says. "The day he passed, he said, 'Meet you at USC,' where we were going to go to a clinic. I was paging him and paging him. . . . We were close. He'd been sick since '97, with fluid buildup; I used to sit and watch him take twenty pills three times a day. He carried them in a pouch he wore around his waist. The kids, they didn't know how bad it was."

Merle III watches the players at their stations, running through their drills. He nods to Charles Owens, down in the stance, going up against Manuel. A mammoth collision and brief flurry of red dust. "Some of these kids, they're hurting so much . . . Charles's mom just passed. He found her in bed. He's so confused, he showed up at practice the next day."

Standing over Charles and Manuel is Don Norford, who has the longest tenure of any coach at the school, twenty-three years. His three children are Poly graduates; for decades he has coached the Poly track and field program, considered the nation's finest, both for boys and girls; he's the only assistant ever to win the NFL High School Coach of the Year Award. He has also just been released from the hospital after a three-week stay due to the complications of diabetes—yet here he is, moving slowly, speaking little, and coaching, not with his hands or his voice, but with his eyes.

His own eyes filling with tears, Merle III shakes his head. "This team has been through a lot: Jaso leaving, Kirk passing, now this. Looking on the outside, you don't see all that."

At the end of practice, Lara addresses the team. "We're prospering," he says simply. "Defense, better get ready for that option. Those L.A. teams, that's all they run.

"Remember Kirk. That's why we keep him in our prayers. Remember what he walked and talked and established here. Those of you who never got to see Kirk in his prime, we're going to see about putting together a highlight film, so you can see what Poly football is all about.

"So we are going to get there. But I've been seeing guys relaxing, talking, goofing . . . There's going to be a point where I'm going to stop that. If you stop it on your own, that's leadership. Our first goal is to beat Westchester. That's all we're thinking about."

The first drill of the following day, coach Tim Moncure ceremoniously calls on Winston and Manuel to open the practice. The two 300-pounders come up, bow to each other with clasped hands, step back, drop into a three-point stance, and then go at each other five times. Each collision feels like an earthquake. People across the field drop everything to watch.

During a water break, someone mentions the trouble last year's stars have had qualifying for their Division I scholarships. Neither all-star Marvin Simmons nor defensive player of the year Ray Tago have been able to make the 820 SAT cutoff score; both their USC offers are on hold. At least Ray will be able to join his two brothers *and* Jerry Jaso over at Long Beach City College. Simmons, whose younger brother Marlin is a Poly sophomore linebacker (and whose twin brothers are on the freshman team), may also end up with the other Jackrabbits.

On days like this, the tremor of SAT nerves shoots through the football program. The coaches stress grades and attendance, the counselors make sure they take NCAA-approved core subjects, the school provides support, and the Poly Moms fiercely exhort the players as they disperse from the locker room after a practice to "study, take that PSAT prep course, don't go out tonight"—encouraging all the kids, not just their own children.

The members of the Sunday SAT club at the Parrishes are trying their best to carry the entire team a little further down the road. Exiting practice, they throw SAT vocabulary words at each other, daring each other to attempt definitions. Each time they get one right, even though it may draw a laugh for the sheer obscurity of some improbable eighteenth-century euphemism, Marcedes, Brandon, Leon, and Darnell are breaking down invisible cultural barriers.

All August the coaches have been installing the offense. Poly starts from an unbalanced line, splitting two receivers out wide on the same side, which forces the defense to detach two defensive backs to cover them. This way, Jerry Jaso has explained, defenses can't "pack the box," the area between the tight ends, with extra defenders. "Now it's nine on nine," Jaso said, and the offense can attack the gaps—or bubbles, as they are called—between tackles, linebackers, and defensive ends. There are seemingly endless variations: sweeps, traps, counters, dives, draws—and those are just running plays. Each week, as the season goes by, more plays and variations and wrinkles are added, some to fool the following week's opponent, who will be studying film from the past games, others to allow the talents of certain players to blossom.

In 1968, the year Jaso graduated, Poly ran a far simpler offense, called a Power-I. Adopted from nearby USC, it was all about running the football without wrinkles or deception. When Jim Barnett brought in the Wing-T, Poly joined the modern age. Now, instead of six basic plays, there are probably sixty to a hundred variations.

In terms of personnel, Poly's one major difference from the glory years of the early sixties, as Herman Davis says, is "the Bixby Knolls kids won't come out for football anymore. We lost our big offensive linemen from there. Now they're our water polo and soccer players. We had a big kid Jaso begged to come out—no. Next year he's a drum major." Winston Justice is the highly visible exception.

The talents and experience of this year's team is providing the coaches a chance to expand the offense in new directions. Like most football coaches, they've attended clinics at various colleges, where the latest schemes are introduced. So, a play like the one Poly is installing today, a quick inside screen pass that the receiver takes and runs at a diagonal behind a picket line of blockers, can seem to pop up everywhere at once. It was last year's favorite during the pro season, and it's in the De La Salle repertoire as well. Now Derrick Jones, the fastest Jackrabbit of them all, a sophomore who just missed being invited to the U.S. Junior Olympic Trials—he ran one hundred meters in 10.6 seconds—is trying to master its quick-twitch mix of fakery and split-second timing.

Coaches and fans have been waiting for Derrick for years. They watched him tear up Pop Warner, then star on Poly's freshman team. Though Poly has a reputation as a team that plays its seniors, it will be tough to resist plugging Derrick into the mix, especially since three starting receivers from last year's team have graduated. As long as Brandon throws a fair share of balls to

Marcedes and junior Alex Watson, everybody should be happy—
except the opposing defense.

Just before practice began, defensive line assistant Herman
Davis talked about De La Salle: "Here's what I think. They've
never played a game like this. They're coming to hostile territory.
It's a real hostile house, Vets [Stadium]. I'd hate to be in their
shoes. We're so deep personnel-wise. We were looking at 'em,
lookin' at last year's roster, and said to ourselves, 'You'd better get
yourselves more linemen.'"

For the Poly defense to function at its best, Davis explains, it
needs seven true linemen to rotate in and out of four spots. If you
only have four good players, they tire in the fourth quarter, which
puts pressure on the defensive backs and linebackers. This year,
Herman has four tackles and three ends. "And poor De La Salle
plays that Landri and that number fifty-five"—Andy Briner—
"both ways." Davis shakes his head.

"Then there's speed. You know what they say: 'There's speed,
and then there's Poly speed'? Well, it's true. I've seen film on
their number twenty, their big man in the defensive backfield"—
he's talking about Nate Kenion—"and let me tell you, he's *slow*. I
mean, when he's running up against our sprinter-speed guys, running eight to ten plays in a row, covering a 10.6 sprinter—he's
going to get *tired*.

"If it's close, then the fatigue doesn't set in. If we're up by
seven or more, or they're up by three, you don't feel the fatigue
as much. But if they fall behind by a couple of touchdowns—
well, fatigue makes cowards of us all."

That same day after practice, the linemen converge in the
weight room, a large but haphazardly organized space with
benches and machines, nothing like De La Salle's House of Pain.
The players trade rumors about the Spartan strength and condi-

tioning program. Upon hearing that the team had kept lifting through their August two-a-day practices, the kids fall silent.

"So what?" a player grunts. "Ain't no difference between what we do and them."

"Yes, there is," says a deep, quiet voice from a corner. Taeao Salausa, a '95 Poly grad who played at Long Beach City College and now is up at Washington State, is lying on a weight bench; he sets the bar in the rack behind his head and rests. "That's a typical Division I program; what you're doing here is nothing like that. There's no comparison. That's what I found out."

The players look abashed. The kid who objected, however, is having none of it. "They're not Superman," he grumbles.

On the first day of school it's hard not to feel a tingle as I wander around the handsome art deco–style quad. The lawns are green, new planters are full of flowers; the school looks a lot better than when I was there.

There are almost twice as many students as in 1970. The quad, second-story walkways, and snack area are densely crowded. The usual logos are in evidence: Fubu, Hilfiger, Phat Farm, Old Navy, and North Face. Against all this khaki and denim the Cambodians stand out, the boys in crisp, ironed Hawaiian print shirts, the girls in bright, skimpy cheongsam-style dresses. Cambodians are the largest group at Poly (the majority of the 36 percent Asian category), but they aren't a majority. As Shawn Ashley has explained, it's a Long Beach truism that as long as no group exceeds 40 percent, schools stay peaceful: minority rules.

Strolling past the 1930s WPA murals in the halls, I find myself in an old team photo in a glass case that looks as if it hasn't been opened since 1970. A reverie of Poly past ripples under the dusty glass: bobby-soxers and bandleaders, adolescent leading men and teenage torch singers. Dorothy Buffum, from Long Beach's first family, departed Poly to marry Norman Chandler, scion of Los Angeles's first family, owners of the *Los Angeles Times;* through philanthropy and will Dorothy would drive the creation of modern Los Angeles, including its Music Center, art museums, and Blue Ribbon 400 social elite. And yet, rounding a corner, I also come upon the ghosts of local hoodlums selling red devils and yellow jackets and demanding my lunch money as a toll for passage; revisit the echoing culs-de-sac whose great acoustics drew generations of a cappella singers and, later, rappers like Snoop Doggy Dogg; stop outside the auditorium to imagine Cameron Diaz practicing monologues in her Poly Pepette uniform.

I bump into coprincipal Shawn Ashley zipping down a hallway and ask if I can tag along. "Sure, I'm just about to give my 'Welcome to Poly' speech," he says. I glide into the back of an English classroom as Ashley goes to the front. After introducing himself and explaining what he and his counterpart, Mel Collins, do, he begins:

> You are really the chosen ones. I had a choice of eighteen hundred kids; that meant seven hundred got left outside the door. We took you because you can do for us what your mom and dad and brothers and sisters did for us. And Poly is a big family. I went to Poly, my wife went to Poly, my six brothers and my sister went. Just like any big family, you have to pull your weight. You can't expect Mom and Dad to do the laundry and pick up your room. . . .
>
> You are sitting in the exact same seats that Cameron Diaz sat in when she was a ninth-grader. She makes $10 million a movie. She didn't think she had anything to offer Poly. When Tony Gwynn was here, he didn't think he had anything to offer Poly. If you work hard, if you do your best—you're doing something for Poly.

Here's what I need from you in the next four years. You need to pass eight English classes to get the diploma. If you don't pass this class, and you make A's and B's for the rest of your career, I will not give you your diploma. So if you're having any kind of trouble, go to tutorial. Tutorial is your best friend.

The LBUSD says you have to pass algebra to get a diploma. You have to pass all four semesters of it, guys. So you really have to put in your best effort.

I need you to meet three goals: (A) to graduate; (B) to graduate on time; and (C) to graduate with honors. I also need you to help out—this is the trash thing. You got to take care of your own trash. When you stand out on the quad after the lunch bell, you'll see very little trash. Why? Because tenth-, eleventh-, and twelfth-graders already know the secret—they take care of their own trash.

Why? Because I want my school to look nice. I don't know where you went to school or what it looked like, but I doubt it looks as nice as ours with the roses and the planters.

Now let's talk about fighting. If something is started, we get it broken up right away. Here's what will happen to you the first time you get into a fight: (A) suspension; (B) a conference with your parents and me or Mel; and (C) the LBPD will cite you for $250 and you'll be before a judge. It doesn't matter what you tell the judge: "She walked up and I was studying for an exam and she called me a ho and called my mother a bitch" [the class goes "Ooooooh!"]—it will still cost you $250.

I don't want violence on this campus. Your mom and dad don't want violence on this campus. If there's a second fight, thank you for coming. If there's a second fight, you're going to leave.

Ashley holds up a blue sheet. "This is a list of all the colleges that are coming to talk to Poly this semester. For all you ninth-graders, listen up:

I want you to go to college. I *need* you to go to college—why? You get a nicer job, a nicer house, a nicer car—and I want these things for you. And you get these things if you go to college.

Join a club. We have over one hundred. We have this Black History Club, but if you're white or Latino, they're happy to have you. Why? (A) They like you, and (B) they want to see their club continue. Kids who are involved in clubs get better grades, are more likely to graduate, and more likely to go to college.

Feel free to participate in running the school. Our names are on the door, and if the door is open, we are there for you to talk to. That's what they pay me a salary for. Your problems are not minor to me. I am here to help you.

Now, about the ninth-grade PSAT. We need you to take it because they take the scores and post them and people see them and see what a good school Poly is. And that's good for everybody who goes here, and for the community.

You know we have standards for dress. Girls, the top and bottom have got to meet, they've got to touch. Some outfits, the top and bottom don't touch until they're in the laundry hamper at night. Guys, it's the hat thing. When do we allow a hat?

A girl says, "When somebody has a disease or something?" After the laughter, Ashley says, "Some kind of condition, yes, but outdoors . . ."

A kid asks, "When it's raining?" Ashley gives him a pink slip for a free Slushie. "What is the definition of *raining*? When water is falling from the sky. Not, the weatherman says it's going to rain. Nope. The water has to be falling. And even if the water *is* falling, you still can't wear hats in the classroom."

After a demonstration of what constitutes sexual harassment—"It's when somebody does something to make somebody feel uncomfortable"—and advising them to respect personal space in the hallways, Ashley begins to wrap up: "We chose you because you have something to offer. You really are special kids. We think you can contribute to this school. When you contribute, good things happen for everybody. That's why we won five CIF championships last year. That's why test scores are up twenty points in the last two years.

"So welcome to Poly"—the bell rings; he waits until it's finished—"and have a great year."

Heading out to the field, I come across Mel Collins, the other co-principal, emerging from giving his "Welcome to Poly" speech. The game tickets have gone on sale, and Mel already has stories to tell. "A man just drove up from San Diego; another gentleman wanted eighteen for his buddies who are coming in from all over. Had some long, black Mercedeses trying to squeeze through the parking lot, can you imagine? And regular fans, not even alumni, coming for the football. It's a city thing: doctors, lawyers . . . a garbage truck pulled up, a sanitation worker got out and bought his ticket."

The game has been scheduled for Veterans Stadium, on the City College campus, where Poly plays its home games. This hasn't gone over well with everyone; some want it at Edison Field, where the Anaheim Angels play, and which seats up to fifty-five thousand. Mel and the others concerned have opted for the much smaller Vets, which seats twelve thousand, but at "the rate tickets are selling, though," he says, "we'll put in the extra bleachers, go up to fifteen thousand. And if they keep selling, well, we'll find a way to get some extra seats in there."

Mel and I split up on reaching the field—he has much to do, on many fronts, not just the game—and I run into Anthony Cobb, a grad and NFL vet, currently rehabilitating from an arm injury and serving as press liaison for Poly. Cobb waves to Collins, his old principal. "Mel's the James Bond of principals," he says affectionately. "He's got all this stuff going on with everybody, all the time. An international man of mystery—that's Mel."

On the sidelines, various old grads, including NFL all-pro Earl McCullough and '64 star Dee Andrews, discuss the drive-by shooting that occurred in front of Compton High on the first day of school. "Where's the respect for the school?" Andrews demands. "That's a community thing, you understand—that could never happen at Poly."

Practice gets under way. On the field is a new face, an older white coach in crisp shorts and polo shirt, scrutinizing every offensive play with his hands on his knees. White hair poking out from under his cap, the master mechanic of Poly's offense, Jim Barnett, has come out of retirement to give his baby a tuneup.

During a receiver drill, Derrick Jones streaks out and runs under a perfect rainbow from Brandon. For a moment the ball lies cradled in his fingertips, then, patty-cake, he loses it. Merle II slams his clipboard on the grass. "I hate sophomores," he growls, loud enough for Derrick to hear. Assistant Keith Anderson starts to speak, but Merle II won't be denied. "Hey, I hated Ken-Yon Rambo, too, and Kareem Kelly, too, when they were sophomores." Rambo was the Raiders's seventh-round pick last year; Kelly is USC's current star.

Anderson hooks Derrick by the arm and sticks his face right up to his face mask. "Hey, I don't hate sophomores," he says quietly. Pause. "I hate receivers who can't catch."

At around five o'clock, the team in full scrimmage mode, a long, loud series of pops, like a Chinese New Year's string of fireworks, breaks out to the left, in the direction of the all-Cambodian ROTC drill team. "Is ROTC having target practice?" I joke.

Reserve linebacker Brian Banks and several others snort and shake their heads at my obtuseness. "Ack-ack," says Brian. "AK-47," another adds helpfully. "Gangbangers," says a third, cocking his head. "Fifteenth, maybe Fourteenth Street." Two blocks south—might as well be two miles. They return to observing practice.

Fourteen

THE SHORTEST SEASON

On Thursday, the tension that has been building on the Poly fields breaks loose like an earth tremor. Yesterday's sideline circus was big; today's is bigger. Fifty people are in the bleachers watching practice and socializing: parents, brothers and sisters, students, Pepettes and cheerleaders and members of the Spirit Guard, members of the band. Two Long Beach policemen, former players, come by to watch. The LBPD helicopter that circles the campus every day when school lets out slides over and hovers above the field. Norm Zink, a 1967 grad who owns a sporting goods store and supplies Poly's equipment and uniforms—everything at cost, for years and years—is here to hear any problems players have about their helmets and shoes. Philip Turner, an alumnus and local businessman who was Dr. Dre's and Snoop Dogg's Pop Warner coach ("Dre was a good linebacker, Snoop a wide receiver, but his real game was basketball"), shows designs for the T-shirts he's going to have printed up for the game, with proceeds going to the school and program. Reggie Benson, sharp in a black-on-black ensemble, rues the betting line on the game—"twelve points, De La Salle"—but does not dispute it. "They're undefeated, they deserve that much." Rob Shock, the tight end coach and head trainer, has a list of people who want sideline passes: 122 names. "This list has grown over the years. There are people who don't show up for games at the beginning who begin to show up at the end, and then all of a sudden you have a mob scene." A Poly assistant has responsibility for making sure the rap celebrities—Snoop, Nate Dogg, Dre, Warren G., and others—get their passes; he'll try to use the opportunity to pass along a freshly burned CD of his original beats.

Coach Lara speaks to the players. "We are not taking backpacks, we are not taking Walkmen, we are not taking radios. We are just going to Vets Stadium to play us a football game. I've been waiting to see you play a game since spring.

"A chain only stays strong when it stays together. One guy getting angry in a game, starts yelling, starts cursing, doing his own thing—he breaks the chain. Remember, great teams don't get freaked out when something goes wrong. In the last four years, our teams have experienced that—something has gone wrong, but the momentum turned. It *will* turn.

"For this game, Hershel Dennis will wear number twenty-two, Kirk Jones's Poly number. Rory Carrington will wear number ten, Kirk's number at UNLV. Before the game, hold your helmet to the side to show the KJ sticker to the TV cameras and the people in the stands. Remember Kirk. Remember what he accomplished. Pray for his family."

Lara leads the team in a prayer. Parent Bob Veach is firing up a barbecue beside the bleachers for a Booster Club cookout. Two of his sons have played for Poly, and a third is on the way. Ruddy and football-sized, Veach tells me that his son Joe, on scholarship at Portland State, will sit with his De La Salle teammates for the big game. Then Freddie Parrish III comes up with a concerned expression on his face. "I've just heard there's no team meal before home games," he says.

Veach nods. "Don't have the money. It's all we can do to pay for the road game meals."

"Every team Freddie has ever played on has had a pregame meal," Parrish says firmly. "I'm going to look into organizing something."

Veach nods; Parrish will figure it out soon enough. Hershel has his lucky meal. Winston eats with his grandmother. A group of Samoans go to Tommy's #2, a Hawaiian-style plate-lunch shack run by a Korean immigrant and passionate Poly sponsor, Yukon Oh. The Poly kids, Jerry Jaso has said, need to get away before a big game.

De La Salle would probably never understand.

"You can talk all you want about ghetto kids," says Veach, "but I was cooking up the barbecue on Labor Day and ninety percent of the guys said, 'Thank you, sir.' I'd rather watch these boys play than almost anything. They have a special thing going here. And these are fine men out here. They push ethics, they push morals."

To illustrate his point about money, Veach tells the story of the great toilet giveaway. The city and Edison Power wanted to retrofit houses with low-flush toilets and decided to make the schools the focal point of the effort. People could pick up their new toilets, then bring their old ones in for a rebate; the school got a cut, too. The football program saw a rare opportunity to make some serious money and mobilized the community. Hundreds of toilets were distributed. But on the day to turn in the old toilets, the temperatures soared into the nineties, and Jerry Jaso and the other Poly coaches had to deal with hundreds of—"Well, let's just say not everyone brought in clean toilets," says Veach. "There were double lines around the block, Jerry and the other coaches were sweating, loading them into the trucks, and, oh, the smell! But we made nine grand."

● ● ●

There's a film session after practice. Then the team strolls out of the dank locker room, onto the asphalt playground, and faces a crowd of nearly two hundred waiting in the near dark. The *Press-Telegram* and *Student Sport* reporters are old hands and know the stars. New press arrivals, including a radio journalist from Germany, grab anyone who looks big and begin interviewing, before noticing the competition has Marcedes, Darnell, or Manuel, at which point they break off without apology and edge in. A couple of fathers shake their heads at the commotion. "It's just high school," says Leon Jackson's father. "This is going to go to their heads."

The crowd moves in a long strung-out line from locker room to the gate to the parking lot. All in a row, greeting players and calling out encouragement, are the Poly Moms. Nearer to the gate is Yvonne Withers, Marcedes's mother, tall and lean and self-possessed as she leans against a pillar. "I decided I wanted to do some fund-raising," she says, "so I went out to where the long-shoremen get their checks down at the harbor, stood outside for six hours, and raised $1,145 for new jerseys. We wanted to have a different color for the De La Salle game—it would still have green and gold on it, with black. But Mel"—coprincipal Collins—"said no to black."

On Friday, September 7, the U.S. secretary of education, Rod Paige, comes to Long Beach. Paige praises the LBUSD for its leadership in implementing magnet programs, leading the way with school uniforms, and championing diversity.

Sportswriter Michael Arkush is doing a story on De La Salle and The Streak for the *New York Times*, which was to have been published yesterday but got held over. Now they want to wait until after the Buchanan game to make sure De La Salle doesn't lose. Arkush says that the *Times* won't decide to do a story on the game until it's sure both teams will come in undefeated. NFL Films, on the other hand, has asked permission to film the Poly team starting the week before the game and do a segment that will air on ESPN. Meanwhile, Ted Kian, a sportswriter at the *Press-Telegram*, says that they are planning intense coverage for the game—"more than we gave the Olympics, which was *a lot.*"

All this background noise, this buzz, is all the louder as the first game nears and with it the Russian-roulette-like odds of either team losing before the first week of October. If that should happen, the whole thing goes pouf. The media will fold up their tents and go home.

Right now, though, the season is shiny, new, and unblemished. It all starts tonight: the unveiling of Poly's latest edition, the beginning of the Raul Lara Era, and the countdown to The Game itself.

Tomorrow night, in the Central Valley town of Clovis, De La Salle faces its own debut.

Vets Stadium feels like a time-warp: the stands are a hunk of bare concrete opposite a set of ramshackle aluminum bleachers; the vast parking lots of the Long Beach City College campus stretch out as far as the eye can see. Nearby is a mammoth Boeing aircraft factory, and a bit farther down is the Long Beach airport. A chill, dank breeze comes in from the ocean at night, even after a warm day.

Westchester takes the kickoff, a good boot by Jeff Hastings. The first play, a run, is stuffed. On the second, the quarterback tries a rollout pass and misses. On the third, he connects on a twenty-yard pass-and-run, but the officials call it back because of illegal motion.

Poly fumbles the ensuing punt, but recovers the ball. The offense trots out, huddles, lines up. Brandon walks up behind the center, looking over the crouched linemen, counting off the locations of the linebackers and safeties. They've cheated up a couple of steps, figuring that Poly will start the season by handing the ball to its all-CIF, Long Beach player-of-the-year tailback, Hershel Dennis. A first play of the season is almost a formality, anyway.

Brandon takes the snap, fakes the handoff to Hershel, drops back, and throws—not a quick flip to a halfback, not a ten-yard out, not a fifteen-yard seam, but the deep fly route, the track-meet pattern. The rotating ball goes up, then dips its nose earthward and descends forty yards downfield into the outstretched palms of the sophomore sprinter Derrick Jones, who never breaks stride, taking it in for a touchdown. A seventy-yard bomb on the first play of the game, of the season, of Derrick's varsity career.

Lara claps his hands together once, says, "So we hit it, huh?"

After the kickoff, Westchester tries a sideline out pass, one of the safest to throw, on second down. Poly cornerback Tyrone Jenkins makes a diving interception. On offense, Brandon pitches to Hershel, who glides for an easy ten yards and then, after he steps out of bounds, is hit from behind and knocked down into the concrete rim of the track. The official throws a flag: unnecessary roughness, fifteen yards; first and goal at the five.

Hershel goes for three yards off-tackle. Brandon takes the next snap and rides the backs of his surging linemen in for the score. The kick is good. With four minutes gone, Poly leads 14–0. After the kickoff, Westchester starts a drive, seeming to settle down. They make two first downs in succession, then fumble. Junior Lemauu recovers. The Poly offense trots out. Rory Carrington goes for five yards. Brandon throws a slant to Marcedes for a first down. Rory takes a handoff going one way, cuts back sharply, and slashes for fourteen yards. First and goal. Hershel bulls it in.

With the point-after kick good, the score is 21–0 after seven minutes.

"It's like Pop Warner," says a sideline observer. The Poly band strikes up "Gonna Fly Now," the *Rocky* theme song. The sideline expert points out that Carl Weathers, the actor who played Sylvester Stallone's opponent Apollo Creed, is a Poly grad and former football star.

The second quarter is a yo-yo, Westchester holding on to the ball a bit, Poly getting it back and sputtering. Then the offense seems to get fed up and Hershel kicks it into gear, running hard and swerving behind blockers. Brandon throws for an apparent touchdown, but the Poly receiver is called for interference. The next play, Brandon drops back to pass, then starts to run. "Tuck it, tuck it, baby!" scream players on the sidelines as he races past, warning him to protect the ball for the big hit that they can see coming. The crunch, amplified by the plastic shoulder pads, is cartoon-loud. Brandon bounds up, grinning.

Hershel wiggles and squirms for four yards. On the next play, he blasts in for a touchdown as the demoralized Westchester defense gives way. It's 28–0, with 2:30 to go in the half.

At halftime the game, for the fans, is over. But for Poly, it is now a laboratory for testing plays and especially players, whose performances will be scrutinized later on film. The locker room is absolutely still: no shouting, no celebrating, no jubilation. Coaches who have acted as spotters high up in the press box come down and diagram what Westchester is doing; then players huddle with their position coaches, studying the white boards and talking over the adjustments marked on them. Water bottles float from hand to hand, trainers bend over ankles and knees, wrapping and rewrapping.

Poly gets the kickoff to open the second half. There's a sack of Brandon, followed by a foul on Westchester: penalties are proving to be the undoing of the L.A. team. Brandon takes the next snap from center, bobbles it in midair, then alertly pitches it to a trailing Hershel. Three defenders are converging on Hershel, but with a twitch and a blur of his quick feet he's off again, all the way down to the goal line. On the next play the announcer's bored tones say it all: "Dennis, touchdown Rabbits." It's 35–0. On Westchester's next possession, they go nowhere but backward, driven on their heels by Manuel's erupting surges. Trying to kick with their backs to their own end zone, Westchester's center snaps the ball over the head of the punter for a safety—two points for Poly, plus Westchester has to punt the ball back to the Jackrabbits. Darnell Bing takes the punt and returns it twenty yards to the 38, easy striking range for Poly.

But the team is done scoring. Even with its excellent second-teamers now in, the coaches call conservative plays, mostly runs, to keep the clock moving. On the sidelines, Fox Sports is interviewing Raul Lara's linebacker brother, Carlos, who's on crutches and hasn't played at all.

Marcedes, meanwhile, is slapping hands with two ten-year-old Pop Warner kids who wear his number, nineteen. A trainer opens a medicine kit, removes a pair of eyeglasses, and hands them to Winston Justice. Putting them on, he glances up at the now empty stands. "The fans are getting spoiled. They left at halftime." He smiles.

Manuel takes a breather on the sideline bench. "A great beginning," he says. "Tomorrow—watch some film and get better. Tonight—go home and take a hot bath."

A couple of reporters and a TV crew gather around coach Lara. "I'm just glad it's over," he says. "Now I get to think about the next game."

The next game is Banning, L.A. City champions, with the only defensive lineman in Southern California to be rated as highly as

Manuel—a 6'3", 290-pound Samoan by the name of Fred Matua. Don Norford says, "That should be some matchup."

Heading north from Los Angeles, funneling through the San Fernando Valley, climbing up the Tehachapi Mountains over Tejon Pass, and then down into the vast, treeless, alkalai-bleached desert of the lower Central Valley, Highway 5 ushers the driver into an older California outsiders rarely experience. Radio stations switch over automatically to pounding, pulsing Norteño, accordion-and guitar-driven, blended with slightly sour mariachi horns; cotton, oil, and raisins are the crops here. Three and a half hours and two-hundred-some miles later, most of it on the arrow-straight, two-lane blacktop of Highway 99, the empty landscape turns urban. Five minutes later and Fresno seems like a 427,000-person mirage. In its place are more empty, pale-dusted fields, more Norteño, migrant grape-pickers working under a giant billboard that says SAVE AMERICA—STOP ILLEGAL IMMIGRATION!

Clovis, the "Gateway to the Sierras," as an antique, swaying sign hanging over Main Street attests, looks like the sort of place Humphrey Bogart would pause in just long enough to fall in love with a waitress at a diner, before careering on to some desperate mountain shoot-out. Amidst the Cattle Rustlers' Steak House, Treasured Memories Antique Mall, and the Olde Town Saloon, there's a museum devoted to Festus, the raggedy hillbilly character in the TV series *Gunsmoke*.

"This place just grew, not because of people moving from L.A. or San Francisco, but with Fresno people who wanted bigger homes," explains Buchanan High's coach, Jim Moxley. The school that opened in 1992 had the luxury of fitting the elementary, middle, and high schools together, on a 160-acre homestead lot. The campus is modern, if incongruous out in the peach orchards: at the corner of Minnewawa and Goshen Streets, the stadium looks like a giant clam, half-open, with a brilliant green tongue for a football field.

"If it's for the children, people here will spend the money," Moxley says. There are four baseball fields set end to end; two enormous outdoor swimming pools; lots of landscaped green space between the corporate-style buildings. One secret to the willingness to spend—in a California that has been downright cruel to children since the passage of Proposition 13—is that the whole community gets to use these facilities. "Our pool goes twenty-four hours, our fields, too," Moxley explains. The other key to the investment is that an entire population of professionals has "hived" away from Fresno, with its troubled school system.

One reason Clovis football is so good is that kids start playing tackle in a fifth-grade school league, which allows everyone to learn the same offensive and defensive systems from cradle to college. "We don't have very many Division I–type athletes here," Moxley said, "but the players understand what a team sport football is." The eighteen seniors on the 2000 team that had come within six points of beating the Spartans had played together since seventh grade—six years.

As it happens, discipline is a major concern in the Clovis Unified School District, which has a strict dress code from elementary through high school. Along with discipline, however, Buchanan offers resources that are eye-popping: Every junior high student gets a laptop, with an option to buy. The laptops are linked via wireless to classroom modules and telephones using the Apple Airport system; most parent communications are conducted via e-mail. And then there are the beautiful facilities to consider, including the sleek twelve-thousand-seat stadium, festooned in arcs of braided red and white helium balloons.

Across the street, the Concord contingent has arrived and is tailgating. Their mothership is a thirty-eight-foot Fleetwood diesel motor-home, awning extended, with deck chairs and a barbecue. Walter and Louisa Binswanger are the captain and first mate, parents of a couple of De La Salle players. In the jovial swirl of tailgaters, a mother comes up and declares, hand on her heart, "What these kids learn from Bob Ladouceur they will take with them for the rest of their lives—his spirituality, his accountability. My son at college already looks back at it as a magical time."

On the grass, opposite the green gate to the stadium, in the shade of a couple of small trees and slightly behind three white police cars parked facing outward, is a distant tableau of figures in shorts and white tank tops. One drops into a familiar stance— arms out, hands balled into fists, butt out, and torso upright, like a man lifting a piano or a safe. It's Derek Landri, along with Matt, Flea, Brian Callahan, Scott Regalia, and some others. On the grass nearby are a couple of plastic plates with partially eaten steaks and a full bottle of Worcestershire sauce—from Buchanan's pregame meal, not De La Salle's.

"It doesn't get any better than this in the Valley: De La Salle on a Saturday night and you're the only game in town," says Jim Moxley. "De La Salle, bless their heart, they treat us right."

In their season opener last week, the Buchanan Bears edged Pittsburg 31–30. "When you have an inexperienced team like ours, that builds confidence." Recalling the first time he saw De La Salle play, Moxley says, "I was shocked. I counted forty-one players, and I don't think they get the greatest players, either. But their conditioning program is almost unreal. And the kids have bought into it. You can say, 'We'll run a De La Salle–style conditioning program,' but that doesn't mean it'll happen.

"It's their coach. Ladouceur is a very mesmerizing kind of person. He doesn't fit the eyeball test of who you'd pick as the winningest coach. It's never an X and O approach with him in the clinics I've seen. It's all about the team game, the bonding. When the kids decide they want to do it, then you can."

Bob Ladouceur makes his way toward the field and is introduced to Moxley. The two coaches immediately start talking about the costs of travel games; Moxley mentions that a trip to play Iolani High in Hawaii hit $40,000. Ladouceur counters that it costs almost that much to go to L.A., "with flights and hotels and stuff."

"You guys are like a gunfighter," says Moxley. "Everyone wants you. I really appreciate you letting us lock in with you."

"You've started a great thing here. They give you great infrastructure," says Ladouceur with a wave at the deluxe stadium.

"They pay extra taxes," Moxley says, "and they get to use it. Hey, we got some food for you and your players. You did a great job for our guys last year. When even your fat kids are complaining that they ate too many burritos, you know they've eaten well. Anyway, make sure you get plenty of those chilled oranges. The hardest thing is your kids get so dehydrated in this heat, and you don't know where to stop on the highway."

This is the way to Ladouceur's heart—to show concern for his kids—and his appreciation shows. But both coaches also seem to know that the time for conversation is up.

As game time approaches, a local reporter shakes his head at the size of the crowd; it won't top seven thousand. "Folks know last year was our big chance," he says. "We graduated *everybody*."

Buchanan kicks off in a balmy night turned bright as day by the massed banks of stadium lights. The first play of the season is Nate Kenion's run for eight yards. Matt Gutierrez is stuffed turning up on the option, then on the next play rolls out and passes for twelve yards. Alijah carries twice, moving the ball down to the 16-yard line. A penalty moves the ball back to the 20, and then

De La Salle is stopped on three passes, one an apparent touchdown called out of bounds by the officials. The secret weapon and point differential of last year's game, kicker James Bloomsburg, comes in and clunks a high, fluttery miss. On the sideline there are sour faces; Brother Chris looks concerned, no doubt remembering when Buchanan nearly broke The Streak on his first-ever game as principal.

The Bears start on their 20, miss an opening pass, gain two yards, then draw De La Salle offside for a five-yard penalty. The third-down play is a sweep. Nate has the angle and rushes in to deliver the big hit, but flies past the runner, who is stopped by Damon Jenkins. Buchanan must punt, does, and Maurice Drew makes a nifty catch and return.

The time has come for De La Salle to make a statement. Matt drops back, sets up for a pass, and throws a perfect tight spiral— right into the path of a Buchanan defensive back. Interception! Bears ball on the 38. The momentum could shift if Buchanan can make something of this opportunity.

First down is a run for one yard. The Bears go offside; loss of five yards, second and 14. A pass goes for two yards. Third and twelve: offside Bears, again. The players opposite Derek Landri are freaking and firing out too soon. Third and seventeen, Landri tears apart the protection and chases the quarterback down after a short gain. Buchanan must punt, does, and Nate takes it on the De La Salle 8-yard line, a risky move.

First down is a Nate run for no gain; second down, a short slant pass thrown a little too low for Flea, Matt throwing in a hurry, under pressure. On third down, a short pass to Maurice Drew becomes a long, exciting sixty-yard zigzag for a touchdown . . . which is called back when a penalty flag is dropped late and far behind the action. The Bear fans cheer.

It's third and five at the De La Salle fourteen-yard line when

Matt drops back and hits a nice pass over the middle to the 32. Alijah rips through a hole for big yards again, and again the Spartans are penalized. Second down, fourteen yards to go for a first, no gain on a run. The Buchanan defense is holding. Third down, Matt drops back to pass, is chased, and turns upfield even though he doesn't have the kind of speed to make up fourteen yards on a converging defense. But he does get ten yards, which puts punter James Bloomsburg in better position.

With that, the first twelve-minute quarter is over, scoreless. After the break to switch sides of the field, James paces off his distance back behind the line, lets the line get settled, then lifts his hands. De La Salle holds and waits, and still the center doesn't snap the ball. James calls out a shift—an adjustment of the backfield. When the backs move, the Buchanan line surges across: offside, five-yard penalty, first down Spartans. Oldest trick in the book.

Matt's slow-motion run now seems fortuitous. De La Salle hardly looks invincible, yet they keep dodging the bullet. The offense trots out, sets. Matt takes the snap, spins, and gives the ball on a counter to Maurice Drew, who bursts through the line, accelerates in a pretty curve along a line of downfield blocks by the wide receivers, then breaks into the clear; it's a footrace, a sixty-five-yard run stopped when an angling safety drives him out at the 13-yard line. First and ten, another counter, this time to Alijah Bradley, and he's in for a touchdown. With the extra-point kick, 7–0.

The kickoff is taken at the 5, but De La Salle's covering gunners smother the runner at the 14. On first down, Buchanan has twelve men on the field, a five-yard penalty; on second down and fifteen from the 9-yard line, another flag is thrown, again for having twelve men. Now backed up on their 4-yard line, Buchanan lines up and calls a time-out, obviously rattled. They run the ball two times for a couple of yards, then punt.

Maurice Drew leaps to snag the ball in his outstretched hands at the 38-yard line, then springs forward as if off a trampoline. On cue, every return player wheels and looks for someone to block, and the Bears are either knocked on their backs or bull-rushed out of the play as Drew tears for the short side of the field, cuts left, cuts back, runs over a tackler, and is standing alone in the end zone. It's 14–0, 9:39 left in the second quarter.

James Bloomsburg's next kick almost goes through the up-rights of the goalpost on the opposite end. The Bears complete a pass for nine yards, run for a first down. The quarterback rolls out, throws . . . a Spartan linebacker, Nick Barbero, snares it as it zips overhead, runs hard back to the 12-yard line. On first down the handoff goes to Nate Kenion, who surfs a big line surge, picks his moment, and slides into the end zone: 21–0.

With 8:50 left, the game settles into the rhythm of a blowout. The Bears go three-and-out on the next series, punting on fourth down. Now in at tight end, Nick Barbero grabs a slant pass for five yards. After a couple of runs go nowhere, Barbero again pops free for a short dart of a pass from Matt. First down. De La Salle runs the ball down, runs the clock down to 21.7 seconds, when Nate slashes in for his second touchdown: 28–0 at the half. It's the same halftime score as the Poly-Westchester game, if achieved a bit more slowly.

The second half begins, and after a few minutes of back and forth, Alijah Bradley takes an interception the long way in, sixty-one yards, for a touchdown: 35–0. Alijah and Maurice and Barbero have waited for their blockers on these interceptions and punts. Patience in running the ball is the hardest thing to learn, because so much can go wrong waiting for the lanes to open up, but Spartan discipline turns good gains into scores.

Buchanan fumbles and goes in reverse for a couple of series, including a partially blocked punt. When Matt takes over, he throws that quick slant pass, this time to De'Montae Fitzgerald, a wide receiver. De'Montae catches the ball five yards deep but at full speed and in stride and sprints the twenty-four yards to the end zone untouched. With the extra point, 42–0. Defensive back Matt Kavanaugh gets a "pick," an interception, again waits for his wall of blockers to form, and scores: 49–0. A couple of Spartans are down with heat cramps, and the Spartan second team goes in. Buchanan's first string scores twice, meaninglessly. De La Salle's Jon Alexander runs eighty-seven yards to score with seconds left in the game, making the final 56–14.

Jim Moxley looks wan and resigned. "I think our inexperience showed," he says. "They hit for the cycle—scored every way you can score."

The lopsided score is a bit confusing. Most people assumed Buchanan would build on their near upset of the previous year. Was Buchanan that bad? Was De La Salle that good? Blowouts muddle the picture, because they can happen to good teams. Asked how this De La Salle team compares to last year's, Moxley says, "Because we lost eighteen starters, I don't know if this is the better team. They're a good team"—he shakes his head to scratch that last remark—"they're a *De La Salle* team."

The program roster bears out how the kids have grown since January: Alijah has added twenty pounds; Maurice has added two inches and gained fifteen pounds, almost graduating from Smurf size; Nate's up fifteen pounds to 200 pounds; Andy up twenty-two to 232; Erik Sandie up thirty-five to 235; Derek Landri up twenty to 280. A few have the metabolisms of supermodels: Ryan "Flea" Eidson, Scott Regalia, the undersized center, and Pedro Cabrera, the wide receiver, have all gained princely amounts: five, ten, and three pounds, respectively.

Nate Kenion Sr. pauses as he's leaving. "They kind of start

slowly until that third or fourth game," he explains, then smiles. "They always peak around the fifth game."

Nate Jr. catches up to his father, still in his hip pads and cleats, and a sweat-soaked undershirt. "A lot of us came here with revenge on our minds, after last year," he says. "Like Alijah Bradley." Alijah overhears this and comes over, his expression resolute. "Last year I had a bad game. I had to come back and redeem myself, that was my focus, my mentality. I had to show what I had." He looks around from the high ground overlooking the sparkling stadium, now virtually empty except for red and white balloons drifting about. "I'm loving this victory. There's nothing better than coming into this house before this crowd and getting this victory."

Andy Briner leans against the outside concrete wall of the visiting team's locker room and eats orange quarters. "Had fun," he says. "Took a hit from a 335-pounder, a whopper. It hurt but it was fun; my heart was beating so fast I didn't feel it." He grins.

Matt Gutierrez isn't so satisfied. "To tell the truth, I was a little anxious. It all began to flow when I calmed down and let the game come to me."

This draws a sardonic glance from offensive coach Mark Panella. "Matt was trying to be too perfect. He's seeing things that he didn't see before, because it's his third year, and that kind of makes him eager to take advantage. In this offense, nothing is predetermined. He's got to read on the fly, but he was seeing things in slow motion tonight. In a couple of weeks he's not going to be pressing. He just has to let it happen."

A group of Buchanan parents and boosters are setting up a buffet table outside the locker room door. There are eighty-five foil-wrapped burritos, cases of water and Gatorade, and boxes of chilled oranges, pride of the Central Valley, for the ride home. These are of particular interest to Mike Blasquez, who spent the night monitoring the hydration levels of his starters, particularly the two-way players. "Some guys lost eight, nine pounds; Maurice Drew and Damon Jenkins, on the field the whole game, dropped ten, maybe twelve pounds," he says. "They really feel it. At least we didn't have to poke 'em with IVs."

Blasquez heads into the locker room, where a drained Maurice Drew sits on a chair, shirt off, head back. He gives a languid, exhausted smile at the mention of his punt return. "It all depends on my blocking; the linemen just broke out. It's a wonderful feeling, to have seven thousand people watching."

Terry Eidson is standing amid the tape, paper cups, and postgame debris, looking miffed. "Both my green and my white shorts are gone! This is ridiculous!" He slides a thick De La Salle playbook and a Bible into a duffel bag, pulls out a video cassette, and hands it to Blasquez. "This is last week's Mater Dei scrimmage for the bus ride." The three-hour trip back to Concord makes a perfect classroom in which to begin preparation for the next game.

Fifteen

PRELUDE IN G(AMES) MINOR

The wisdom and appropriateness of holding sporting events, whether amateur or professional, was one of the lesser topics of debate following the events of September 11, 2001. The NFL canceled its games, in part because New York Jets quarterback Vinny Testaverde announced that he would not play that Sunday. Major League Baseball did the same. Division I-A college football also canceled its games, but most of the lower echelons played, not having the financial wherewithal to reschedule. At the high school level, a dozen cities that were not directly affected by terrorist attacks chose to idle their athletes; for most, the games went on, bedecked in flags and carried out amid solemn ceremony, the events serving as collection points for charitable contributions.

When the Los Angeles Unified School District decided to cancel its games, it meant that Poly would not face Banning High. Some might have regarded this as a blessing: the L.A. City champion had been charged with so many personal fouls in its season opener, leading to the suspension of several players, that a highly ranked opponent, Newhall Hart High, had already announced that they would not play Banning.

Yet Poly was bitterly disappointed. They are such an intimidating team that it's hard to scare up the kind of hard-edged—and even nasty—competition that they need to make them stronger, and to test their nerves. The Jackrabbits do not relish playing gang-ridden or violence-prone schools, but they play a couple that straddle the borderline. With no budget for games against faraway teams, Poly does not have the luxury of picking only well-behaved opponents with orderly fans, precisely the criteria that De La Salle can afford to employ. Indeed, when the Jackrabbits face Moore League opponent Compton High, the team employs a drill it has developed for getting on and off the field in hostile situations—when fighting breaks out in the crowd, when gunshots are heard—heading straight for the bus inside a cordon of police and security guards moments before the game clock winds down to 00:00.

Midweek, Newhall Hart called Poly offering to play an impromptu game that Friday, but Mel Collins said no. Their little plan was obvious: Hart would bump off Poly, then an enraged Poly would beat De La Salle, leaving the pollsters no choice but to give Hart the number one ranking. *Nice try, boys,* said Collins's smile. Too much was at stake for Poly to risk everything on a whim—and Hart was dangerous, a pass-first team with a Division I-A recruit at quarterback. Poly would resume the following week against Narbonne, another L.A. city school, but not much of a test.

De La Salle would go up against Mater Dei. This was their fourth meeting in a row, and the last year of the contract they had signed with such hoopla in 1998. But this rivalry, which had begun with such intensity—not just a national championship on the line, but bragging rights between Southern and Northern California, as well as among the state's Catholic schools—had unexpectedly sprung a leak. Like Buchanan, Mater Dei had gone into the 2000 season loaded with talent and nearly upset the Spartans. Unlike the Bears, who went on to win every game and their league and district championships, the Monarchs of Mater Dei sputtered. They'd lost their game after De La Salle, then got knocked off in the play-offs. At Mater Dei, a 9-3 record is a disappointment.

The 2001 season began with turmoil at Mater Dei, after a tough loss to Mission Viejo High on September 14. That very night Mater Dei's former top defensive back and running back, Camron Carmona, quit the team, after being replaced in the offensive lineup by a transfer from Loyola, Rafael Rice, whose arrival had sparked gossip. On Tuesday, September 18, Carmona transferred to Fountain Valley; by Friday night he was in the lineup and playing. One such transfer in a season raised eyebrows; two, under these circumstances, gave the appearance of chaos.

Word of team strife reached De La Salle's ears, of course. The coaches entered practice week determined to combat complacency on the part of the Spartans.

"Be a Spartan, get off your knees. Suck it up. Suck it up, suck it up, suck it up. You know what it takes, guys, you know what it takes. I guarantee you, Mater Dei is not taking a day off!"

Terry Eidson pauses, ready to blow the whistle for another forty-two-second gasser, in which players run the width of the field and back. "Hey, straighten up, Maurice!" somebody calls. Maurice Drew complies, his face drawn in agony.

"This is the tradition," Eidson says. "This is what we've done, year in and year out. This is one of the biggest games here, and this is how you push yourself. It's mental. Not physical. Right now you're feeling sorry for yourself—that's mental."

Terrell Ward, expressionless, hands on hips, drawls like a drill instructor, "You're sandbagging."

"Given the number of things that happened in the country this week, this football game isn't such a big deal," says Eidson in the same loud, uninflected voice. "But it's about your individual goals and what you do with adversity.

"When things get tough in life, how are you going to respond? When things get tough in school, when you get D's and F's—how do you respond?

"I sincerely believe this program instills discipline and an appreciation for hard work. It's something that stays with you all your life. It builds character. All of us standing here have done what you're doing."

Mike Blasquez joins the other two, looking just as grim: "Don't expect to go out there and have a good time. You're setting yourself up for a miserable experience."

"This game is their season," says Ward. "If you're sandbagging, Mater Dei's gonna eat you up."

Water break. Andy Briner is dragging his leg, in severe pain. He's coming off Vioxx, a prescription anti-inflammatory drug. Andy didn't want to stay on it continuously. "I'm going back on it tomorrow," he says with a wince. He had the experimental ultrasound treatment in Canada, but it didn't work. Nothing to do now but play the whole season in pain.

The kicker, James Bloomsburg, is off by himself with a net sack of footballs and a couple of different kicking tees at his feet. "I'm not kicking well at all," he says. "My timing is off." James is trying to coach himself out of this slump. He has a coach over the Donner Pass in Reno, four hours away, but no one here who can really help him.

"I'm getting my Mater Dei red on," says Pedro Cabrera, talking about the De La Salle game-week tradition in which a few players gradually deck themselves out in the opponent's colors. Mater Dei wears red, so it will be red socks on Monday, a red jersey Tuesday, maybe a red helmet Wednesday.

The offensive and quarterback coach, Mark Panella, is sitting in the bleachers working the cell phone. Panella is a broker at J. P. Morgan, and sometimes the two jobs intersect, such as now, as he concludes a call with a promise to put in an order for tickets to The Game.

After the last whistle, Ladouceur walks with a herd of sweating, drained players. "Mater Dei always plays us hard," he says. "They're physical. They'll grind you down. They got guys Derek's size. I don't know how much conditioning they do, but when you only go one-way, you don't have to be in as good shape as when you're going two."

This sounds logical, if also the usual noblesse oblige all winning coaches engage in. Watching the players, though, particularly the linemen, the main difference between the Spartans and the other wide-body teams such as Poly, Mater Dei, Kahuku, and St. Louis becomes clear: on the fields of those teams, a little flesh jiggles—something unseen at De La Salle. With only forty-five players dressed for the game, there are no breaks for anybody; the kids must be able to go for entire games if necessary. Big bodies, wide bodies, aren't treated differently, allowed to discount their Jell-O bellies as ballast for blocking, leverage for the trenches. At De La Salle, fat is fat and lean is lean, and never the twain shall meet.

"All the games but one with us, we jumped out ahead and they"—Mater Dei—"came back," Ladouceur continues. This year, though, is different. "They just mowed over Fallbrook, but Fallbrook self-destructed, too. Lots of fumbles. But that Mission Viejo game—boy, it wasn't even close. Mater Dei had, like, four first downs. It was ungodly. I'll have to see the film on that."

Ladouceur heads over to change clothes. "Have to do a fundraiser tonight," he says with a grimace. This year the school finally prevailed upon their main draw to add rainmaking to his official duties. He's had to drop his religion class because of it and seems sheepish about that. He understands that fund-raising enables the school to pursue its mission, but, for Ladouceur, teaching *is* the mission.

The next day, at 11:30 A.M., Terry Eidson holds a defensive film session in an upstairs classroom. The kids are clustered around a balcony, talking about homework, checking out the Carondelet girls (most respectfully, of course). Senior defensive back Lawrence Raman has his jaw wired—broken in practice. He won't think about missing the Poly game. "I'm still lifting and running," he says. Raman already has the distinction of having lost part of a finger in a weight-lifting accident. "My mom wanted me to quit after that," he admits with a tightly wired grin.

The film session consists of watching a grainy video of a game run herky-jerky, backward, forward, backward, while the coach points out certain tendencies or sets to the player concerned, then quizzes him on what he should do, while the others chime in with calls or predictions: "counter," "inside screen," and so forth.

These kids know football; it's a second language to them, a grammar of stasis: spacing, positioning, alignment—all before the ball is snapped, all capable of being read and interpreted. After the ball is snapped, the syntax switches to active: reading, reacting, separating, closing, hitting. Eidson wields the remote, lecturing in the dark. "After a big play Mater Dei likes to run a double reverse, tricky stuff. Here's a fake punt: instead of the kicker, the blocking back gets the snap, runs up, puts it underneath the butt of the interior blocking back, who runs with it." Adds Eidson, "That's the fake punt Monte Vista ran to beat us, fourteen to thirteen." This play is a bit of ancient history, easily a dozen years old, and it tickles the players. Football has such lore.

The class buzzer goes off. "We gotta get to the bomb, the one that got them back in the game," Eidson says. "One more and I'll let you go. Here's how they scored on this one: bring tackle over, put the tight end in motion, which means the tackle is eligible. So, it goes motion, then"—after the snap, pointing to wide receivers on the screen—"slant, slant, out. The out is wide-open." As he clicks off the video, students race for the door.

Practice starts with a touch of fashion: kicker James Bloomsburg in full Monarch red. Red socks, red jersey, helmet spray-painted red, red tape across his pants and socks. For a flourish, the name and number of last year's kicker—who blew the game for Mater Dei—is in white tape on his back. "That's cold," says a teammate.

Mark Panella and the two quarterbacks, Matt and Brian, will study game film tonight. After Mark takes a call from his wife, Sue, on his cell phone, he comes up to Matt. "Pork loin," he says, kissing the bunched ends of his fingers. Sue, a professional caterer, has just informed him that she will prepare dinner.

Panella addresses the running backs, Alijah, Maurice, and Nate: "Here's what I want to see from you today. I want you to pick it up. I want you to finish your runs. To lower the boom—deliver some hits. Don't stop. Keep those feet moving, keep your motor moving. And we need good play fakes. The way these Mater Dei guys roll up, they're gonna go off our first steps. So I want good play action and follow through on your fakes."

A roll call of play names: Blue Wham, 38 Power Pass; Strong left, Red Lamb, 16 X Counter; Slot right, 52 Escalade—the last using the name of the popular hip-hop SUV. One Orchid Screen Wheel. The offense executes as if it has an extra gear, faster, sharper.

Ladouceur stops to correct a lineman. "Come on, iron this shit out now. If the linebacker doesn't move, think, 'Where am I supposed to go?'" Matt Gutierrez, under pressure, lofts a ball over the middle, above the grasp of a receiver. "You know if it goes over his head, it's a pick!" The pressure mounts to get it right, until it feels like game pressure. Balls are dropped, players bounce off each other like pinballs.

During a water break Nate Kenion describes his schedule: precalculus, economics, civics, marine biology, and an elective, Classics of Horror. "We're reading *Frankenstein* and Poe right now." Apparently *Frankenstein* has every single SAT vocabulary word in it.

A long bomb is caught over-the-shoulder by sophomore Cameron Colvin. "Let's end on that one!" says Joe Aliotti, dean of discipline, line assistant coach, former Pittsburg High quarterback and all-American at Boise State.

"Go for one more," says Ladouceur. The snap sails over the head of the quarterback. Another. Chris Lucas beats his man, stops the play, adding one more point to his tally. If Lucas gets to ten, Derek Landri has to buy him dinner. Another play, the ball lying on the ground. "You've single-handedly ruined our offense," Eidson says. One more; QB Brian Callahan is sacked. Another—his throw is picked off. Eidson laughs. And that's how it ends.

Ladouceur says, "That was—okay. Wasn't great. When you see film of the Mission Viejo game, you'll see a team that wanted it more. You must be ready to play like that, or a Mater Dei team is going to beat you."

Before trudging back to the lockers, the staff gathers by the bleachers for a drink of water. Talk turns to Mater Dei. "We should feast on those guys," says one. "I read every single play based on their feet. Our linebackers are going to *feast!*"

Someone else remarks that Matt Gutierrez's hand hurts. "He's with the trainer?" asks Panella. "Looking very serious," says a coach. "He was doing this"—he flexes his hand back and forth—

"a lot in practice." A crease of worry divides Panella's brow. Matt's passes have looked less crisp, the long balls have fluttered. If the broken bone hasn't fully healed . . .

Matt and Brian Callahan and Panella hop into their cars and head down Treat Boulevard, onto the freeway at the height of rush hour, zipping in and out of on-ramps and passing lanes. Panella's house is on a tree-shaded street of relatively new, upper-class homes. His young daughters, Sophia and Francesca, greet their daddy with chatter and demands, to read a book, start a video, fix a toy. Sue Panella is putting the finishing touches on pork loin with apples, mashed potatoes, caramelized carrots with brown sugar, green beans, fresh rolls, gravy. The boys linger around the kitchen.

Dinner is eaten on a gleaming dining table set with cutlery, plates, napkins, and a pitcher of ice water. Everyone's talking: Brian mentions that there's a football team in Alaska that practices on slate; Matt asks if anyone has noticed how much coach Ladouceur is smiling these days: "In film class he's hysterical, keeps breaking me up." Coach Panella shakes his head: "He never cracked a smile all the years I played here." After fifteen years of hyperintensity, and a scary perfectionism, Ladouceur seems to have relaxed a little—without losing his edge, of course.

Talk turns to 9/11. Brian says that he's thinking of doing ROTC in college, maybe even joining the air force. Mark Panella looks at him as if he can't believe what he's hearing.

The talk turns to choices: personal, career, moral. It's a free-ranging conversation, not hemmed in by pieties, but throughout, Panella, who is a coach after all, manages to slip in offhand, insistent reminders of the consequences of every decision. Sue reminisces about when she and Mark first got together, and he casually adds, "We were living in sin." Matt remarks that he ran into one of his play-off opponents the other day, now nineteen and selling cars. "He had lots of Division I offers," says Matt, "but he's got a baby now."

"What does that tell you?" Mark Panella asks. "What does that suggest to you?"

The men retire to the living room to watch film over cookies and milk.

Everybody chips in with terse observations. "See how the backers set up? Four-three," says Brian. "We could seventeen that all day, fourteen that all day, too," adds Matt, referring to plays he can run. Panella points out that, after a big running gain, Mater Dei switches to a 5-2, meaning five linemen and two linebackers up front. "We're gonna see something like this," he says, clicking the remote from the comfort of his leather recliner. He points out that the strong safety is reading the tight end for cues as to what kind of play will develop.

Film sessions are character studies. A trait or flaw is noticed, and the offensive scheme is tweaked to exploit or counter it. A Mater Dei linebacker, all agree, is vulnerable, he's "just in space and undersized," says Panella. A defensive end's attack technique is scrutinized: "If you feel pass pressure from this guy," he says, "give him an escape move, a head fake, or shoot underneath, and you'll get right by."

Matt and Brian take no notes, but they're all eyes. Mater Dei goes on defense again, blitzing linebackers through the gaps between the battling linemen. Mark looks for a way to key the blitz, to anticipate it. The Mission Viejo quarterback escapes by bootlegging, running counterflow all alone; he's fast and scores. "Wish we had one like that," says Panella. Matt grunts at the dig. The group debates whether coaching or players make the difference in a program—Panella comes down on the side of coaching.

All agree that Mater Dei's strong safety is good and can hit. Then he gets blown up twice in a row. The Monarchs are looking inconsistent, as advertised. "We'll be seeing a different team out there," Panella says as daughter Francesca appears in the doorway, pouting. It's nine-fifteen, and Brian has other studies. "Say good-night to Sue," says Panella. "She's in the bedroom."

At the start of Thursday's offensive practice, Panella and Mike Blasquez debate what to do about Matt's arm, watching as he takes snaps from Scott Regalia and drops back, without throwing. "Footwork's a little off," Panella says, calling out a correction.

"I want to keep him out today," says Blasquez. "We've got to implement bouts of recovery during the week or that arm's not going to have any snap in it."

"I've never had a dead arm," says Matt.

"You forget that you had three months off due to your wrist surgery," says Blasquez. "You've probably never had three months off in your entire life. If I'm hearing you correctly, one day it's there, the next day it just doesn't have that snap."

"I still don't have that one hundred percent strength feel," Matt agrees.

"Every baseball practice you ever went to counted your pitches, right? We could do that."

They decide to hold Matt to seventy plays today.

On the field there are seven red jerseys, and players are even impersonating individual Monarchs. Several discuss the film they've watched and ponder the mystery of Camron Carmona. "I don't get it," says Regalia. "He was a starter. He had a good game. Had an interception. Third-year varsity. It's mind-boggling that he'd transfer."

After school the next day, Friday, comes the first of three traditional rituals, rites of bonding and commitment, that De La Salle goes through before every game. These are sacred and private moments for the players and coaches; former players whisper that this is the secret heart of De La Salle football.

As school lets out, the parking lot is filled with boys and girls and cars, a froth of pent-up adolescent energy released by the 2:30 bell. The school chapel is in a quiet brick annex, not very big, with a sunken central area, an altar at one end, seven sliver-thin windows, muted wall-to-wall carpet. The players enter quietly and spread out in the shadows, some sitting, others lying on their backs staring up, others facedown on pillowed arms.

Each week a couple of players come with texts to read, songs to play, and lyrics to ponder. Lyric sheets for a Metallica song, "Nothing Else Matters," are handed out, then the song is played: somber, acoustic guitar, big bass.

Terry Eidson invites responses. Players speak of the importance of trust, of challenging yourself. "Losers make promises they always break," says one. A coach brings up the example of Jim Valvano, the North Carolina State basketball coach whose team won the NCAA title in a great upset, only to die shortly after. A player adds, "He was ninety percent certain it was bone cancer, but he attacked the only way he knew how: with all his energy."

A Bible verse is haltingly read by another player: "About the fourth watch of the night He cometh unto them, walking on the sea, and He would have passed by them: but they, when they saw Him walking on the sea, supposed that it was an apparition, and cried out. . . . But he saith unto them: Take courage, it is I, be not afraid." A coach responds, "Powerful readings, powerful song. The last stanza of the Metallica song, 'don't care what they say, what they do'—that's how we should approach Mater Dei. Another line, about trust: trust Chan to make the right calls, trust Regalia to make the snap, trust Matt. Since January we have been taking it week by week. We're not looking ahead, we're looking at Mater Dei. But we know at the back of our minds there's our ultimate goal—a U.S. championship."

A minute of silence goes by. A player speaks: "The way we talk, in our chapel, our team dinner—the way we open to each other, from the heart, not just to be cool."

Then a minute, almost two, before another player responds, "Every single one of us made a commitment to ourselves, to each other, to our coaches. We've worked hard for it."

Another cites the complementary Bible story of Paul walking on the water toward Jesus, growing afraid, and nearly drowning: "Maybe like if against Mater Dei we might lose faith; we have to have faith in each other or else we'll sink as a team."

Eventually a coach speaks: "I'm not going to spend a lot of time talking about last year. But I will say, about this song, that last year's team had an attitude that said, 'Nothing else matters.' Not the whole team, but enough so that Spartan tradition was imperiled. Enough went along. The attitude was 'If we win, I can be rude, I can be selfish.' That attacked the core of Spartan tradition.

"I haven't felt that about this team. As you go through life, you won't meet many people you can trust. But if you look at a teammate and say, 'I completely trust that person,' that is awesome. With the World Trade Center event, you can lose some faith. We have worries. We hope our government won't make this a holy war. We don't have a lot of control over events. The best you can do is, show your faith. Become the person who you were intended to be. Because, like the old Jim Morrison book says:

" 'No one here gets out alive.' "

Prayers follow—for family members, for a sick parent, for a father traveling on the road, for all the people involved in "the event," for an injured player. After each prayer comes a group response. A coach gives a long, personal prayer that ends, "Thank you, Lord, for the opportunity to grow together as a team and to play this great game."

The Lord's Prayer ends the chapel, followed by hand slaps, and hugs.

Terry Eidson walks out to the field. "The thing about last year's team," he says, "they would sit in silence through those readings. Maybe one guy would speak. One. They had a real attitude problem. Oh, they got through the season undefeated all right, got it together to play one great game against Mater Dei, but mostly they relied on the stars who did care, to pull them through. This team has the spirit; these guys really show their love and trust in each other."

After a walk-through practice, the players return to the locker room—it has been transformed by a mischievous and, it would seem, perverse hand. There are signs and banners on lockers and walls reading: "RED Attitude—GO Monarchs!" "The Streak—It Ends Now!" "Prepare to Meet Your Maker, Spartans! The Streak Is Over!" This last has a photo of a smiling Mater Dei coach Bruce Rollinson. Though parodic, the scene is also a vision of a locker room four hundred miles south in Santa Ana, among those who dream of breaking The Streak.

The evening is only half-over. The players hop into their cars and race through a golden sunset-lit landscape of rolling hills and steep ravines, on a country road that wiggles along until it comes out before the wide, watery plain of the Sacramento Delta. Here, at the modern ranchette home of player Anthony Salvador, Spartan parents are waiting with a barbecue, complete with red-and-blue checked tablecloths, forty pounds of tri-tip steak, twenty pounds of pasta, Caesar salad, and homemade ice cream sundaes. "It's good to do this," says Teresa Tabacco, mother of Dan. "The boys are so private and into it we hardly see 'em until the season is over."

Indeed, after the meal the team withdraws again, inside the Salvador garage, which is large enough for a couple of SUVs and maybe a tractor. Once the garage door is shut, the intensity returns: a briefing for tomorrow's routine, discussions of key assignments, and then a second psychologically fraught encounter session. Kids admit their weaknesses, pledging to do better; players who aren't starting vow to push the starters harder in practice, to make them better. Part sweat-lodge rite, part late-night bull session, part Chinese reeducation camp, this hour of fire is where the bonds of brotherhood are given their final tempering.

The faded stadium at the University of the Pacific in Stockton has known its share of football glory. Amos Alonzo Stagg—one of the greatest minds in the game, inventor of the tackling dummy, the concept of the shift, and the man-in-motion and end-around plays—coached here for fourteen seasons, before retiring at age ninety-eight. But UOP dropped football in 1995, and now the stadium is available for anyone with a team and a dream. Stockton is two hours from Concord, but De La Salle schedules its big home games there.

In an open-air press box, rows of Bay Area and Southern California sportswriters, newscasters, and radio broadcasters kvetched to each other about the tight deadlines they faced. "If De La Salle gets ahead and Mater Dei starts throwing the ball, it may go on until midnight," groused one reporter.

The Spartans took the kickoff and proceeded to play as if making sure the reporters got an early night's sleep was their main concern. Alijah ran for six yards on the first play, for sixty-seven on the second, and Nate scored on the third: 7–0. Mater Dei got a good kick return, but couldn't move the ball and punted. The Spartans moved the ball up to the 50 and were forced to punt, but a roughing-the-kicker penalty on Mater Dei gave them the ball back. Three quick first downs on runs later, Matt lofted a pass to Ryan the Flea in the left corner, who made a tough catch: 14–0. The first quarter ended with De La Salle in command.

In the second quarter, however, Mater Dei's defense stiffened to snuff a screen, sack Matt, and halt the Spartans's reverses and fake reverses. De La Salle had to punt twice on successive possessions. As the teams lined up for the second punt, the press box collectively opined that Mater Dei was ready to make a run, that the meat grinder of its big linemen was already taking a toll.

And then James Bloomsburg's punt was blocked.

Or was it? It all happened so quickly: the ball arrived in James's hands, his foot swung up, ball and foot met just as the butt of the blocking back came into the picture as he backed up (a no-no), and the ball spiked down to the grass, bounced directly into the hands of the other blocking back, Damon Jenkins, who dashed straight ahead, seventy yards for a touchdown.

Or was it? The officials said yes. Mater Dei and Rollinson said no. The press box couldn't decide and called their editors to look up the rule. But the official's call was right: while a blocked punt cannot be advanced by the punting team, this ball hadn't traveled past the line of scrimmage, so technically it was the same as a running play—a weird running play, to be sure.

So the score was 21–0, and Mater Dei never recovered. Final score, 34–7; the four-year contract between the schools was up, and with it much of the Monarchs's mystique.

As the Spartan players headed up the tunnel, a Mater Dei coach approached Ryan Eidson. "Excellent game, number eleven." Flea thanked him. "Did I see you at the Stanford combine?" the coach asked. Flea shook his head no. "Really? I thought I saw you."

Flea shrugged, saying, in a clipped voice, "Too small."

The Mater Dei coach seemed taken aback at first. "Well," he said firmly, "you played big tonight."

That same weekend, Poly beat Narbonne, 28–6, but an outcome that in days past would have been cause for exultation was treated as a disappointment. Nothing the coaches said beforehand could get the Jackrabbits to believe they had anything to worry about. Unlike Ladouceur and Eidson, who could point to Mater Dei's prowess, pride, and history of upsets, Poly coach Raul Lara and his assistants couldn't cry wolf about the Narbonne Gauchos. After Hershel Dennis ran sixty-eight yards to score on the first possession, and Marcedes Lewis caught a sixty-two-yard touchdown pass from Brandon a bit later, Poly played as if it only had half a mind on the game. "I thought we were lethargic and unfocused," said Lara after Monday evening's practice.

Practice ended with film of the Buchanan–De La Salle game. Afterward, Marcedes and his mother, Yvonne, sat near the parking lot entrance, facing each other, their backs against pillars, long legs stretched out along a low wall, the soles of their tennis shoes pressed together.

Yvonne debriefed her son about the game film: "Do you think we have a chance? I hear they're pretty good."

"They looked fast," Marcedes said. "They execute. That quarterback, Matt Gutierrez"—he slowed down and pronounced it like an announcer—"he's like a college QB in his footwork and his reads. He's a heck of a nice guy. Reminds me of Brandon."

"Brandon is going to have his work cut out for him. You know what they're going to do, don't you? They're gonna shut Hershel down, put nine men in the box."

Marcedes nodded. "That's what Narbonne did. Blitzing on every down, right from the first play. Coach said to me, 'Think you can get behind 'em?' And that's what we did, went over the top."

The team filed past into a night bejeweled by taillights and fog lamps; players shuffled into the warm clusters of parents and friends or else set off for home. There were no comments of "We're going to crush them," none of the bravado normally present. Everyone looked sobered up.

That was how the coaches wanted it. During the following week the Poly coaches worked a sort of schizophrenic magic, simultaneously preparing the players for a weak team, Fontana, and an awesome one, De La Salle. The coaches had to build Fontana up as an opponent to be respected, or else the players might come out flat and lose—the worst possible scenario for The Game. At the same time, the coaches didn't want the kids to get so pumped up that they peaked too soon. "Against Fontana I'd rather play a lousy game, and win, then play a great game," Herman Davis said.

Friday night arrived, and with it the last test before De La Salle. Located out at the outer edges of Los Angeles near San Bernardino, Fontana once had all the prerequisites of a great football town: a steel mill, a high school, and a chip on its shoulder. In fact, the Fontana Steelers competed for a string of Southern Section championships and won a national number one year-end ranking in 1987. But an expanding population base led the Fontana District to open three new high schools, and these lured away the best athletes and students. Even Fontana's coaches left for the new schools. Still, the area bred tough players—you had to be tough to play ball in an industrial wasteland where summer temperatures hit one hundred degrees for weeks—and the Poly coaches hoped Fontana would be motivated by a chance to upset the nation's number one-ranked team.

At least the Poly players would have no trouble getting up for Fontana, because as a rare travel game it meant a visit to the Hometown Buffet, one of a chain of all-you-can-eat cafeterias.

When the kids arrived, their coaches stood by, as if to reassure any patron who might possibly be intimidated to find herself amid seventy teenagers, some of them on the large side; the Poly players didn't need more than one or two whispered reminders before their manners kicked in. Players stood aside, smilingly ushering patrons ahead of them.

The food on display soon vanished, however, creating a moment of consternation and, among the other patrons, awe at the sight of an entire buffet cleaned out in under five minutes. But reinforcements were on the way, as the buffet workers, mostly young Hispanic women, came giggling forward bearing a steaming bounty in their arms: steel bins piled high with fried shrimp, fried chicken fingers, fried okra, greens and ham, mashed potatoes, peas and carrots, roasted potatoes, corn succotash, blackened catfish. The boys seemed torn between flirting and eyeing the food—and in the end did both. At the carving tables, two carvers in white toques dispensed slabs of prime rib, turkey, roast pork. Darnell Bing strolled by, an entire plate of mashed potatoes filled with a crater lake of gravy in his hands. "I love the country greens," said Maurice Murray. "The shrimp," said Leon Jackson. Coach Tim Moncure indulged in strawberry shortcake (real biscuits, real whipped cream) and tapioca.

And then it was time to go. The Hometown's manager stood at the door, insisting on shaking each player's hand. "This is the best-behaved football team we've ever had here," he told coach Lara.

On the first Poly possession, after Fontana can't get off a punt on their own 20, Rory Carrington runs for six yards. Then Hershel Dennis takes a pitch and dashes for the touchdown, flattening two Fontana defensive backs. After a second Fontana punt, on first down Brandon throws long to Derrick Jones, who sprints seventy-five yards for a touchdown. On the third Fontana punt, defensive back Kevin Tapp bobbles the ball, then returns it sixty-odd yards for a touchdown. After an exchange of fumbles, Fontana punts again. On the first play, Brandon throws the quick inside screen to Derrick, who races along a picket line of blocks on a diagonal for another sixty-yard touchdown. And that's just the first quarter.

It's 28–0 with three quarters to go. Herman Davis turns with a sorrowful expression and waves toward the empty bleachers. "Where *is* everybody?" he asks. "Fontana didn't show up." Tim Moncure overhears him, nods. "They used to shut down the steel mill at three o'clock and everybody would walk down to the stadium—there'd be food stalls, bands, it was the only show in town. They had great football. They had all those desert kids, gritty and tough."

A security aide walks past and shakes his head. "Two years ago this was a big game. Four years ago this was a *giant* game." A reporter for the *Riverside Press-Citizen*, John Murphy, stares at the Steelers's ragtag band. "Two years ago Fontana came out with one hundred players."

Though Lara needs to give his regulars practice for the showdown next week, the Steelers are offering less resistance than the Poly junior varsity. Even with subs in, the game ends at 70–0, but Poly isn't happy. Hershel, who touched the ball six times, scored four times, and gained over a hundred yards, paces the sidelines in frustration. "Man, I wish we could play somebody better before De La Salle," he says.

Herman Davis feels the same way, although he conceals this from the kids. "You know what worries me? We haven't had a game yet. Westchester wasn't a game, Banning was canceled, Narbonne wasn't a game, and now we got to play *a game* and look who it's against—De La Salle. How do you motivate the kids when they win seventy to nothing? How do you critique them? We've got to have that gut check. And we've got to deal with the circus."

Poly makes a swift exit, straight up the ramp, click-clack in their cleats, into a welcoming crowd, their families mostly. Not a lot of students want to drive out through three hours of rush-hour traffic to see a blowout.

Coach Lara doesn't even bother to go through the motions of a postgame interview. "What game?" he asks. Then he smiles. "I got enough of a workout; the kids sure didn't. Fontana wasn't a test for anything. I just hope the kids don't think we're ready."

Sixteen

SEVEN DAYS

Saturday morning at nine and the Jackrabbits are back in the gym for film study. In the movie-house twilight the trainers move from player to player, applying ice to bruises and bumps, fixing it in place with several twists of Saran Wrap. Coaches hand out Nestlé's Crunch bars to players who've made big hits or pancake blocks. Leading off the bunch is kicker Jeff Hastings, who'd tracked his own kickoff and made a nice hit; Jeff gets a round of applause. A blasé Darnell Bing pauses while reading the sports pages to accept his two Crunch bars.

The tape of last night's game against Fontana starts, and Lara's first point isn't long in coming. It concerns the linebackers, his own area of specialization before ascending to the head job. "They're going to screen the hell out of us," he says, referring to the short-delay passes used to punish an overaggressive defense. When a wide receiver streaks across the middle, Lara cautions linebacker Paul Lepule not to let him do so unimpeded: "Hug up, Paul. If you don't, they're gonna kill us."

Lara reruns tape of a Manuel Wright sack. "See this, guys, this is proper. Manuel gets his tackle, then helps the QB up. I want you to do that. Help the player up."

Adds Herman Davis, "So you can knock him down again." The point is emphasized again and again: the upcoming game is a showcase for Poly, for the community, and for themselves. Anger, payback, unnecessary roughness, have no place on the field.

Up on the screen, Poly is now on defense. "Manuel Wright is high right here," Lara says, referring to the grizzly's upright stance. Herman Davis snorts, saying, "Manuel Wright is taking a break." A Top 5 rating doesn't cut any slack with Davis. Then the linebackers come under the microscope: "Are we hugging *up?*" Lara asks the room, his voice growing more piercing with each word.

The short session soon ends, and the lights go up on the sleepy, slumping bodies. "This week is going be hectic with the media," says Lara. "They're going to ask you all kinds of questions, anything to suck you into a controversy. Make sure you do not make any kind of comment about how you're going to kick De La Salle's butts—because you're not. This is a very good team you're playing."

The team straggles out into the bright sunshine of an empty Poly campus, faced with a few hours of precious spare time. When you're the number one team in the nation, heading for the biggest game in high school history, and you're only sixteen or seventeen years old, and half a dozen girls giggle at the sight of you, life is sweet—even if you're walking around with a couple of pounds of ice wrapped in Saran Wrap on your shoulder.

Sitting on a bench outside, Darnell Bing talks about what his days are like: "Not much time for a life, really. Practice, homework, eat, sleep. Weekends are for games, Sunday for SAT class."

The Top 5 have been invited to attend USC's game against Stanford this afternoon as sideline guests. The USC invitation is special; four former Poly players are already on the Trojan squad: DeShaun Hill, Kareem Kelly, Mike Pollard, and Darrell Rideaux.

If they'd been able to make their SATs, Ray Tago and Marvin Simmons would also have been Trojans. Winston Justice is definitely going to the game, Manuel and Hershel are thinking about it.

But Darnell shakes his head: "My niece turns one today. I'm going to her birthday party instead."

Back in the football offices, trainers Rob Shock and Jessica Wasko are organizing and repacking first aid equipment and materials, and discussing 9/11. "The boys wanted to play Banning," says Rob. "They were ready, they understood the game plan. After Wednesday's practice when they heard that L.A. Unified had canceled, the expressions on their faces were angry, sad, frustrated. Instead of sitting in front of the TV watching the Trade Center go down, over and over and over, they wanted to play. For these younger people, to have everything shut down was traumatizing. Not to trivialize it, but some of these kids deal with this stuff on a daily basis in the neighborhoods in which they live."

Jessica drawls, "It's not like they haven't seen anybody die."

"The thing is," Rob says, "our kids have seen death and destruction all their lives. Our terrorism is gangs. They can take a life anytime, and we know it. And we've lost talented athletes who'd rather be gangsters than play football."

"I think it would have been good to play that game just because it would've given the kids a shot of something normal," Jessica says. "I mean, that was my first Friday night off in September in seven years. I didn't know what to do with myself. I sat at home and watched HBO."

On the other side of the training room's glass door is Raul Lara's football office, a thruway always full of coaches, trainers, and players. A wall is devoted to SAT test dates, target scores, and an index of grade point averages needed to qualify for a Division

I-A scholarship. There are quotations of Scripture, from Proverbs 3:5–6, Psalms 51, and this, from Philippians 4:8:

> . . . whatsoever things are true, whatsoever things are honest, whatsoever things are just, whatsoever things are pure, whatsoever things are lovely, whatsoever things are of good report; if there be any virtue, and if there be any praise, think on these things.

Today is not a day for praise. Since the Narbonne game, Lara has been displeased with the communications between coaches in the press box and coaches on the field, as well as concerned with play-calling on offense and defense. Lara has off-field issues, too. Like any harried new CEO, Lara has had to tread softly yet act boldly to untangle old channels and break with old habits; yet he still has to invite input from Poly's informal board of directors, former coaches such as Al Nogi, Bill Mulligan, and Dave Levy, as well as more recent chieftains such as Barnett and even, it is rumored, Jerry Jaso. "I appreciate their advice and always listen to what they have to say," he says, "but that doesn't mean I will always act on it."

Other distractions are job-related: "My job as a probation officer takes precedence over everything. For instance, one day last week I had a kid call me up and threaten suicide. That's what I had to deal with for a couple of hours. No way I was going to be thinking about football." Lara gives a wry, what-can-you-do glance. "I am trying *not* to think about what it means to be coaching in a national championship game, the *first* national championship, in only my fourth game as a head coach."

And of course he has De La Salle to worry about. "I saw the Buchanan film and, wow, they're good. No wonder they're undefeated. They're so fundamentally sound it's ridiculous. That seventy-seven is a damned good guy," he says of Derek Landri. "I'm a little worried about whether we can control him. He's the real deal. He likes to go over center and create madness. He's a mission for a couple of kids."

Outside, the quad is being invaded by cameramen with giant battery packs. Technicians lay down black cables to television trucks parked around the corner. Television and newspaper reporters sit at the Rabbit Snack Shack's lunch benches discussing camera angles or details of the campus, ears pressed to cell phones. The *Sports Illustrated* writer is on the phone while en route to Poly from a golf tournament he's covering, speaking to the *New York Times* stringer, who has just arrived.

The game is clearly a media event. And the media will now take control, at least partially, of the event, narrowing the idiosyncrasies of the schools and their multifaceted kids and coaches into stereotypes that will be easier to package and sell to the largest possible audience.

Poly's offensive strategy is fine-tuned in a plain room equipped with a blackboard and a film projector. "Little Merle" Cole III, the new offensive coordinator, and Tim Moncure, the offensive line coach, huddle in front of the play frozen on the screen, speaking almost in whispers. On the board are diagrammed three versions of De La Salle's 4-4 defense.

Merle III runs through ways to attack the first two versions of the 4-4. "Brandon throws a quick screen left, then has the option later to throw stop 'n' go," says Merle III. "Or, he fakes this"—he demonstrates a quick pass—"and does this"—he drops his right hand down by his hip, slipping the ball to Hershel on a draw.

The two men stare hungrily at the third diagram. There's an inviting gap, or bubble, between the left defensive end and the tackle, who is lined up over the center. They are figuring out ways to attack it when Jim Barnett, the coach emeritus, strides in briskly, playbooks and papers clamped under one arm. The white-haired guru in tennis shorts immediately points to the huge gap. "They're not going to let you have that big-ass bubble," he says. "Let's not outthink ourselves. Let's work on our shit."

Merle III murmurs the name of a play. Barnett shakes his head, but Merle III persists: "We ran it good all week."

Barnett is unmoved: "If you get a defense from De La Salle that looks screwed up, it's not. They have a discipline. Don't be misled—they will have it plugged."

The men draw circles on the board, rub them out, mark over them, moving the running backs, Hershel and Rory, around like pieces on a chessboard. "Bodies on bodies," says Barnett, boiling down the Poly philosophy. Moncure draws a blocking scheme. "See, from what I heard that didn't work, only Hershel found a way," says Barnett. The curse of having talented athletes is that they can make a team look good for the wrong reasons. When your team finally meets a tougher opponent, your tactics may be unmasked.

The talk shifts to using Hershel's initial step to control the Spartan linebackers, assuming that they will be reacting to Hershel's every move. "It's a real subtle thing, and some backs can't do it," says Barnett. "But if you get those backers thinking, 'Oh, here it comes again,' and then solid block—boom! That poor sucker's hung out to dry."

They weigh putting Marcedes and Hershel on the same side as receivers, with Darnell as tailback. The target: Alijah Bradley. "Number twenty-seven, he's a good athlete, but he's little," says Barnett.

Merle III agrees: "We've got to keep on hitting him." They draw up plans to use John Williams, a 225-pound reserve fullback, to batter the smaller Spartans, as well as to block for Brandon.

Tim Moncure raises a question: "I haven't seen 'em on goal line?"

Barnett shoots back, "They haven't been on goal line!"

The three laugh heartily, if a bit ruefully. There seems to be some question as whether *any* team has scored on the Spartan first-team defense this year.

"Does their free safety go both ways?" asks Moncure, referring to Maurice Drew.

"He's their tailback," says Merle III.

"It's getting to the point that we're almost too predictable," says Barnett. "Let's give them a little different look."

Almost every team will put in a new trick play for a game, one that takes advantage of an opponent's weakness or overaggressive tendency. Poly has nothing against being clever, but doesn't resort to tricks to win. Trick plays are tricky: If you make a big deal of installing one, it can send the message to your team that you don't believe you can win without fakery. This game would likely be decided by the team whose will stayed strongest the longest. Barnett makes a halfhearted suggestion: "If your blocking tight end is Marcedes, he'll always be open for the double pass," a play in which Marcedes would catch a screen pass behind the line of scrimmage, then throw in turn to a streaking receiver. Nobody is interested in spending much time on it, not against De La Salle.

A game-plan consensus emerges at Monday's film sessions. After watching De La Salle slice through Mater Dei for two touchdowns in the first quarter, Big Merle growls, "De La Salle came out really prepped. They set you down in the first series. But they're not used to being scored on. If we come out and shock them, it'll take them right out of their game."

This is an idea that will stick, along with the belief that De La Salle's two-way players will tire in the fourth quarter. Another area of vulnerability is noted when the Monarchs complete a pass to cornerback Damon Jenkins's side of the field. Little Merle crows, "Sophomore! Pick on a sophomore!" (He's wrong—Jenkins is a junior.) Cornerback Willie Glasper, however, is a sophomore, and he bites on a fake, but the Mater Dei quarterback misses a wide-open bomb. "Number thirty-one is my man," announces Little Merle, of Glasper. "I'm gonna introduce you to a couple of friends, Mr. Derrick Jones and Mr. Marcedes Lewis."

At times the room is optimistic, almost gleeful. The offense likes what it sees, imagines rolling Brandon out left and right, tiring the two-way players, Derek Landri and Andy Briner. They envision pounding Hershel and Rory, wearing down the Spartans the way Mater Dei did in the 2000 game. They see Derrick and Marcedes stinging the inexperienced sophomore cornerback.

Still, when several coaches comment on how slow key Spartans seem, Big Merle will hear none of it: "They move out on you quick, real quick. They go all out these first few series, try to put you out of the game. They go up on you *fast*."

Don Norford echoes the caution as he steps outside for a breather. "You can see why they're good," he says of De La Salle. "Their emphasis is on discipline and on the footwork of their kids."

The game itself "is a blessing," he says. "I've been coaching twenty-five years and this is something you dream about. This is one of those games where you get a win and a loss on the scoreboard, but nobody ever really loses. The school, the community, the kids—they learn so much about themselves to be in a game of this magnitude. The game teaches you about yourself. The kids will remember this for their whole lives."

He surveys the cluster of media. "I've run teams against the best in the world in track, before eighty thousand people and all that. But this is the first time the two best football teams in the nation will ever meet. I wish I could suit up and play."

As Norford speaks, a Cambodian woman in light blue silk pajama pants and a conical straw hat glides past, while in the shadow of the wall an Indonesian woman, wrapped in batik with a baby on her back, waits for her ROTC-member son. The media gawks and puzzles over these seeming apparitions; then Marcedes Lewis lopes by wearing his trademark white, fuzzy headband, so tall and graceful, and the cameras and notebooks flow toward him. Norford smiles. "When Marcedes was ten, I would come down to the Pop Warner field and pull him out of games to meet pros like Willie McGinest, Leonard Russell, Omar Stoutmire. They'd sit him down and tell him about life, school, the pros." Mentioning that a number of college scouts will be attending the game, he adds, "Colleges, all of them want Poly, whether you're Division I or NAIA—you just got to get you some."

Monday afternoon, the team assembles in the film room, waiting on the head coach to give his official here-we-go speech. Suddenly coach Lara enters striding rapidly between two uniformed guards armed with walkie-talkies. He looks pale, stressed. "I'm late," he explains softly, out of earshot of the players. "I had to take care of a situation with a kid—a life-and-death situation." A student parolee has threatened suicide.

Turning to the assembled players and coaches, Lara raises his voice. "You have got to remember that there are more things than football," he says deliberately, his voice now calm. "Do not take life for granted. Don't get caught up with drugs. Do not give up on life. If you ever, ever feel like you're that down, talk to me."

The team heads out to the field for practice. Five minutes into coach Lara's guided tour of how to shut down the De La Salle offense, coprincipal Mel Collins approaches Don Norford on the sidelines and the two begin a quiet discussion. Half the team turns to watch.

"This is it," announces Lara with the air of a man who has just had a revelation. Heads swivel back. "I've got it figured out." Lara's tone is borderline angry. "Two people talking on the sidelines and you can't pay attention. What are you going to do with twenty thousand people on Saturday night? We've lost you. We've lost you."

Now that he has the team's attention again, Lara makes a few simple statements: "You are going to watch a lot of film. You need to get to know the guy in front of you. Matt Gutierrez is one of the best quarterbacks in the country. But we want to stop the run. If we stop the run, we force him to throw. We *force* him to throw, we start to have fun.

"Number seventy-seven"—Derek Landri, "is one of the best in the country. Number twenty-one"—Maurice Drew—"their rover on defense and a running back, is a very good football player. Number twenty-seven and number twenty"—Alijah Bradley and Nate Kenion—"are very good runners and need to be contained.

"Guys, our goals are the same every year: to beat every team and be CIF champs. This game does not change that. So be humble and be ready for a fight. No matter what happens, be proud and be grateful."

Later, Keith Anderson, the fireman who coaches special teams and is a major provider of heart-to-heart talks for the players, is asked what he really thinks of De La Salle's offense. He glances around to see whether any kids are listening. "What they do, they do very well," he says. "If they play that kind of football and beat us, then we deserve to lose. But I don't see them running away from us like they did against Mater Dei. So what's been an eighty-yard gain will be a five-yard gain. But"—he pauses to sigh heavily—"I have been around here long enough to know there ain't no definite nothin'.

"I just want us to play an A game. But if we don't, then it could be tough. If they get a lead on us, and then they get conservative, run the ball, run the ball, then we may be in trouble. I really like what they do and they do it well.

"I don't want a good game. I don't want the crowd entertained. Nail-biters do nothing for me. After the Loyola game"—the CIF championship the previous season—"I didn't celebrate for two weeks. Then I said, 'I guess it's okay now.'"

Overhearing this, Herman Davis prefers to accentuate the positive: "If I was De La Salle, I'd hate to play Poly. You have to be real sharp with the checks and reads. If, for some reason, the game is twenty-one to nothing Poly, you have got to change your game plan. Go out passing and do it quick. But there's one problem—our rush. Nobody's been able to block Manuel for two years!"

Davis wonders how De La Salle can truly prepare for Poly. "How do you simulate Poly in practice? That's De La Salle's problem. How do you simulate Winston? Manuel? Marcedes?"

On the sidelines of the De La Salle practice field, Ryan Eidson is looking sharp. He's not representing, though—he's *simulating*, wearing the green and gold with pride. A green-and-gold towel hangs down from his waist, he has tall green socks, green-and-gold armbands, a white, fuzzy headband. Yes, the 5'10", 155-pound Flea has come to practice intending to role-play 6'7", 225-pound Marcedes. It turns out he'll have to take a number. Everyone wants to be the tall tight end with the ebullient smile.

The temperature is ninety-six degrees; here it is the first week of October, and it feels as if summer has only now arrived. Everybody is suffering. Maurice Drew and Alijah Bradley pause to catch their breath. "What we're looking forward to," Maurice gasps, "is for once not being taken out of a game in the second quarter. Man!"

A flat pass to the player impersonating Hershel Dennis, Gino Ottoboni, produces a nifty cut and run that leaves the defender, Alijah, grasping. "Alijah, Hershel will break your ankles, for sure," says Terrell Ward. They run a play where the Hershel/Gino starts on the wing and outraces a linebacker deep. "Think we have a mismatch here?" asks Ladouceur. Aliotti nods. Ladouceur turns: "Okay, Poly, let's get a drink." After the scout team has trotted to the side for water, Mark Panella and Ladouceur talk about the many first steps of Hershel Dennis—just as the Poly coaches had predicted they would.

Ryan knows Poly has been watching him and the other Spartans on film. "What did they say? They talk shit?" he demands. Hearing that this is definitely not the case—at Poly, as soon as someone starts up trash-talking, the coaches and players come down on him hard—Ryan actually looks disappointed; like his uncle Terry, he'd prefer it if Poly showed fewer manners. They'd be easier to get up for.

Coach Ward talks about the heavy community scene in Long Beach. "Yeah, they're tipped for the game; I have friends in Long Beach, they've all been calling. That school has a history. And the thing is, they come back. They all seem to come back.

"This game's gonna be great. It's gonna bring our kids up to the highest level. It's like the Ali-Frazier fights. Those fights brought out the best of both Ali and Frazier. These kids, now"—he nods to the Spartans squirting each other with ice water—"there's no bigger game anywhere. For some it's the biggest game they'll play."

In the locker room, there's a big picture of Winston Justice on the wall, plus his quote: "We're not overlooking anyone, but our whole team's purpose is to play De La Salle. They're a great team, and if we can beat them, it would be huge for us and our whole program. We want a national championship." Underneath it, someone has scrawled in red marker: "How BAD do you want it!"

One more film session at the Quarterback Club; but first, before the work of deconstructing Poly's defense can take place, there's another of Sue's feasts (barbecued brisket, caramelized onions, roast potatoes, two salads) and dinner table conversation. "Cameron Diaz is *so* hot," Brian says wistfully. "But I don't suppose she's going to the game." Matt is more interested in Snoop. He's curious about his athleticism, which has been on display in various videos and MTV specials. "He's so skinny, he can't be a ballplayer," he decides.

Then the film begins. Clicking the remote back and forth, Panella leans back and pronounces expansively, "Sharkey's gonna have a big game." Sharkey is center Scott Regalia's nickname.

A couple of plays later, Matt says, "I don't see any flat coverage."

Panella nods. "I tell ya, they have none. And see how they're getting tired? Manuel gives up his swim move in the third quarter. It's all gonna come down to Sharkey. If we can trap these guys, we'll be okay. If we can't, we're in for a long night."

A fresh tape is put in, of Poly's game against Westchester. Matt notices something immediately in how Westchester's receivers attacked the Poly defensive backs: "What if the receiver moved over? Would they move with him? What if they didn't move over with him?"

Brian says, "If he did that, the Oregon Wheel would work. That's a touchdown sure."

Panella clears his throat, like a teacher in a senior seminar letting the students know they're going too far: "That's a hard throw to do. Now, 38 Power Pass Throwback might be better."

Then they hunch forward and watch a couple of Darnell Bing hits, like fans at a baseball game. "Bing." "Bing." They seem to enjoy the sound of the name. A Poly runner escapes a tackle. "Hershel will make you miss," says Panella.

Matt corrects the teacher: "That's Carrington, not Dennis."

Panella is unperturbed. "They make the first man miss, and that is very dangerous."

Now they turn their attention to the linebackers, Raul Lara's own greatest concern. A full month ago, after he'd first seen film of Poly, Ladouceur had made a bland comment that now seems prescient: "In this game, if you've a weak component on your team, it's going to be discovered. So if you don't have a linebacker corps, it's going to be discovered."

Poly's weakness has been discovered. Pago Togafau they like. The others they eye the way a great blue heron does an unsuspecting frog on a lily pad. One jab—boom! "If we run fourteen when it looks like thirteen, that one there will be playing pitch," says Panella. "We'll go straight up. Probably be Drew."

Brian adds dreamily, "The flats are so open."

The evening ends with two plays to Maurice Drew being added to the honed-down repertoire for Saturday night: a pass in the flats and a fake-pitch counter. Like Poly, De La Salle's offensive guys are absolutely convinced the other team can be had.

Seventeen

TWENTY-FOUR HOURS

Raul Lara is thinking about everything that has transpired these last few months. Hard to believe that back in May Jerry Jaso would suddenly resign, that Kirk Jones would die not two weeks later, and that Lara would find himself head coach—and all with the prospect of the first-ever national championship game looming.

Nevertheless, Lara is coaching in that national championship game, and it's only his fourth game as head coach. He can't help but wonder what Bob Ladouceur makes of it; Ladouceur is coaching his 252nd game and he's only lost fourteen times in his entire career, going back to 1979.

Lara has Ladouceur's home phone number—he'd once called the Spartan coach to offer any assistance he might need. Of course, aside from film exchange, there wasn't anything De La Salle needed—a local Poly rival, St. John Bosco, was providing all the aid and comfort a fellow parochial school could want: practice field, lockers, a chapel service. Bosco hasn't beaten Poly in over a decade, but if De La Salle prevails, that would be enough for Bosco.

So while the Spartans and Ladouceur are embraced by their

compatriots in faith, Lara still feels somewhat isolated, despite the depth and breadth of the Poly family. USC's head coach, Pete Carroll, and his entire coaching staff did fax over a cheerful signed letter of support, but the Moore League hasn't been sending any valentines, that's for sure. The burden of being Poly is a bit much at times, and now Lara can see what Jerry Jaso had to go through, and how much he achieved under such pressure.

So Lara's impulse to get to know his opposite number has grown; he wants to talk to the only other person who could possibly fathom what Lara is going through. That leads him to dial the home number. Ladouceur answers, seems pleasantly surprised, but genuinely welcoming. After an exchange of compliments, Lara asks him about his philosophy, and Ladouceur does the same. They're just talking, not parrying or playing mind games— a couple of sincere and decent guys who are about to climb into the ring together. Every time one says something good about the other's team or a particular player, the other answers in kind. Ladouceur talks about his short career in juvenile justice, and Lara tells the Spartan coach what it's like to have 46 high school probationers in your care, along with 150-odd football players.

Afterward, Lara realizes he's never had a conversation like that before, not with a coach of an opposing team. But then, reminding himself that this is his first head-coach job, he thinks that maybe this is what all the head guys do. So he asks Jerry Jaso if he ever had a conversation like that with a coach.

"No way," says Jaso.

The Spartans have arrived unannounced and unheralded, flying to Los Angeles International Airport and going straight to practice on the Bosco field. They're staying at a Marriott convenient to the airport. A contingent of parents and fans has also checked into the hotel, so they'll be able to do the ritual Thursday meal, the chapel, the meetings, just as they do in Concord. Best of all, there's almost no way the media will find them.

At Poly, on the other hand, even the student paper is hot on the story with a well-reported game-day edition. The *High Life* asks, "How do you prepare for a game?" Darnell listens to 2Pac's song "Hit 'Em Up." Hershel saves all his energy: "I just think about what I've got to do to improve." Winston, with his customary poker face, says, "I jump up and down while shaking my hands chanting, 'I'm the best offensive lineman in the world.'" Rory, with his customary lack of egotism, speaks for the team: "We all pray for Kirk Jones before every game."

Long Beach begins to fill up with people from all over the United States. Junior Lemauu will have fifty family members in attendance. Defensive back coach Doc Moye has bought thirty tickets for family, but laughs when asked if this is close to a record. "Don Norford has one hundred and thirty tickets," he says. "That's almost fourteen hundred dollars." Rumors are flying, too. Jaso will be up in the booth at Vets, calling offensive plays. "Count on it," a member of the sideline circus says. (It is shortly announced that Jaso will do color commentary for the radio.) A second rumor is that Cameron Diaz is coming to the game. "Naaahhhhh," says a sideline roué. "She's gone uptown." Another rumor is that one of Lara's probationers attempted suicide last week—a Cambodian kid who set himself on fire.

The media is starting to back off a little, giving the players room. The main exceptions are Fox Sports Television, which will be broadcasting the game, and NFL Films, whose trademark shots require in-your-face camera angles. But among most of the media there seems to be, even in the midst of a feeding frenzy, an element of protectiveness.

●　　●　　●

Friday morning over breakfast at Hof's Hut, still the high school after-game hangout, Jerry Jaso laughs at how wild, intense, this whole thing has gotten. "Poly's always been a community school. It's been a beacon for a lot of years, and at no time has it been a greater beacon than now."

"There are a lot of people who don't understand where Poly was, what troubles there were, and how we set it right. The times were difficult. In respect to racial animosity in the late sixties and early seventies, black people were rightly upset that they didn't have a say in the governance of the school. Now all the glass ceilings are down. Now there's a full buy-in by the whole school and community. And, let's face it, economically we're in a better place. People are getting the jobs they want."

Jaso disagrees with those who say Poly is doing something wrong by combining high academic achievers, creative talents, and great athletes—some of whom are average students, a few of whom might have been troublemakers in the past: "Jim Barnett always said he had to give the tough kids a place to be successful. Poly is proof that it's not the surrounding neighborhood that makes the difference, it's the success you're able to generate that changes everything.

"Bob Ladouceur said something that tells me why they're so successful. 'I don't try to make all kids alike, from one cookie cutter. I want them to be individuals.' That's exactly right for me.

"Coaches like to say, 'You've got to treat everybody the same.' Well, you *don't* treat everybody the same. Everybody is different. You've got to be flexible to let them make their mistakes and correct those mistakes. And coaches can sometimes be the only figures to show these guys who haven't been parented, or maybe grew up with a single parent, who haven't had the time or opportunity to learn how to live right, how to go in a positive direction." Jaso sighs. "I think coach Ladouceur has to do less of that."

On this day before The Game, Jaso again sidesteps the question that has never really gone away since last May 24: Why did he leave? "Do I have regrets? Wouldn't it be fun to coach against Bob Ladouceur? Sure. As an athlete, you'd want to play in it. Sure.

"But I don't regret leaving Poly. I love my new job. Raul's a great guy, a sincere guy, and he cares about players well beyond the playing field. I feel good handing the program over to someone with strong values—my values, but his values, too. He's more than a football coach.

"We've taken the program to where it is the premier program in Southern California. We had fun with it. It was a great ride. And I was happy to turn it over to somebody who was a great coach." Then he adds a curious afterthought: "Raul was too valuable to lose."

At Poly on Friday an outdoor stage is ready for an 11 A.M. pep rally, but the atmosphere is flat, students hardly pausing on their way to class. Thirty years ago on a big game day, drummers would've started up at 7:30 A.M., making repeated circuits of the campus, rattling their sticks together, then rapping them on the steel rims of their instruments, sketching out the Mighty Rabbit beat, which would then slowly mount in intensity and volume, adding snare to tom-tom to the big base drums—twenty drummers deep—a solid hour of percussion to get the blood moving.

The rally would begin with an elaborate mummer's parade and some sort of skit, enacted on a platform under the Administration Building clock. Then the yell leaders would bestir themselves, their languid poses, passed down for generations, deliberately echoing that of Jonathan Rabbit, whose blasé but peevish expression as he leans against the letter *P* sums up the infuriatingly superior attitude of Poly athletes and students. Handsprings, mystery tableaux, gnomic hand-signs, stylized 1920s gestures to accompany metronomic chants—it amounted to a body of arcane knowledge, now lost, a victim of Poly's academic rise.

If today's spirit does seem a bit wan, who can blame the kids? The racial turmoil, the necessary overthrow of the school's white fraternities and sororities, and then, in 1976, the populist tax revolt of Proposition 13, smashed the old idols and broke the channels by which the arcane mythologies had been transmitted. Before the tax-cutting of Proposition 13, Poly's marching band had numbered 130 members; ten years later, the music program was fighting for its existence. Today's cheerleaders and yell leaders try their amplified best and manage to draw a crowd, but the cheers sound suspiciously pro forma, even ironic. Still, it's a nice diverse group, a bright sunny day, and things pick up when Marcedes, Brian Banks, Brandon, and a couple of other players hop up on the stage in response to a hula hoop challenge from the cheerleaders and yell leaders. Both Brandon and Marcedes show some Division I hoops talent here, bumping away while all the yell leaders and cheerleaders drop out; the crowd gets going, shouting and clapping. One by one the contestants drop out, everyone is gone—except for Marcedes, who keeps his 6'7" frame in syncopated undulation while Brian adds a second, third, and fourth hoop to his gyrations. A major talent, this Lewis kid.

Out on the field, the crew from NFL Films is omnipresent, trailing huddles and coaches with big boom microphones and deploying a number of cameramen. NFL Films doesn't do television; they do movies, with a voice-of-God narrator, shooting real film stock, not video or digital. They've been here a week, burning miles of tape for this segment, which will air on ESPN. Within minutes the former NFL All-Pro, future Hall of Fame safety Mark Carrier arrives, joining former Poly stars Eugene Burkhalter and Anthony Cobb. All three are in natty urban uniforms—gray turtlenecks, charcoal sport coats, dark slacks—as if they have coordinated beforehand. In a way they have, not in the choice of clothing, but in coming here as examples of prosperous young men who've seen the world and have come back to show today's players how far they can go. Carrier was enrolled in Poly's Center for International Commerce (CIC) and says, "It was the greatest experience, one of the greatest academic programs in the state. At Poly, you get used to other cultures. I entered the greater world prepared."

The practice is short, a walk-through. Coach Lara gathers the team once again. "You guys have a big task ahead of you, but I believe you will be ready for this game. This is new territory for us. So on Saturday I want you to stay together. Stay together. Do not fall apart. It is going to get nasty at one time out there. When it happens, be ready. If the offense needs some support, go and cheer 'em on, do it. If the defense gets scored on, go and give 'em a bump.

"And finally, men, have fun. That's the main thing." He steps aside and calls up the former players, who speak briefly, without histrionics. Mark Carrier does address the importance of playing for the school. "That was the thing that made me so proud— when I put on the colors, I represented them. *I am for the green and gold.*"

Merle Cole II steps forward: "Tonight, you guys keep Kirk Jones in your heart. He really wanted to be here for this game. And you know what? *He will be here.*" And with that straightforward Merle, never one to embroider or mince words, steps back.

Raul Lara wraps up: "After the game, go straight into the locker room. Don't hang around on the field. Inside the locker room, it will be just us. Nobody else. We need to talk, do our prayer. If there's anything to talk about, we'll talk about it. Then we go straight back to Poly.

"I want you to have fun. Don't let this stuff affect you. If we lose, nothing happens to us, we don't lose a seed in the CIF playoffs." He pauses, regards the upturned faces. "Now, this team has not been tested as regards character." Pause. "When it starts getting thick, will we stick together? Will you guys stick together?" Long pause. "In my experience, the guys, here at this school, do."

In a silent meeting room at the Marriott, located somewhere between Los Angeles Airport and north Long Beach, the coaches of De La Salle are quietly pacing in front of the players, taking turns telling them what to expect, how they will feel, and what the game plan will do to make the odds go in their favor. *This is the game you've trained for since January,* Mike Blasquez will be saying. *Tomorrow night is going to be the hardest workout you've ever had. You'll have guys outweighing you by twenty, thirty, forty pounds. You'll be fatigued. In the third and fourth quarter you'll have to be able to give it everything you got. So get mentally ready. Nate, Alijah, Drew, you guys have to take what you did to Mater Dei and make it better. Keep your feet going, get four or five extra yards.* Bob Ladouceur will second that: *Keep your feet. You have to run through a lot of arms.* Blasquez won't let up, he wants them to understand what they're up against: *You're going to be in pain, you're gonna be tired on Sunday. These guys are big, they're strong, they're gunning for you. The only way you can overcome that is come out with intensity.* Terry Eidson will growl: *You linemen, Landri, Briner, Carlos—you have to pursue away from the play or else Hershel Dennis will reverse field and take it all the way. Backers Ottoboni, Barbero, Smith, and Hanks, you got to keep Hershel from going north-south, string him out.* This will be Terrell Ward's cue: *And then you d-backs got to do your job: keeping Hershel out of the end zone. No easy trips to the house. Make 'em work for it.*

Ladouceur: *Offensive guys Sandie, Chan, Regalia, you got to stay on those blocks from the very first play to let Maurice and Alijah and Nate get past Manuel and Murray, and those ends—Lemauu and Tauanuu. However you pronounce their names, they're big and they're good. But they can be beat.*

It won't go on long, it never does. Ladouceur will wind it up: *It doesn't matter who you play—you're going to go out there with a huge target on your back. Tonight it has number 116 on it. Whoever puts that 1 next to that 116, what does that make them? That is gigantic motivation. What's Pittsburg's claim to fame? The last team to beat us. That's still their claim to fame to this day. When we signed Mater Dei, they said, "We're going to give them a taste of SoCal football, Southern Section football." Well, we've given them a taste four times of Spartan football. Now this other SoCal team says, "Wait a minute, we're the real SoCal thing." They just don't get it. They just don't get it. But after tomorrow night, I think they will get it.*

Eighteen

A PARADE

In front of the Bixby Knolls junior high, Charles Evans Hughes, the football players and fans begin to trickle in. The surrounding neighborhood isn't what you think of when you think of a parade—it's quiet, residential, sedate. The prosperous two-story houses are fronted with lush and well-tended lawns, the street lined with forty-year-old sycamores, the gutters and sidewalks immaculate, the window shades drawn.

The idea for a parade came about as a result of a brainstorm between coprincipal Shawn Ashley and Steve Hastings, Star Jewelers owner and father of kicker Jeff Hastings. Bixby Knolls should do something for Poly, said Ashley.

This is the result. As everyone musters up, the parade doesn't look like that big of a deal, more of a stroll, albeit with the brass section of a marching band (out of uniform), a majorette (likewise in mufti), and a motorcycle police escort. But with a whoop of a siren and an outburst of brass, Bixby Knolls is transformed from a buttoned-up suburb, where each perfect dichondra lawn has its yellow Armed Response sign, into a Norman Rockwell small town.

The silent, shuttered houses throw open their doors. In slacks and khakis, pastel oxford shirts and cardigan sweaters, the largely white, upper-class homeowners come out on their lawns to wave, their children joining the crowd on skateboards, bicycles, or just skipping along.

Strollers with babies take up the rear, along with a Poly grad from 1970, Larry Austin, pushing his son Terrence, an eighth-grade Poly Pop Warner star, in a wheelchair. "Fractured an ankle in practice," Larry says. "Scored five touchdowns in two games, too. But he'll be back."

Bright lights, small city. A parade at dusk for the big game to-morrow. Parents trailing their almost grown-up sons. Coaches with their wives and babies. There's even a tight ensemble of drummers to put a polyrhythm in your step. Yes, and it's all taking place in front of the middle school known for keeping blacks out, in the neighborhood where a cross was burned on the Terrys' lawn.

Asked if he'd be at the parade, Herman Davis snorted. "Are you kidding? An invitation to Bixby Knolls doesn't come along every day."

Though six years separate us, Herman and I grew up straddling the same civil rights divide. When I was a boy, I knew I was never supposed to venture south of Wardlow, although, of course, I did. When Davis was a boy, he knew black kids shouldn't ride their bikes north across Hill Street. Davis didn't push those limits, be-cause that was where the Bixby Knolls white people drew the line and the Long Beach police enforced it. "The thing was, I used to bike right up to the line, Twenty-first Street and Hill, we called it Jungletown. You know why we called it that?"

This has been a theme the entire summer between Herman and defensive coordinator Jeff Turley and Tim Moncure, running down the roots of the names for various Long Beach neighbor-hoods: Dogtown, J-Town, Northtown, and now Jungletown. "Something to do with the ghetto?" I hazard.

Davis shakes his head. "For the billy goats." In the no-man's-land of oil derricks, oil sumps, rills and ravines and rickety sheds and pump houses that separated the Poly district from Bixby Knolls, there had been a herd of billy goats that young Herman loved to visit.

This jogs my own memory, of how at age eleven I would bicycle down daily from the opposite side to visit a mule. "A mule?" asks an incredulous Davis. "You visited a *mule?*"

Joking as we go, Davis nevertheless takes pains to sketch in the world as it existed on the other side of the Signal Hill divide—the true Hill Street Blues. There was the stricture never to cross into white people's neighborhoods, not just Bixby Knolls; the memory of getting a new bicycle as a ten-year-old only to be pulled over by a squad car and held at gunpoint under suspicion of theft; the rousts and threats that made life feel endangered, liable to violent intervention on a whim; the economic struggle of everyone around him.

Davis tells the story of the time he was sure he was going to die, just for crossing Hill Street. "I was home from the service," he recalls, "and driving the night before I'm due back on duty, to go off to Vietnam. I'm a grown man, I've seen a bit of the world in uniform, and I guess I was feeling a bit cocky, because I stopped off in Signal Hill to buy a soft drink. You remember how Signal Hill was, don't you?"

Of course I do. Even a mischievous teenager who'd had his share of run-ins with the Long Beach police would never confuse their ironfisted ways with the downright scary centurions of that tiny oil pimple of a town. Signal Hill was formed by a breakaway city manager and his cohorts who saw a way to get rich and control the oil wealth of an area; who, essentially, stole the heart of Long Beach. Signal Hill's story is a classic of L.A. corruption, and Signal Hill was where Raymond Chandler wrote his first stories, working as a small-time oil executive. When you read about Chandler's crooked and murderous cops or watch the climactic shoot-out in the movie *L.A. Confidential*, you're looking at Signal Hill—even into the mid-eighties.

If we white teenagers had our Hill Street rules, which included never taking any kind of shortcut across Signal Hill, a black teenager's were even more strict. Davis thought his uniform would protect him, but he calculates that it was only that he had already left the liquor store with his soda in his hand that saved him. The cops waiting outside had their guns trained. "They had looks of actual disappointment on their faces," Davis remembers.

Davis endured a thirty-minute search and roust before being allowed to go. Once in his car, however, he was too shaken to start the engine; gradually, he became aware that the police were sitting behind him in their car, as if waiting for him to leave. Davis was convinced that if he pulled away, they would promptly run him down. "Shot while resisting arrest," he says. "That's what they always say."

Signal Hill made national headlines in 1981 when a Cal State Long Beach football star, Ron Settles, was stopped driving through the city and arrested for possession of cocaine. Somehow, according to the police, Settles managed to beat himself in his empty holding cell and then to hang himself. Settles had no history of drug use, and his death caused enormous unrest in the community. In the lawsuit that followed, a young former assistant DA and black attorney, trying his first case in private practice, got Signal Hill to settle before trial. His name: Johnnie Cochran.

Not long after, a black newscaster for a local television station had himself trailed by a film crew while driving on the Hill. He got a little more than he bargained for, being stopped, manhandled, and then thrown through a plate-glass window of a store by two policemen. Even with the incident on film, no charges were brought against the cops.

Lawsuits and years of bad publicity resulted in a restructuring of the Signal Hill police department, but what really changed the rogue town was that the oil dried up. As hundreds of derricks fell idle and began to decay like a diseased forest, they and their tank farms were dismantled. Offering concessions on property and commercial taxes, Signal Hill lured a dozen large car dealerships, then big department store outlets. In the end, the 391-foot-tall butte became a luxury real estate development—albeit one built on fantastically toxic soil.

When Davis looks back on his life, he sees the close calls and knows how it felt to be overlooked, to burn with helplessness. But, he says, "My life was changed by a coach," a green-and-gold coach who happened to be white. At Poly, Davis was ready to quit football when then coach Bill Mulligan overheard him complaining. "He poked his head around the corner and said, 'Everything's going to be okay.' And after that it was. Just having him acknowledge me made the difference, taking the time to know my name." Davis would play, graduate from college, and enter the Peace Corps, where, in Ghana, he met his future wife, Lisette.

My life was changed by a coach, too, I tell him. "A Japanese coach."

Davis laughs. "A mule *and* a Japanese coach—you Bixby Knolls kids just got to be different." Then he sighs. "Now the shoe's on the other foot. There are kids here I don't even know by name. For some of these kids, we coaches are their fathers. But you get him for six hours, the street gets him for eighteen."

Does Davis remember the cross-burning on the Terrys' lawn in Bixby Knolls? He nods—"I knew Dr. Terry, and his son, Tony"—and says that it gives the parade tonight an added freight of symbolism, although he's not sure to what extent the current Bixby Knolls residents are aware of it.

The parade route goes down Roosevelt to the busy thoroughfare Atlantic Avenue, which links so many of the ecologies of Long Beach: Queen's Way, Downtown, Poly District, Wrigley District, Dogtown, Oilfields, Bixby Knolls, J-town. If this parade keeps going, it will eventually reach Compton and then South Central. But that's for another night. With a fanfare of ruby lights and Jackson Five tunes, the crowd surrounds Arnold's Restaurant, cheering, hoisting signs, while the team enters. The band follows, taking up positions against a wall and launching into the complete abridged oeuvre of the Jacksons. After this cheery, brassy prelude and a prayer by a local businessman, Bill Murray, the team goes to work on a prime rib dinner.

Star Jewelers owner Steve Hastings talks about how it feels to suddenly become the father of a football player: "Three months ago, they plucked my son off the soccer team. Three weeks ago was his first football ever, in his whole life. No flag teams, no Pop Warner. Only touched a ball on Sundays. Now he's in the biggest high school game in history.

"And you know what? He's very calm. I'm the one who's a wreck."

Jeff almost didn't get his father's approval to play, however. "He and I made a trade-off," says Steve. "He's a struggling student. If, I told him, he does this football thing—which would make him a three-letter guy, golf, soccer, and football—he'd have to pay more attention to his grades. After back-to-school night his teachers gave me only glowing reports."

As the "Beef Bowl" dinner breaks up, some of the adults head over to a local sports bar, E. J. Malloy's, in time to see Barry Bonds hit No. 72 out of the park. Suddenly a promo comes on for

The Game and another cheer rises, bigger even than the one for Bonds's home run. People start pounding the tables, chanting, "Go, Poly!" until the room is rocking.

Saturday morning, Game Day, the *Press-Telegram* puts a picture on the front page of Marcedes and Brian Banks gamely doing their hula hoop fun for the student body, goofing to keep a pep rally from going flat.

On the sports page, however, De La Salle gets the big picture, photographed from above and behind in the chapel at St. John Bosco, seated in pews in tight rows, kneeling, at prayer, in uniform, with a priest in his surplice at the altar and Christ on the cross looking down piteously upon the righteous. Then, way down at the bottom, is another shot of laughing Poly players with their balloons and hula hoops.

The players and many coaches are angered and embarrassed by the paper's choice and placement of the photos. They see racial stereotyping. They feel betrayed.

Up north, *Contra Costa Times* columnist Neil Hayes quotes Ladouceur on football: "The game as it stands by itself doesn't stand real tall. Without the intangibles, in a certain sense, it's barbarism. The brutality of the sport isn't what draws me to it. It's getting all those guys to play together and get along with each other."

Both newspapers are now breathlessly inflating the number of Division I scholarship candidates on the Poly team: up to twenty-five in the *Press-Telegram*, twenty in the *Contra Costa Times*. The David vs. Goliath theme, so strangely inverted given the Spartans's perfect record over the past nine years, is alive and well—and yet another example of Ladouceur's genius at motivating his kids and demoralizing his opponents: just let the media do it.

Nineteen

VETS

Signs reading "Go Poly!" line windows and trees on the long boulevards leading to Veterans Stadium. Within the parking lot are rows and rows of early arrivals who have come to open their tailgates and show their colors for the old school. There are young and old graduates. Barbecue smoke fills the air with the odor of burgers, hot dogs, teriyaki marinade, the Portuguese linguiça sausage favored in Hawaii. The entire Poly Student Commission munches on a ten-foot-long submarine sandwich. Buckets of fried chicken and potato salad pass from hand to hand. Hopeful fans wander by asking if anybody has tickets for sale—someone yells out that he saw a pair on eBay for $165.

In the cramped locker rooms and out in the concrete tunnel, Poly's players are getting spatted and taped. Darnell Bing smiles in anticipation. "Before I go out, I try to picture what I've got to do out there. I picture what my first hit will feel like. Hopefully, tonight my first hit will take somebody's helmet off. Not hurt them or anything, but deliver a message on the first blow. I did that once or twice last year." Brandon Brooks is listening, as usual, to "Danger" on his Walkman. Trainer Tabitha Romero is writing all the names of the dead on his arm, plus "R.I.P.," plus

"Danger." Brandon nods at the names. "This is for my mom and grandmom, who didn't have a chance to watch me play. But they're watching it from up above. And for Kirk." Marcedes puts on his lucky socks, a pair he has worn ever since his first game. Marlin Simmons dons a lucky shirt that he, too, wears at every game. "My cousin fringed it; he passed away."

Matt Gutierrez and the rest of the De La Salle team can't believe how dingy and airless the visitors' lockers are at Vets; they assume Poly has stuck them here on purpose, when in fact these simply are the best Vets can offer. But they quickly block out any distracting thoughts, the way they're trained to do.

Matt has never seen the coaches so serious. They begin the last talk, stuff everyone has heard before. *I know these guys are seriously good,* Matt thinks. *But we play highly touted teams every year. It's just not that big a deal. You know, when we watch film, the coaches always say, "These guys are good, real good." Then, just before game time, the coaches say, "You're capable of dominating."*

Matt realizes that the coaches sound different this time. *Hey, they don't sound so confident. They sound as if they know Poly can do some things to us.* Matt waits for the usual wrap-up, but the meeting ends without it. No coach says, *You're capable of dominating.*

Apparently not tonight. Slowly both teams rise in their respective locker rooms and bring their heads together for a prayer. Then they shuffle out, click-clack on the concrete of the dark tunnel, forming two lines next to each other.

Other teams, especially championship opponents, would never be placed together in such tight confines moments before a game. It would seem like a dare, would risk an outbreak of taunting or a brawl. But the Poly principals, Mel Collins and Shawn Ashley, discussed with Brother Chris Brady the sort of evening they have in mind, and displays of sportsmanship are high on their list of priorities.

Some, if not most, of the De La Salle players expect to hear some trash-talking, maybe a murmured diss, certainly to get hit with a cold, hard ghetto glare. Nothing of the sort occurs. Poly is silent. De La Salle is silent. They hear the bands out on the field, the aimless cheering and the rattle of the noisemakers.

Matt casts a covert glance at the players alongside him. As the tallest Spartan, he's used to being a sort of human yardstick, and it's always interesting to see which players have oversold their height on the official roster to attract recruiting attention. *Man, he thinks, these guys are huge! They're all legit 6'6" and 6'7", not padded one inch!*

"Okay, De La Salle, move it out!" The Spartans start up the tunnel and emerge between double lines of student commissioners and cheerleaders. A wave of applause starts high up in the stands, but lower down, near the tunnel, a storm of booing breaks out. It's so loud Matt is startled. Most of the time when De La Salle plays away, he expects people not to show much affection, but this booing is different. The crowd is so into it.

"They're *booing* us," Ladouceur says with a mock-shocked smile. Eidson is apoplectic; booing, he shouts to anyone who will listen, is *specifically prohibited* under the CIF's "Character Counts" program, and at that moment Mel Collins gets up and takes a microphone in hand. "There will be no more booing. That's it." The announcement is greeted with a huge cheer. And there is no more booing.

"Hey, look up in the stands," a player shouts in Matt's ear. He glances up and then can't look away. For a moment Matt lets it all go, the tension, the hype, the butterflies in his stomach, and turns around to take it all in. It's a conscious decision: *I will remember this. This is the one. You are in the game of the century, the sort of game you've always read about and dreamed of being in.* Then he takes a deep breath and blanks out the crowd, the stands, the yellow noisemakers, everything.

Then from deep in the tunnel, a falsetto trills. Silence, then a moan, an ululating sound, eerie, not something from the standard cheerleader's songbook; it's the Samoan chant. And here come the Jackrabbits.

The crowd screams as the band plays "Poly High," the school fight song. Everyone sings along, young and old, everyone knows all the words. With the thunder of cavalry the team crosses the track and heads out to their end of the field.

Twenty

THE GAME DON'T WAIT

Lines of fans snaked slowly up the aisles and wiggled past those already seated, looking for any kind of place to squeeze into. The carefully thought-out seating plans had collapsed under the post-9/11 security requirements and the usual stadium bottlenecks. There was no reserved seating section, except for the VIP rows, where the mayor, Beverly O'Neill, the superintendent of schools, Carl Cohn, and the school board were sitting, and even they were packed in with stray fans. A mass of Poly supporters had staked out a huge wedge of seats in the front and center rows and were shaking elongated yellow plastic noisemakers. But parents, students, and fans from both schools were squeezed together. Traditionally, fans and families are kept separate to avoid incidents and preserve school spirit. But tonight there was nothing to be done: once in, no one was going anywhere. Either people were going to get along, or they weren't.

Outside Vets, an estimated seventy-five hundred waited to see if any tickets would be available or followed the game on radios and portable televisions. Some were distraught at not being able to get in; others were happy to relax and barbecue.

• • •

Jeff Hastings stands in the hyperreal glow of center stage, eyeing the leather ball tilted at an angle on its plastic tee, his teammates spread like wings on either side of him, waiting for the whistle. On the opposite end of the field, Maurice Drew stretches his torso, leaning left, then right, taking in the spacing and placement of the return-team players arrayed in front of him. The ball leaps off Jeff's instep and starts its downward fall, tumbling end over end, descending from its apogee into the cradling hands of No. 21, Maurice Drew, at the 8-yard line. His teammates race toward him; seeing him catching the ball, they instantly decelerate, pivot, and curl into a return formation, forming a wedge. Maurice explodes forward, aligning himself behind the moving pyramid. Sprinting toward them are Poly's green-and-gold cavalry, outliers to pinch in, wedge-busters coming up the middle to shatter the phalanx.

Maurice reaches top speed as the collisions begin taking out the wall, just as he catches up to it. Gaps open up, bodies hurtle in space. With a feint left, he tries to throw off the oncoming hordes; a hand scrapes his thigh; he hurdles a falling body and pops through the wall on the right side, legs pumping, bouncing off a tackler angling from the left side. He's past the 35-yard line, outrunning the coverage, sensing the last line of defense desperately closing—another second or two and he's loose, gone for a touchdown, and Poly is *toast,* let the blowout begin. Maurice hurtles into the closing gap, twisting sideways, feet pumping, chopping even faster, as he's been taught—long-strided runners are easy to stop, as easy as jamming a stick into the spokes of a bicycle wheel.

Boom. Pinballing, Maurice is bounced violently sideways, slammed into the grass, and buried under a rapidly expanding pyre of bodies. The last man got him. But he's advanced the ball nearly to midfield, to the 45-yard line.

On the sidelines, All-NFL and future Hall of Fame candidate Mark Carrier claps his hands. The hardest-hitting safety in football until his retirement this year, Carrier whistles and shouts, "That's not high school hitting! That's not high school speed!"

First and ten. Maurice and Alijah, side by side, crouch down six feet behind Matt. Scott Regalia, the 185-pound center, thinks, *Well, here he is.* All spring and summer in the weight room, Derek Landri has been whispering in his ear, "Manuel Wright, Manuel Wright." Now the 315-pound Top 5 defensive tackle is across from Scott. At the snap, Matt reverse-pivots, seeming to race right past while sticking the ball into Maurice's gut as he explodes left. Scott's assignment is to back-block for the pulling guard, so he drops back a step and squares to face a charging Ernesto Villasenor, the other 300-pound tackle. On the left side, Alijah seals off the linebacker while the tight end ties up the defensive end. Maurice scoots through the gap for eight yards. In the tangle of bodies at the line of scrimmage, Scott gets up and gives himself a shake.

Second and ten. The same formation, only this time when Matt gives the ball to Maurice going left, Poly is ready and follows the play. The receiver on the left wing, Damon Jenkins, steps back from the line and starts running to his right, passing behind Maurice, who slips him the ball. A door opens, courtesy of Poly's overreaction. Damon races through, picking up nine yards.

The reverse is a trick play, and this one, used on the second play of the game, installed especially for Poly, caught the Jackrabbits overpursuing. It's no fumble-rooski—Poly's safeties recovered in time—but enough to sow doubt, give the defense something to think about.

After this first down, De La Salle tries a veer series. Matt takes the snap, stutters toward the left, hands to the back plunging past him for four yards. Scott Regalia introduces himself to middle linebacker Pago Togafau, firing out and hooking him out of the play. Like two men caught in a revolving door, the two whirl around and then Pago slips free and gets in on the tackle. *Hey, he's pretty good with those hands,* Scott thinks. Matt tries a variation of the same play to the opposite side: four yards. Poly is trying not to get frustrated: with its whirligig of three possible runners—and a dozen options off those options—the veer is always good for a couple of yards. The trick is to shut down the first- and second-down plays. If the offense has to get five or more yards on third down, the veer becomes much less of a terror.

This down, though, third and two, is made for the veer. Alijah bolts through on the dive option. First and ten on Poly's 27-yard line. The Jackrabbits are experiencing the famous De La Salle opening blitz, a little like trying to slap mosquitoes with one hand tied behind your back.

Being sliced and diced makes a defense edgy; it's easy to become reckless, desperate, and that's when you give up a score. It's De La Salle, however, who gets overanxious and jumps offside. The five-yard penalty backs them up: first and fifteen from the 32, an obvious passing down. For the first time, Manuel the grizzly will be able to charge in without having to worry about some little scatback slipping past and making him look silly. The Spartans put three wide receivers on the right; it's called a package: when the play begins, they'll do their own bobbing and weaving, crossing and curling, describing a geometric nest of angles intended to put them in a certain spot at a certain time, along with, they hope, the ball. Matt keeps just one back in with him, Maurice, to block and serve as a running threat to keep the defense honest.

At the snap Matt dashes back in a seven-step drop, the move of a quarterback going to throw to a streaking or crossing deep receiver. This is like waving a red flag to the defense. Scott and Andy Briner are tandem-blocking Manuel, who sees a double-team on nearly every play. They contain him, but the ends, Junior Lemauu and Joshua Tauanuu, push in from opposite sides at a terrifying rate and overwhelm the blockers. It looks as if Matt is going to get sandwiched. Only he cuts short his drop and with a flick underhands the ball forward to Maurice, who has drifted up after pretending to block. It's the shunt-screen pass, well remembered from John Elway's time with the Denver Broncos.

This shunt should be the perfect way to mousetrap Poly, but even as Maurice's fingers close around the ball, a massive presence engulfs him: Manuel, not fooled a bit. "Fumble!" shouts the rapper Warren G, pacing the Poly sidelines. "That's a fumble!" But it only looks like one.

Second and thirteen, ball on the 30. Two wide receivers line up on the left, one on the right, and one back sets behind Matt. Before the snap, one of the left-side receivers begins to jog right, which forces the free safety to mirror him, jogging parallel behind the defensive line; a single offensive player is allowed to go in motion without incurring a penalty.

After the motion receiver has passed him, Matt takes the snap and stutter-steps right, trying to draw the defensive end toward him, at which point he'll pitch out to the trailing tailback, who will follow the blocking motion receiver. It's a veer in disguise, but again Poly doesn't bite, so Matt turns up into the gap between the battling tackles and the wary end. He's hit immediately, and yet, churning his feet as he falls, he manages to get five yards.

As the play is winding down, Scott Regalia slows up after doing his dance with Pago, who's managed to get loose once again. *The guy never quits.* Scott only sees the golden helmet out of the corner of his eye, rushing toward him like a comet, then, boom, he takes a hit in the jaw that lays him out. For a moment he thinks his jaw is broken. When he gets to his feet, Scott finds himself eye to eye with Darnell Bing. They stare at each other for a long moment. Scott thinks he sees Darnell nod, as if to say, *That's on.* Scott nods back: *Bring it harder.*

Now it's third and eight on the 25, another obvious passing down. The drive has taken four minutes and is now subject to the Law of Football Entropy: the longer a march, the more things fall apart. Either the offense or the defense could collapse—it all depends on the psychological states of each. A long drive can be demoralizing for a defense, for instance; but it can also put the pressure on the offense, induce a breakdown or provoke a mistake, if the nerve of any one individual should fail. Any drive longer than seven plays can feel long for those on the field.

De La Salle is at a disadvantage, because down and distance are against the Spartans. Poly can expect pass and has seen enough not to be fooled by a draw, a screen, or a shunt. The big boys can come on strong, letting the shallow linebackers take care of any funny business, while Darnell and the defensive backs shut down the deep routes. This is when Poly feasts.

On the Spartan sidelines, James Bloomsburg kicks into a net, warming up for a field goal attempt should the next play fail. On Poly's side, the offense and punt return units are bouncing up and down on their toes, getting ready for their introduction to the Spartans.

An official from a handpicked crew of Southern California refs places the ball on the right side of the field, the "near" side, on the right "hash." These white-chalk hash marks are an element of football arcana that high school has retained; the pros have streamlined them out of existence. The hashes divide the width of the field into thirds, and where the ball ends up after a play determines its starting point, aligned on the nearest hash mark, for the next. Unless the ball is on the center hash, this results in one side of the field being quite cramped and the other side extremely wide-open. The tendency for offenses to run plays to the wide side is counteracted by the tendency of defenses to shift safeties to the wide side, which, in turn, is counteracted when offenses fake to the wide side and run plays into the narrow corridor. When a team gets close to the goal line, this equation is complicated by the fact that a field goal kicker working from either of the side hashes has a difficult angle. It seems likely that De La Salle will hedge its bets by running left, to the wide side, toward midfield. If the play fails, James's kick will at least be straight-on.

This down, this eighth play of the first drive, is a perfect example of why coaches and commentators love to refer to football as chesslike. It involves lots of guessing and second-guessing. Unlike chess, its moves must be figured out and initiated within thirty seconds of the previous play.

The Spartans line up a receiver on the left "far" side, with another in between him and the nearest offensive lineman. Behind Matt is a single back, Maurice; to his right, split off from the offensive tackle on that side, a wide receiver and a slot receiver. As Matt counts off cadence, the receiver in the slot starts jogging left, to the wide side. A Poly safety follows, mirroring.

The play looks to develop on the left, and at the snap Matt rolls in that direction, raising the ball and looking at the three receivers. Maurice, the halfback, takes off to the right. The defense, seeing Matt roll to his left, has rolled toward the middle. Maurice looks like a decoy out in the flats, but Matt's look left is just a look. He circles around to his right, taking three quick steps that alter the shape and dimension of the play; coming out of his turn he fires a screen pass to Maurice, who takes it in stride. The linebacker on the narrow right side, Rory Carrington, thinks he has a play on Maurice, only the wide receiver has cut his route short, catches Rory unawares, and smothers him. Maurice zigzags past the line of scrimmage and slices up the narrow corridor toward the end zone.

From Poly's point of view it still seems under control; two defensive backs are cutting off Maurice's angle. But Maurice's burst of acceleration so surprises the first back that he lunges for a flying tackle and Maurice's ankle rips through his fingers. The second defender, Tyrone Jenkins, has a moment to adjust and make a hit, but gripping the muscular Drew is like squeezing a tennis ball—Maurice just bounces back, feet churning, and the goal line is in sight.

Then Maurice does a funny thing, a seemingly un-De La Salle-like thing: a somersault. In full stride, having broken two tackles, on the verge of scoring the first touchdown of The Game, knowing that the CIF is severe with taunting and celebrating, Maurice still can't help it. He springs off an imaginary trampoline and tumbles into the end zone.

He's mobbed by his teammates. A penalty flag is thrown. Darnell claps his hands, thinking it's a penalty on Andy Briner, who finished the play by chopping Darnell off at the knees. But, no, the flag is on Maurice, and the score stands. The extra-point kick is marched all the way back to the 25-yard line, the distance of a serious field goal. Perhaps this is where Maurice's exuberance will cost the Spartans, but James Bloomsburg, warmed up for a field goal anyway, nails it.

As the Poly defense comes off the field, coach Lara claps his hands together, leaning forward and staring into the faces, repeating, "See? I told you they were good. I told you, I told you." The funny thing is, he's smiling.

And he's not the only one. Despite the shock on the Poly sidelines, a lot of faces are wearing a sort of cockeyed grin. The speed and abandon with which both sides are playing is almost surreal. It feels far, far faster than the average high school game, even an average Poly or De La Salle game. Adrenaline is in the air.

Warren G isn't smiling; the rapper shouts to the players coming in, "Don't let 'em get ya out ya game!"

James Bloomsburg tees the ball up on the De La Salle 40 for the kickoff. The coaches have decided not to give Poly any deep kicks to return, at least early on. James plans a squib, a burner along the ground, which will allow the Spartans to swarm the returner and maybe even cause a fumble. He lines up, hears the whistle, throws his weight behind his leg—the ball shanks sideways and hops out of bounds at the 35, a five-yard penalty. His second kick is a pooch, high and soaring, intended to allow the Spartan gunners to stop the return before it gets started. It succeeds, and then some—two Poly players collide trying to catch it, fumble the ball, and only barely recover.

Here come the Jackrabbits, from their 30-yard line. Hershel and a tight end, Jonathan Johnson, line up in the I formation behind Brandon—a trick formation. Out on the far right side are a slot and a wide receiver. Standing up and surveying the defense, Brandon sees what he has dared to hope for and also feared: the Spartans in man-to-man coverage, with only a single safety, Alijah, deep in midfield. Moving deliberately, Brandon steps up under the center, calling for a shift. Jonathan moves to the right end of the line. With Marcedes anchoring the left side, the Jackrabbits are in a strong running formation.

In chess terms, Brandon has forked the defense. With two tight ends in, the defense has to look first for a running play. That means keeping a strong safety in close, and leaving the free safety, Alijah, alone in support of the two defensive backs, Damon Jenkins and sophomore Willie Glasper, who are separated by twenty yards. Alijah lines up thirteen yards deep and splits the difference, but he also has to keep an eye on those two very tall tight ends, either of whom could slip his block and go out for a pass. If Marcedes can get behind the three linebackers, who will be looking for a Hershel run, that could be a touchdown.

It's a game of chicken. Brandon sees that the Spartans are willing to risk leaving a single cornerback, and a sophomore at that, on the Poly sophomore Derrick Jones. The De La Salle defense is calling his bluff.

That's exactly what happens. Brandon takes the snap, Hershel bolts for the near left side, and the quarterback slips the ball into his gut, then pulls it out, continuing back in a semicircle, setting up to throw in one smooth motion. Poly's two tight ends block, slip off, run five yards deep, and then cut right. Poly's wide receiver and slot receiver on the right, Derrick and Alex Watson, explode in tandem like matched greyhounds. Then Alex jerks and cuts toward the right sidelines; he's open, alone. But so is Derrick, streaking straight between Willie and Alijah.

Derrick and Brandon have done this before; still, it's no easy thing, timing a throw so the ball will arrive in the hands of a 10.6 sprinter in full stride so that he doesn't have to make a single adjustment to catch the ball. Brandon's throw travels sixty yards in the air. Derrick doesn't have to make a single adjustment.

For a moment it's in his grasp, then the torque of his pumping legs and vibrating body seems to whip up his arms into his fingertips. The ball pops out. No catch. No touchdown. No shock to De La Salle's system.

Second and ten. Two wide receivers on the wide right, an I formation with Hershel and Rory. It's a straight handoff, blast left, the type of play that De La Salle expected Poly to open with, and four defenders bury Hershel. On third and ten, with wide receivers on either side, the two backs go in opposite directions at the snap, Hershel behind a wall of blockers for a screen on the near side, Rory into the far-side flats. Rory has 20 yards of open space in front of him, but the play is designed for Hershel. The linebackers arrow in and stop it well short of a first down.

Poly's first punt, by backup quarterback Leon Jackson, is a good one, and Maurice has to spin around and catch it over his shoulder at the 25. As the Jackrabbits line up on defense, they are in a situation every one of the Spartans's last 116 opponents is familiar with, the sinking feeling that all their fine plans are coming to naught, accompanied by a haunting refrain: Is this when the blowout begins?

But Poly never panics—a Jackrabbit can take a punch. What counts is solving the riddle of the other team, then going on the attack.

Warren G is pacing anxiously, definitely wrought up, but the number one rapper fan of the Jackrabbits hangs his head when asked if he played for Poly. "I went to this junior high that wasn't in the Poly district, back when the jurisdiction was locked tight, so I had to go to Jordan. But my heart is with Poly, I had a lot of friends who went there. These are my niggas."

The Spartans come out in a full house, three backs in a triangle behind Matt, another variation on the veer, the same formation Narbonne used to bedevil Poly. Matt pitches to Maurice, while Alijah blocks sophomore linebacker Marlin Simmons, who slips past and tackles Maurice for a loss. On second down out of the full house, Matt reverse-pivots to his right, handing the ball to Maurice as he runs past; the other two backs carry out fakes to the left side, while Maurice pops through a hole on the right that opens when Manuel is hooked by the tight end out of the play and a linebacker fails to fill the gap. Maurice gets nine yards before Pago Togafau drags him down at the 37.

Third and two, time out De La Salle. This is a tough down for Poly, hard to defend. Matt fakes a handoff to a back on a dive, then, seeing a rush coming, throws a pass sideways to Nate while retreating. Nate drops the ball just as Manuel arrives with a head of steam to scoop it up. Poly thinks it's a fumble—a pass behind the quarterback is officially a lateral, which means it can be picked up and advanced by the defense. But the officials rule an incomplete pass (which it is, by about a foot).

Fourth down. Poly crowds the line, putting on the rush for a block. James Bloomsburg's punt veers to one side and bounces, but Kevin Tapp takes it on the hop and races up the sideline. A penalty flag on an illegal Poly block, however, brings it back to the 20-yard line.

Now it's time for Poly to go to work. Poly lines up in the Wing-T, with a wide receiver and a flanker out on the far right side, and a wing receiver and a halfback behind the tight end on the left. Hershel takes his stance, bent slightly forward, hands on his thighs, behind Brandon. At the snap Brandon pitches the ball left to an already sprinting Hershel, who plucks it out of the air and is racing up the narrow near-side corridor behind a perfect wall of blocks. The play is working so well that Hershel has two down-field linemen just ahead and to his right as escorts. Only Alijah stands between Hershel and an eighty-yard touchdown run, and center Hercules Satele, 6'3", 240 pounds, is homing in on 5'7", 167-pound Alijah.

Except that Hershel is accelerating to escape the pursuing Spartans. Alijah stays low and holds his position. Hershel tries to hurdle him, just as Hercules arrives. The little guy wins.

Still, Poly has a first down on the 50, and the game now has a thirty-yard classic Hershel run in its highlight portfolio. First and ten, out of the same Wing-T setup, Brandon takes a short drop and throws a hard, high pass to the right-side slot receiver, Alex Watson, who stretches up to snare it in stride and keeps going until he's forced out of bounds. First down, plus a face-mask penalty on De La Salle on the tackle, moves the ball from the 35-yard line to the 22. Poly is moving.

Poly comes out with triplets, three receivers, on the near right hash, one back behind Brandon. Marcedes is the wide receiver, for the first time in the game. The slot goes in motion left; at the snap, Brandon turns his back to take a deep drop, and only when he starts his pivot does he see four De La Salle players in hot pursuit. Derek Landri has exploded the center of the Poly line, allowing linebacker Cole Smith and Maurice Drew to race in on a blitz; Maurice hauls Brandon down for an eight-yard loss.

With this blitz, De La Salle's Terry Eidson had gambled, correctly, that Poly would try to pass again on the reeling Spartans. Now Poly's in a hole, second down and eighteen from the 30. Brandon pitches to the back, Hershel, who's stopped after four yards by Brendan Ottoboni. Now it's third down and fourteen, and Poly's drive, which had begun so exuberantly, faces long odds. Brandon sprints back for a seven-step drop, not even bothering to fake to his two backs. He's looking deep all the way, to Derrick again. From the left wide side Derrick streaks straight, cuts right on a post pattern, then immediately cuts back left toward the red-coned end zone, leaving Damon Jenkins behind. Brandon's throw, however, doesn't have enough arc on it by about a foot, and instead of being burned for a touchdown, Damon springs up and gets both hands firmly around what is going to be a costly interception. But Damon grips the ball so tightly as he draws it toward him that he ends up dashing it down into the grassy field; then he clutches his helmeted head in his hands, like a man who has just dropped a Ming vase.

Fourth down, and Poly is effectively out of scoring range. Poly will either pass or try Hershel on a draw, and they know the Spartans will not be surprised; or they'll try to chip-shot a punt down to the 2- or 3-yard line. The one thing they won't try is a field goal.

Or will they? Here comes Jeff Hastings and the kicking unit. A forty-two-yard field goal is beyond the distance of most high school kickers—James Bloomsburg's personal best is twenty-five yards—and Jeff has yet to attempt any field goal in his entire four-game football career. De La Salle's defense can't believe Poly is serious—it must be a trick play. Then they hurry to the line.

Jeff keeps his head down, checks the goalposts once, steps back and over to the side, and waits for the ball to appear in Leon's hands; even as Jeff begins his approach, Leon is spinning the ball on the point of an index finger so the laces face outward. Then it's up, and . . . it's . . . good. The first field goal of Jeff's life, in the game of games, is a forty-two-yarder, a respectable distance for the pros. On the sidelines kicking coach Ryan Downey is shaking his head at Jeff's cool.

An appreciative roar of relief pours down from the stadium. It may not be a touchdown, but it feels big. A little doubt might have crept in, you never know.

On the kickoff, Jeff chip-shots a high ball that Poly covers perfectly, three players blasting aside Spartans while one behind picks off the football and starts for the end zone. Instant touchdown—except the whistles are already blowing. Poly was offside, and back it comes. The next kick is a boomer that forces Drew to make an over-the-shoulder catch, but he's able to pivot and spring upfield so quickly no Poly player can get near him until the 20. He finally goes down at the 30.

Maurice trots up to the huddle still buzzed from his touchdown. Ever since his dazzling punt return against Buchanan, he's been waiting to have a breakout game. Alijah Bradley had his breakout against Buchanan, then went berserk against Mater Dei, exploding for 260 total yards. Right now, Maurice feels very good, ready to rip.

In the middle of the field, Matt hands off to Maurice on a quick inside pop that gets eight yards before the Poly grizzly bears can throw their blockers aside. Out of the same set, Matt stutter-steps down the line, fakes to his fullback diving inside, fakes a pitch to the tailback, then leaps into the gap and gets the first down. On the next play, again out of the same set, Matt fakes to the dive-back again, but this time sprints back and sets up to throw deep. He lets fly a rainbow to De'Montae Fitzgerald, who's sprinting downfield with Kevin Tapp, only 5'7", matching him stride for stride. One bump and the official will call pass interference, but Kevin's footwork is immaculate. The ball is long by a couple of yards.

On the next play, the Spartans set up in an obvious pass set— one back, four receivers on the right, what's called a quad package. Matt drops back as if to throw, before slipping the ball to Alijah. Three of Poly's biggest, 6'5", 300-pound Maurice Murray, 6'3", 260-pound Joshua Tauanuu, and Manuel, pounce on the 5'7" Alijah like grizzlies on a leaping salmon.

After this loss of three yards, the Spartans face third and thirteen, a definite passing down. Poly can smell this one. The set is Poly's favorite Wing-T, with Maurice on the left wing. As the two wide receivers on the right go deep, Maurice fakes a block, slides forward a couple of yards, and runs parallel to the line, to his right. Matt gives the deep men a glance, then takes the sure thing, a crisp pass over the charging linemen to Maurice, who catches it just as linebacker Rory tackles him. But Drew keeps his feet, churning them until he busts loose, and zooms up the right flat and sideline for twenty yards.

Poly doesn't have time to get mad at themselves. The Spartans line up at the 35-yard line on the right hash. Matt drops back, handing the ball to Nate Kenion at the right half, as Maurice crosses in front. The Poly defense follows Maurice for a step, allowing Nate to steam toward the left flat with room to move. It looks like another big gainer, with the linebackers sucked out, but Tyrone Jenkins, Kevin Tapp, and Darnell Bing arrive like a volley of crossbow bolts. Nate is knocked flat and lies on his back, legs flopping, arms outstretched. After an eight count, he is helped up, wobbly but okay.

Second down and four. Nate's run moved the ball to the left hash. Matt fakes a counter handoff to his two backs, rolls right, looking deep. The receivers are covered, so he tries to dump it to the tight end, Nick Barbero, but the throw is behind, leaving Nick vulnerable to a smack from Darnell as he turns in midflight to try to make the catch.

Third down and four, on the 31-yard line. The next play is the eighth of the drive; the last time De La Salle scored was on the eighth play. This is a make-or-break down, and the Law of Football Entropy kicks in, as if on cue. With two backs behind him, and two wide receivers on the right wide side, Matt drops back to pass. When he looks up, a Poly rusher is in his face and he has to run for his life, straight back. About to be sacked for a fifteen-yard loss, he throws the ball forward at the feet of a Poly rusher. There isn't an eligible receiver in sight. This would normally be a penalty, intentional grounding, except that Matt has thrown directly in line with a receiver ten yards downfield, making his intent a matter of debate. There is no flag; it could be that one of the best throws Matt will make all night is this one.

The Spartans have escaped that little disaster, but still face fourth and four. The safest play would be to pooch a punt, pin Poly inside their 5-yard line, and tell the defense to hold them, hoping to get the ball back on a short field. That's the percentage call, the one most coaches would make. The second option is to try for a field goal; the distance from the goalposts is the same as it was for Jeff's field goal, and James Bloomsburg has hit them in practice from forty-five yards. But a miss would give Poly good field position, and Bob Ladouceur believes his offense should be able to get him four yards anytime he asks, regardless of what down it is; it's a matter of attitude. However, with the entire defense keyed on stopping the Spartans shy of those four yards, he and offensive coach Mark Panella realize it will actually be easier to go deeper. But then they are faced with another assumption: If they believe ten yards will be easier than four, why not try for twenty yards, or even thirty? What's holding them back?

The Spartans trot out to the left-side hash, two split backs and one wide receiver on each side. At the snap Matt rolls right, to the wide side, as the two backs cross in front of him. Maurice heads for the left side as if to block, Matt looks deep downfield to the right. But Maurice doesn't stop; he shifts gear and zooms at full speed up the narrow alley on the left. It's the 38 Power Pass Throwback; Matt's fake spins the defense in one direction while a single back rotates in the opposite direction. It takes nerve to call it in this situation, and trust to run it; moreover, it needs a perfect route and a perfect pass, no hesitation.

Poly strong safety Chris Davis never sees it until the ball is coming down. Maurice's feet are a blur, his hands are outstretched, fingers soft, almost pliant, so there's less chance of an abrupt move or flinch. The spiraling ball alights, Maurice tucks it in, and scores.

And so, instead of maybe getting four yards and a first down, Bob Ladouceur has gone thirty yards for six points. With James Bloomsburg's kick, the score is 14–3.

The boisterous crowd has fallen into stunned silence. Mark Carrier whistles. "This team is showing why they haven't lost in the last eight years. I'm impressed with their quickness. Lots of guys are quick, but these guys are organized and very disciplined in what they do."

Twenty seconds are left in the first quarter. The twelve minutes have gone by so fast people in the crowd are clutching each other, dizzy and breathless.

Poly has every right to be devastated. High school kids, having taken a shot like that—on fourth down, too—might be forgiven for slumping. If this were a Super Bowl game, it would be time to open another beer and turn one's attention to the guacamole.

On the kickoff, De La Salle continues to deny the ball to the deep return men, Derrick and Hershel. Pago Togafau spears the squib kick and tucks in for a ten-yard return to the Poly 45-yard line.

A run goes for two yards, and the first quarter ends. After the two teams switch sides of the field, Hershel takes a handoff and follows his fullback's seal block through a gap, is hit by Maurice Drew, breaks loose with a complete spin of his body, lunges forward, and twists to a first down. On the sidelines, and in the huddle during time-outs, Spartan coach Mike Blasquez eyes the players for signs of injury or excessive dehydration. They're breathing hard, but nobody's gassed—yet. Briner is limping; the groin pull is probably acting up. On the next play, Brandon pitches to Rory to the right side, who slashes for ten yards. Poly's big front—Winston Justice, Hercules Satele, Maurice Murray, and Julai Tuua—is moving the pile. On first down from the De La Salle 30, Brandon sets up and throws a deep ball to the corner of the right end zone, but nobody's there. The intended receiver, Marcedes, is still ten yards away. Second and ten: a pitch to Hershel, who again twists through a thicket of arms and slides between lunging bodies for six yards. On third down, Derek Landri collapses the entire right side of the Poly line, blasting through 6'5", 300-pound Maurice Murray to grab Hershel with one big arm. Hershel falls forward for three, leaving Poly one yard short.

Fourth and one on the 21, the seventh play of the drive, and here is another moment of truth. Jeff can trot out and try a field goal, but three points at this juncture just doesn't feel like much of a statement, and he may miss, too. It's Mighty Rabbit Time. Out they come, no deception, everybody knows what's coming. Tight end Jonathan Johnson, center Hercules Satele, and big Winston provide a huge surge, with Maurice Murray sealing off any pursuit. Brandon surfs over their backs for six yards. Ordinarily called a quarterback sneak, this play ought to be called a parade.

First and ten at the 15, the eighth play of the drive, and when Brandon hands off to Hershel inside, Andy Briner and Cole Smith smack him down for no gain. On second down, Poly comes out in the same set, Marcedes at wide receiver on the right, a slot receiver between him and the tight end. At the snap Marcedes sprints out exactly five yards as Brandon drops back exactly two steps, sets, and throws. Even as Marcedes turns, the ball is arriving, as is Maurice Drew, but Marcedes stands aside like a toreador and then drives for the goal line, splitting Cole Smith and Alijah. Cole finally gets him down.

First and goal at the 5. Poly comes out in a full house backfield for the first time. Brandon pitches to Hershel sweeping right, to the near side, behind tight end Jonathan Johnson's 6'6" frame. A surf of churning humanity trails the play, bodies crashing as Hershel struggles for the orange cone of the goal. Second and goal at the two. Brandon tries to sneak it, finds a crevice in De La Salle's line behind Maurice Murray, and gets his helmet—but not the ball—over the line.

Third and goal, the twelfth play of the drive, and for Poly it's quite simple: the game depends on the next two plays. Some teams might try something fancy or simply run wide on a pitch or blast, but as Jerry Jaso likes to say, goal line is all about attitude. After Brandon calls the play in the huddle, Marcedes reaches out and pats him in the small of the back. At the snap, supersized fullback John Williams drives in behind Hercules at center, right into Derek Landri. Brandon smashes across, over their backs, two yards into the end zone, but he pays for it, as Landri grabs his waist and linebacker Brendan Ottoboni his legs. A moment later Cole Smith applies a crushing blow to the quarterback's head and chest, bending him backward. The pile collapses on him.

The crowd goes wild, scattering programs and confetti, smacking the yellow rattles against each other, screaming. Down on the field there's a rawer screaming as Poly's players dive into the pile and start yanking De La Salle players off Brandon. The refs are blowing their whistles while tugging on De La Salle arms and pushing Poly players back, trying to prevent a brawl. Everyone knows what's happening. Brandon has dared to poke his nose one too many times into the heart of De La Salle's line, and now he's paying the price. Anything could be happening inside that scrum, gouges, twists of ankles and knees, fingers jabbed into eyes, even biting—one college player was suspended this year for biting another player's *genitals* in a goal line pile.

The Spartans roll off one by one, looking sleepy and surprised, *Oh, is there somebody under me?* Landri takes his own sweet 280-pound time. Brendan Ottoboni, now lacking a helmet courtesy of an angry Rabbit, peels off. Way at the bottom, Cole Smith finally relinquishes his grip. Football has just shown its origins in the Old English melay, or melee, the Shrove Tuesday tug-of-war, the scrum played with the head of a Dane.

While the trainers and team doctors work on a collapsed Brandon, checking his sprained right knee, the Poly offense huddles on the 15-yard line in prayer. Brandon gets up and then breaks into a trot off the field, to cheers. Jeff comes in to kick the point after.

The snap is high. Leon has to stretch way up to even catch it. Damon Jenkins and a wave of Spartans smother the ball. With

7:56 to go in the second quarter, the score is 14–9.

On the kickoff, Jeff chips a pooch shot and three Poly gunners run "knockout"—not even looking for the ball, they pick a man near where the ball is planned to drop and blow him back. Perhaps they're a little too well trained: if even one turns around, the ball is there. Kevin Tapp gets a hand on it, but De La Salle recovers.

From the 36-yard line, Nate Kenion takes a handoff and twists and slashes for nine yards. On the next play, De La Salle seals off one side of Poly's line and Manuel misreads the direction, charging blindly, while his partner, end Junior Lemauu, is a second too late to collar the passing Alijah. Ernesto Villasenor runs him down from behind after a thirteen-yard gain.

Matt takes a two-step drop on first down and fires out to Ryan Eidson, whose fast route, sharp cut, and precise timing leave him all alone at the sideline. The defender, Tyrone Jenkins, lies sprawled on the grass as the Flea turns upfield for even more yardage, perhaps a touchdown; then he slips on the Vets's shaggy turf. Still, the seventeen-yard reception, the sum of his total output last year, backs Poly up to its 30-yard line.

Joshua Tauanuu, the junior defensive end, goes offside and then bangs his head on the grass in frustration, piquing Manuel, who reaches out and yanks the 260-pounder's jersey, bringing him up for a nose-to-nose reminder that the Jackrabbits do not carry on in public. Matt keeps the next ball to himself for two yards. On the play following that, Manuel demonstrates what the recruiters have been raving about. He's walled off by two blockers, yet sticks an arm between them and makes a one-handed grab of the runner's ankle as he flies past, turning a big gain into chump change. On the next play, though, Matt sneaks for the first down, down to the 17.

The seventh play of the drive. Once again, despite having had over four minutes to rest, Poly's defense is "feeling the power," as the NFL slogan of the moment would put it. On the right hash, Matt stutter-steps to his right, handing to the dive back, Maurice, who slips between the defensive end and the tackle in a blink. Racing over from deep on the left side, Derek Landri and Erich Faustman come across like a pair of drag-racing Mack trucks. Darnell Bing is closing on Maurice, arms wide. Maurice looks into his eyes. Darnell looks back, lowering his shoulder for the hit, as Maurice contracts every muscle in his body into a hard rubberlike shell. This is called "loading up." Just as the two players meet, Landri appears out of nowhere, throwing himself between them, burying Darnell and popping Drew out of his grasp.

The moment Maurice is in the clear, the crowd emits a loud, "Oh!" They know.

The 5'7", 180-pound junior scampers in to score his third touchdown of the night. The point-after kick makes it 21–9. John Chan is hurt on the play, and Bob Ladouceur comes in and, with Alijah Bradley hovering nearby, gives him a shoulder to lean on as he limps off.

There are four minutes and ten seconds left in the half, about the amount of time each team has taken to drive and score.

The kickoff is a squib that bounces through into the end zone for a touchback. As Brandon steps under center, everyone wonders whether he's hurt. He drops back, hits Rory Carrington on a flare to the right for ten yards. He drops back again, sees nothing good developing from the left-side receivers and instantly bootlegs right. Brandon's quick, but he runs like a quarterback, a little too upright to be safe, especially when Cole Smith and Nick Barbero are closing in, with Alijah to apply the love tap. Somehow Brandon avoids the direct shot that might knock him out of the game. On the next play, Brandon looks left and, forced to wait and step around a cluster of struggling linemen, threads a pass to Hershel a moment too late. By the time Hershel slips past the first tackler, Derek smacks him into the grass.

On third down on the Poly 37-yard line, Brandon drops back again and, after looking at his wide-side receivers, fires a quick, high pass over a closing Willie Glasper into the hands of a leaping Hershel. A big first down at the 47, 2:10 left in the half. On the next play Rory takes the pitch going left, accelerates, and blows through two arm-tackles, spinning down to the 38. Next, Brandon drops back to throw, sees nothing, dips up and dips out, weaving around knots of struggling linemen while edging his way upfield. Nate Kenion drops him short of the first-down marker.

Hershel gets the first on a straight-ahead surge to the 35. Again Brandon tries the rollout pass. Every time a linebacker starts to close on Brandon he pump-fakes the ball as if to throw, freezing the backer, and in this way runs all the way to the sidelines to stop the clock. Hershel takes a pitch for five yards. The clock is running down—a minute left, and Poly sends in big John Williams as a deep tailback. De La Salle takes one look at the 5'9", 225-pounder and figures he's in to block for a pass, but Brandon pitches him the ball and John takes aim at the first-down marker like a charging rhino. First down, and John stops the clock, too.

On the 27-yard line, Brandon rolls, sets; he hesitates a moment before throwing deep in the right corner to a cutting Derrick Jones, whose speed has once again gotten him open and into the end zone—and into the spotlight. The ball comes in low and will be late, forcing Derrick to put on the brakes and fall to his knees facing it—but there's no doubt it will arrive. Defender Damon Jenkins, having spun around to catch up to Derrick, sees the ball and in an instant launches himself forward, contorting his body in midair. He's too late, too short, but extends an outstretched hand, a splay of fingers, into the ball's flight path. Contact! His fingers barely brush the ball, but he does alter its trajectory at the very last second and it flutters to Derrick's left. The sophomore shows good concentration and lunges sideways to gather the ball to his chest. In another second of possession it will be a touchdown. Jenkins, however, while still flying through the air, has redirected his missile of a body so that its momentum carries him into Derrick, who loses his grip in the collision. Give Damon credit for *two* great plays on a single bound.

The next play starts off as a Poly fizzle. Hershel takes a hand-off and plows straight into the left side, right at Derek Landri. He vanishes into a pile of bodies. It looks like a one- or two-yard gain. But the pile is moving. Yes, the Poly linemen are pushing the entire squirming ball of arms and legs and butts and torsos, and somehow in there Hershel is burrowing like a mole until he pops out, astonishingly, nine yards downfield. If sophomore Willie Glasper hadn't been there to wrap him up, he would've gone the distance.

As wonderful as the play is, it's used up a lot of time. Poly's players race back to the line and set, waiting for Brandon to call the play without a huddle, calling it out as he stands over center. It's a quick toss to Hershel, who cruises left behind the highlight-film blocking of Hercules Satele. Hercules methodically knocks aside three Spartans while leading Hershel to a first down on the 15-yard line that also stops the clock.

Fifteen yards in twenty-some seconds with no time-outs remaining means at most two plays, maybe three if the ball carrier gets out of bounds. The Spartans are holding out with all their might, Derek Landri bench-pressing six hundred pounds of struggling Poly players on every play. If they stop Poly here, they go into the locker room and rest having done their job, having played to the game plan as laid out by Terry Eidson back in December of 2000, when the very idea of this game first got serious.

It was at O'Kane's Sports Pub, a few hours after the NCS-CIF championship game. Ladouceur, Panella, Blasquez, Aliotti, Geldermann, plus an old friend, Pat Hayes, were sitting around for the one night of whoop-de-do they allow themselves. Talk turned to the new year, and to the proposal to swap Bishop Amat for Poly. On the back of the proverbial napkin, Eidson made his calculations for Poly. "Get me twenty-one points and I think we can hold them," Eidson had said that night at O'Kane's.

If Poly doesn't score here, in the second half the Spartan offense will run the veer on the Jackrabbits, nickel and dime them while letting the clock tick away. The veer makes teams crazy; they get impatient and self-destruct. While Poly crumbles, De La Salle's defense will be able to play loose and aggressive with a two-touchdown advantage, knowing that even if Poly scores twice the Spartans can still win—that missed Poly point-after kick suddenly looms large. Poly will still need two touchdowns to win or, should they miss their extra-point attempts, even tie. The pressure will be huge, especially if the Spartan defense keeps forcing Poly into these long marches.

Meanwhile, the offense will have the entire second half to summon its strength for one more drive. There's no way Matt Gutierrez won't get them into the end zone, or at least put James Bloomsburg into position for a field goal attempt.

Bottom line: the next two or three plays will determine the game. Some twenty-seven seconds are left when the Poly offense breaks and trots up to the line. The Jackrabbits are showing run all the way, two tight ends in a jumbo package. Even the nominal wide receiver is a tight end: Marcedes, split out all alone on the right. He'll probably crack back on a safety.

So it's a total run, and that alone should tell the Spartans something, but De La Salle is nonetheless surprised when Brandon doesn't even fake to Hershel, but takes a two-step drop. Marcedes races forward five yards and stops on a dime, causing the defensive back shadowing him, as well as the safety racing along the goal line, to slip as they try to recover. Brandon zips the ball so that it arrives the moment after Marcedes makes his cut, and the 6'7" tight end with the principal dancer's body pirouettes and springs toward the goal as the safety and defensive back converge on him. In fact, he actually slides over Damon Jenkins's prostrate body to get the ball over. Up go the official's arms: 21–15.

Confetti flies, fans go berserk, the band launches into the "Trojan Fight Song," which Poly always plays after a score—a bit of tradition going back to Jackrabbit Morley Drury, USC's first football great. The relief of getting this touchdown after the tension of the long bolero of the drive sends Poly's players into an uncharacteristic frenzy. They mob each other and Marcedes, who leaps about in triumph. He starts pounding his chest like King Kong, hollering and marching in the direction of the stands—until he comes face-to-face with an official. The CIF has been strictly enforcing that excessive-celebration rule, and so, having penalized Maurice for his somersault, the ref pretty much has to throw the flag here.

The penalty moves the point-after kick, normally a chip shot, back to the 25. As the De La Salle rushers collapse his blockers, Jeff pushes a weak boot to the right. No good. The score remains 21–15.

Jeff's kickoff is short, taken by Damon Jenkins at the 20. He gets behind a wall of blockers, going left, and is at the 40 when a tackle jars the ball loose. Poly's Tyrone Jenkins—no relation—recovers the fumble. Suddenly Poly has another twelve seconds to try to score, time for two or three plays. It's a long shot, but one twenty-yard pass play puts them within Jeff's range. A field goal here will erase those two missed extra points and send De La Salle reeling into halftime, momentum gone, game-plan shot.

From the 47, Brandon takes a deep drop. The Spartans blitz from his left, the blind side, and Brandon fails to check for a blitz before looking for his receivers. He never sees linebacker Nick Barbero, who buries him.

The sack deflates the momentum, and two Hail Mary passes later the teams head for the locker rooms, marching in ranks as television and NFL Films cameramen backpedal before them. Up in the stands, the air is alive with the sound of noisemakers: ancient flails, hollow gourds filled with pebbles, and the ubiquitous yellow plastic kazoo.

Twenty-one

GO TELL THE SPARTANS

First in on the Poly side is Jim Barnett, with a sheaf of plays under one arm and a stern expression on his face. He's joined by Tim Moncure, the offensive line coach, and John Williams, the big fullback. They spread out charts on a portable table in the tunnel and go to work, right out in the open, ten feet from the entrance to the De La Salle lockers.

Inside, Rory sits on the cold concrete floor and studies the air. Next to him, Hershel sits cross-legged, expressionless. Lara motions to the coaches, as well as to Manuel and Junior. "This is what we're going to do," Lara says. "They're killing us with the dive. I don't know what's happening with the tackles, but we need to get penetration. Other than that, they're beating us on the line of scrimmage. We are not controlling the line of scrimmage. This is the game I expected. It is a tough one. It will be our time in the fourth quarter. Be aware. Be aware.

"Try to get the ball. If Gutierrez comes running in there again, try to strip it. And let's make some tackles. That number twenty-one is so strong; Darnell, I think you went high on him. We have to start hitting him in the legs—same as Grootegood in '98, same

257

as McNair in '97. There are just some runners, you cannot tackle them high. Now, let's get a break."

The defense gathers and begins a chant I haven't heard before, probably because Poly hasn't trailed at the half this year. "Hey, hey, it ain't over! / Hey, hey, it ain't over! / Defense!" Then they break into crooning song: "You ain't going anywhere . . ."

The scene in the De La Salle locker room is the opposite of Poly's: chaotic, steamy, full of shouting men and desperate-looking kids. It's like a segment of *ER* set in a Turkish bathhouse. In a tiled room off the lockers, on a tilted board held up by a straining Mike Blasquez, lies Javier Carlos, in just a towel, passed out. Scott Regalia and two others are standing over Carlos, redirecting air from the fan by waving playbooks and clipboards. Brother Chris is watching from one side, a look of deep concern on his face. Eidson and Ladouceur, instead of diagramming plays, are helping to distribute bags of ice over Carlos's supine form. An assistant coach on his knees is jury-rigging an IV.

Blasquez is clearly upset. Under his program, this shouldn't be happening. But the intensity of the game, the energy of the kids on both teams, plus some other unknowable factors, perhaps a bad lunch choice, or poor hydration—something as seemingly innocuous as a diet cola—has led to this.

And it's not only Carlos; there's an epidemic of cramping. In this season of Korey Stringer and Rashidi Wheeler, athletes who died amid questions of supplement use, the thought undoubtedly passes through the adults' minds that, despite every warning and prohibition, some of these kids might have taken supplements. Teenagers are always tempting each other with secret potions, whether to cure acne or turn themselves into mini-Schwarzeneggers, and they will take crazy risks in highly pressured situations.

Take Andy Briner, for instance. Ladouceur is standing over

him, jaw agape in a caricature of astonishment: "You did *what?* Tonight of all nights?"

That limping that had everyone worried wasn't the result of a Poly hit or Andy's strained groin. Andy's wearing new shoes. Everyone stares at his red, raw, ruined feet. "Are you out of your mind?" Ladouceur looks as if he's about to burst into laughter, and a couple of coaches cover their faces with their hands.

By the urinals, John Chan is walking back and forth, back and forth, his cleats click-clicking on the tiles, eyes straight ahead, lips moving. His muttered words run together without punctuation or affect: "God grant me the serenity to accept things I cannot change courage to change the things I can wisdom to know the difference . . ."

Terry Eidson stops on his way past the toilets. He observes for a moment, then steps in front of Chan. "What's up with you?"

"Going out and doing better, Coach," says Chan in a flat voice. Eidson nods and rolls his eyes, but moves on. Chan continues pacing.

A referee pokes his head in. "Five minutes!"

"Get fluids!" shouts a coach. Players are in agony, in attitudes of collapse. Derek Landri is bent over at the waist, a trainer kneading his calves while he sucks water out of a tube. Nate's head is completely covered in a wet green-and-gold Poly towel. "More ice!" someone bellows.

"Quiet down," Ladouceur says. The room grows still in seconds, except for the sounds of the team working on Carlos. The coach gazes at the faces staring up at him, arrayed along the double benches. Half are in sweat-and grass-stained jerseys; half are in gleaming white, like contrasting sides of a detergent commercial. "Some of you guys standing on the field will be helping out in the second half. Everybody's gonna pitch in. Everybody's gonna go." He pauses.

"Don't let down. Go all out."

Ladouceur turns back to the room where Carlos lies, his pep talk—if that's what you call those twenty-nine words—over. The team heads out to the field to stretch. When they're gone, Ladouceur asks Blasquez, "Is he doing all right?"

The improvised IV is going in. Someone stands on a bench, above Carlos, holding the fluid bag. A couple of minutes pass; Brother Chris has closed his eyes and appears to be in prayer. "He's doing okay?" Ladouceur asks, breaking the silence. Blasquez, fingers on Carlos's pulse, nods. "He's doing much better."

Ladouceur turns and walks steadily to the door. He pushes it open, and a dull roar enters the locker room. The amplified voices of Poly cheerleaders soar above the crowd's cheering: "Are you ready to rumble?" The answering cry is loud and hungry.

Twenty-two

STILL TIME FOR A HERO

For much of the media, used to big-time pro and college sports, the pace of the first half of the game, without the sclerosis of beer and car advertisements, was astonishing. A play ended, players untangled themselves, moved briskly to the huddle, then trotted up to the line. There was none of the interminable, almost scholarly debate over play-calling that goes on in the professional games, as ads and time-outs combine to create five-minute lacunae. There was no instant replay on a huge JumboTron screen, as in college and professional stadiums. There was no recorded rock 'n' roll or rap blasting the eardrums: the crowd brought the noise. There was no voice-of-God announcer filling dead air with cheesy rhetoric: what you got as a spectator were your neighbor's comments, your row's, and maybe you made your own. At Vets, this was football—straight up, no chaser.

The first half had seen something close to high school perfection: nine possessions, consisting of two punts, six scoring drives, and one end-of-half flurry of Hail Mary passes. There had been no quick scores, no blown coverages resulting in an easy touchdown; both offenses had showed grit and ingenuity. There had been one turnover, at the half, and thus inconsequential. There had been no questionable calls by the refs; the two excessive-celebration penalties, one on Maurice, the other on Marcedes, seemed deserved. The only errors that could be seen as costly (besides giving up touchdowns, of course) were the two foiled Poly extra-point attempts. These lost points were certainly going to affect strategy in the second half.

The responsibility for the perfection rested with the players themselves. The lumbering pace of the pro game gives coaches time to diagram minute variations of plays on both offense and defense. Here, the decisions were being made on the field. Both quarterbacks, Brandon and Matt, had the authority to change plays at the line, and in the veer offense Matt had a tree of options to run through at every snap of the ball, as did the linemen. As they settled their knuckles on the grass, centers called out the gap and spacing of the defenders, tackles on both sides barked out their coded adjustments, linebackers checked off formations, and running backs and ends made tiny shifts in their stances—all without an adult whispering in their ears. Not that they didn't pay attention to the coaches: right up to the snap of the ball, defenders would look over at their position coach, or to Eidson and Lara, to see if a special stunt or blitz was being called.

"We want our kids to think," says Lara of the defense, "whereas kids at other schools just do what the coaches tell them to do. It's like a chess game. I love when the kids control the game, when they call it."

To most in the stands the second half probably seemed to promise more of the same, a high-scoring affair that would end up being decided by a kicker's foot, a last-ditch touchdown, or a goal-line stand. But partisans of De La Salle and Poly—those who were shouting "Reverse!" and "Draw!" as plays developed on the field—knew that the second half would be another game entirely. The Spartans struck fast and hard in the first half; now they

were going to dig in and hold on, with an occasional quick coun-
terattack. And the Poly Jackrabbits, shrugging off their opponent's best shot, would keep grinding. Both teams and their fans
understood that by the fourth quarter, the pace could change
again to an all-out assault, especially if the Poly barrage was successful in beating down the defenders.

At the kickoff, a tricky Bloomsburg squib goes past the Poly
returner and out of the end zone. Starting at their 20, the
Jackrabbits send Hershel straight ahead for one yard. On second
down, Brandon drops back and waits for the aggressive Spartan
rush to create an opportunity for a screen to Alex Watson. Instead he finds himself trapped and forced to throw the ball behind for an incompletion. On third down and ten, the Jackrabbits
are exactly where they didn't want to be: forced to throw, on the
verge of surrendering control of the ball to De La Salle. On top
of that, if they punt from their twenty they'll be giving the Spartans great field position, setting them up for the knockout punch.
It's a little early to be calling this a turning point, but it has the
makings of one.

Brandon comes to the line hoping his blockers can hold off
the Spartan rush long enough for his receivers to solve the riddle
of the defensive backs, but he has to be worried. He's been hur-
ried or sacked on every obvious passing down, which is a little
galling when your linemen outweigh theirs by fifty pounds.

At the snap Brandon drops back, and even before he sets his
feet, the pocket of blocking collapses. Buying time by rolling to
his right, Brandon looks for his receivers, hoping to see one break
out. But the chase is on, lunging defenders clutching at his heels,
clawing at his jersey, and so the undersized quarterback goes
straight for the first-down marker, ten yards away. At first there's
no way he can make it; then, with 6'2", 235-pound Erik Sandie
and 5'10", 215-pound Erich Faustman converging on the line,

and Maurice Drew charging in for a big hit, it looks as if this is going to be Brandon's swan song. As Brandon nears the line, Sandie gets a hand on his jersey from behind, pulling him upright and wide open for Drew's shot. But then Faustman flies in, tagging Brandon but messing up Drew's timing.

It's a big first down, even if Brandon limps away favoring his right knee, the one twisted in the pile in the first half. The next play is an inside handoff to big John Williams, who carries four men on his back as he staggers away from the line. Then Rory tries to drive up the narrow left side. The De La Salle defense knows they have to get a defensive stop, to shut down the Poly steamroller before it gains momentum. On third down and nine yards, Poly doesn't even think about passing: Brandon fakes to Rory right then gives the ball to Hershel, who cuts inside a mammoth block, makes Drew miss, twists out of the grasp of Jon Alexander, and eludes an Alijah Bradley tackle. Hershel has just planted his leg for a solid explosive burst that will kick off a seventy-yard touchdown run when Nick Barbero pursues from behind and knocks him down. It is, however, another first down.

Hoping to be less predictable, Poly passes on the next play, but Brandon's soft toss to Rory is broken up by Nate Kenion. On second down, however, a short pass to Marcedes is complete for six yards. Darnell Bing now comes in on the wing, one of the wrinkles that promised a Poly advantage. Darnell slices for three yards, but a sure Cole Smith tackle brings up a fourth and one on the Spartans's 46-yard line.

Poly's made a dangerous living on fourth downs so far this game. Up in the stands, the Poly fans are gasping in excitement; some of the older ones, who've flown or driven in, partied last night and tailgated this morning, are getting a little gray in the face.

Fourth and one. Brandon pitches to Hershel, and it's clear

sailing to the left sideline. As Hershel escapes the containment, Andy Briner spins out of his blocker's grasp and gives chase. The orange marker is right there as Andy dives and Hershel cuts, as Andy's fingers brush Hershel's heel. But Hershel's through, and after he plants his right foot, he'll be able to turn upfield.

The right foot comes down, but the grass gives way. Hershel knows what's happening, and as the momentum begins to carry him out of bounds, he plants his white-gloved right hand, knuckles on the first-down line, intending to use his upper-body strength to levitate his legs long enough to get his left hand, carrying the ball, over the line. The ref is standing right on the sidelines, staring down at this sea-level gymnastics routine, waiting to see whether any part of Hershel's legs will touch the ground before the ball crosses the plane of the first-down marker. The feet land first. It's De La Salle's ball.

The Spartans have dealt themselves this break before they've gotten worn down, early enough to make something good happen. With Matt and the running backs, it should be no problem getting a couple of first downs to rest the defense. Then they can go for the kill. One more touchdown and Poly will be looking up a very steep mountain, especially with those two missed extra points.

Matt does a quick drop and fires a pass out to De'Montae Fitzgerald, but it's knocked away by a defensive back. Matt goes to the dive, which had been good for five yards or more in the first half, but Poly has switched around responsibilities for the backs and the wrong linebacker is blocked. No gain. On third down, Matt rolls out and tries again for De'Montae, but the junior can't make the tough catch.

De La Salle has to punt. The Poly defense has risen up at last.

Stanford quarterback Chris Lewis, watching from the sidelines, gives a shout. "Aw, man, I wish it was me out there! I wish it was us," meaning the '98 team that had so much talent. After a short return to the 25, Poly gets down to the business of letting Hershel find a way. Through the right side he goes, for seven yards. "He's close to breaking one," says Lewis. On the next play, Hershel takes the ball inside and, when the hole closes, runs in reverse like a backed-up film strip, out of the hole, swerving around and escaping Drew's tackle, ducking and diving in and out of promising cracks in the defense. From all the way over on the left, he dips and spins all the way over to the right, switching the ball to his outside hand as he sprints, just as it's taught. He's finally run to earth after twenty-seven yards.

On the next play, Rory takes a pitch left for three yards. A couple of the Division I scholarship players on the sidelines shake their heads: "Marcedes needs to hold his blocks longer." Poly goes offside and is penalized five yards. Leon Jackson comes in for a play at quarterback, but under a big rush throws a screen pass away. When Brandon rolls out to pass on the next play, he waits and then zips in a hard pass to Alex Watson, who has run a crisp pattern and found a hole in the defense. However, he's tackled before he can turn upfield. The De La Salle defense, which now includes a couple of kids whose shirts were white at halftime, has brought Poly right back to the edge.

Once again it's fourth down. "We need some second and shorts," says Chris Lewis. Fourth and one can be done, although not without risk, as Hershel's slip shows. Fourth and six is heart-attack territory: the odds go down below 50 percent, maybe to 25 percent or lower against a defense like De La Salle's.

The players' focus is solely on the next play, they don't hear a thing, don't spare a glance for the band, the cheerleaders, or the fans in the stands. But the game is happening up there in the bleachers, too. This is where the Boot at the north end of the stadium plays a part. It has been in motion the entire second half, criss-crossing every row, as regular as a shuttle on a loom, left, right, left. There is a Boot for every bleacher section, carried by a member of the Long Beach Fire Department and used to collect donations to the families of New York firemen killed on 9/11. This particular Boot seems to dance for Poly, darting along with the drive on the field. As the players trot to the line of scrimmage, fingers fumble unseeing in purses and pockets for spare change to feed the floppy black rubber maw.

Standing half-crouched deep behind the quarterback, hands resting lightly on his thigh pads, Hershel Dennis's impassive expression doesn't give anything away, but his eyes are clicking, reading the feet of the linebackers, the shoulder tilt of the defensive ends, and noting the shifting defensive backs. De La Salle's first thought must be for Hershel, but six yards is so long they're probably guessing pass—perhaps a fake to Hershel, then a flare to him or a slant to Marcedes.

At the hike Hershel's feet dig with short, chopping steps, instant acceleration, but his center of gravity remains back; on a six-yard run he doesn't want to commit early, has to pick his hole, read his blockers, take a fleeting precognitive snapshot of the converging linebackers and safety, and only then explode. He doesn't look for the handoff; Brandon is so smooth and reliable the ball is suddenly just there, right where it should be, and Hershel's fingers clamp down. He sees that the linemen in front are surging forward in such a solid, unbroken wave that he can scoot behind them for a couple of yards, feet jitterbugging, eyes tracking the backside pursuers, before he has to commit, blow up the left side.

First down on the 30. The fans release a deep, pent-up sigh. It's a sign. Propitiating the Boot has made a difference. Hershel Dennis is in the building. Poly's going to take it to the House. This long agonizing bolero is the point, after all. Let De La Salle almost stop you, then grind it out; let them hope, let them despair, let them tire, let them lose. A touchdown will make it 21–21, an extra point will give Poly the lead. De La Salle has only trailed once in the second half in nine years. They won't know what to do, and they're running out of time—this quarter is almost over, three minutes to go.

On first down, though, Poly goes for the kill, not just the crush. The linebackers are creeping up to stop Hershel. Poly has seen how the De La Salle defensive backs have shaded over to cover Marcedes, leaving Jonathan Johnson, the other tight end, free to release. So with only a pro forma fake in the direction of the running backs, Brandon drops back and fires a dart straight over the middle to Jonathan as he splits a seam, going right up the line of shared responsibility between safety, linebacker, and cornerback. It's a timing throw, a bit high, but not too high for a leaping 6'6" Jonathan, who gets his hands on it as two defenders converge, dragging at his jersey. Perhaps he's distracted; perhaps the ball, thrown hard, arrives a tick late; it slips through his fingers after a tantalizing nanosecond.

On second down, the handoff goes to Rory, who is hit by player upon player in succession, each one latching on to a body part. Somehow, snorting like a young bull, Rory carries four defenders on his back for five yards, showing the kind of big-game grit college recruiters notice.

Third and five. At the snap, Brandon drops back to pass. The play includes a slanting end and two receivers flaring into the right side, but the De La Salle linebackers and defensive backs are like a net stretched in front of a fleeing shoal of fish. Brandon has no one open and is forced to run for it. He's brought down by Andy Briner and Cole Smith for a five-yard loss.

One again the Spartans have done it, brought up fourth down. This time it's fourth and ten, and Poly's got to pass. The consequences of getting away from the run on first and third down are severe for a grind-it-out offense. Though the Rabbits are within range for a field goal, nobody likes the odds of Jeff hitting two forty-two-yarders in one game.

Up in the northern section of the bleachers, a group of students can't wait for the Boot any longer. A girl in her teens rises to her feet and shakily tosses a handful of change. Others take up the change, add their own, toss it on down.

In a moment the crowd changes. They begin throwing coins: dimes, quarters, pennies, nickels. A shower of coins arcs through the air, descending like a copper-silver rain on the fireman, who realizes he can do nothing but stand there, holding the Boot out, its mouth open.

People dig in their pockets. Girls are begging their friends, then absolute strangers, for coins. The copper-silver rain falls faster and faster, bouncing off the chest of the fireman. It's something from archaic days, when statues of saints were paraded in village streets with thousand-lire notes pinned to their robes.

Fourth and ten. All the arms make throwing motions, even if they haven't anything left to throw, a gesture of *Go!Go!Go!* With 1:19 left in the quarter, Brandon steps up under center, eyes the defense, sees the seam he wants to exploit, and confidently barks out the cadence. At the snap he starts his drop, only to realize in horror that the ball hasn't arrived. The center has short-armed the hike, and the ball falls to the grass, where Brandon can only cover it.

The Poly crowd is devastated. De La Salle voices rise up in triumph.

Matt brings the Spartans up to the line. But there's confusion as the receivers line up, and De La Salle takes a delay penalty. Could it be they're slipping, too?

Matt takes the snap with an empty backfield behind him, a

clear passing set, and is immediately chased by Manuel, who evades his blocker and closes with a sprinter's speed, incredible in a 315-pounder. Matt gets the ball off to De'Montae, but Darnell is right there for the stop. On the next play, Matt rolls left and throws back on a delay screen. There's a solid wall of blockers in front of De'Montae, but again Manuel flies in, squeezing between bodies and dragging him down. Still, the play gains six yards.

The third quarter ends. On the Poly sidelines, former players are slipping in, talking their way past sympathetic security guards. The college and pro guys know what is happening here, even if the clock says that there are twelve minutes left. Poly has left De La Salle an opening, and nobody expects the Spartans to go three and out this time. In comes a tight trio of receivers, and Alijah alone behind Matt. Alijah goes in motion wide, Matt takes his one-step drop and hits Nate, the middle member of the trio, for a first down.

De La Salle looks sharp, but Matt is aware that this game, unlike any other he's ever played, is so fast there's no comfort zone. It's like everyone is being shot out of a slingshot. And the hitting is cartoonish, *ka-pow!* He thinks, *It's so cool.*

But the increased speed, however thrilling, carries risks, as when Matt misses a handoff on the next play and is tackled. On second down, he fires out a short pass to De'Montae for five yards—a junior, De'Montae is having a career day, thanks in part to the defensive backs' concentration on Ryan Eidson. On third and three at the 49-yard line, the play comes in from the sidelines.

It's a honey of a play, too. The Spartans are sucking air, they're cramping, but they understand that if they can put this one over, they may just get some breathing room.

Matt lines them up. Third and three is a luxury, because if it fails, then at least there's fourth down. On third and three you can take your shot at a long bomb or dig into your bag of tricks, and Ladouceur has rummaged deep in his bag for this one. At the snap, Matt drops back to pass, getting a big pass protection effort. In fact, there's too much protection—on the left side, Derek Landri and tight end Brendan Ottoboni are joined by a couple of other Spartans in tandem blocking—and too few receivers. The deep-streak guys are covered. The Poly linebackers and the safety see what looks like a broken play, the middle's wide open, nobody's there, just Derek and Brendan double-teaming some poor soul way over on the left, drifting downfield and riding the guy like he's a sled. Tick, tick, tick. Suddenly Brendan stops, slides behind Derek, and steps into the huge bubble at the precise moment Matt delivers the ball, chest-high, in stride.

The sixteen-yard gain stuns Poly. It came out of nowhere. De La Salle is now on Poly's 35, and here comes the counter, Maurice for five yards; then Matt keeps it for two. On third and three, Poly's defense gives each other The Look. *Are we going to stop this thing?*

Matt hands off to the dive back, Alijah, and Junior Lemauu and Maurice Murray roar in to blow back the pile and hammer him down. Fourth down and three—Poly has risen up one more time. A stop here and the momentum will turn, plenty of time for a game-winning drive, to squeeze the air out of De La Salle's exhausted defense.

Two backs line up behind Matt. Nate is on the right, Alijah on the left. At the snap Nate cuts in front, going left with a fake, while Alijah takes the handoff going right, slotting himself behind the duo of Erik Sandie and Derek Landri. With a quartet of Poly players hanging and banging on them, the threesome rumbles for two yards, then Alijah spurts through for the final thirty-six inches and a first down.

It's the eleventh play of the drive, De La Salle's longest of the night. For the first time the body language of the Poly defenders reveals frustration and despair: someone lying on his face pounds his fists on the grass.

De La Salle doesn't futz around. They know this is the money drive. Up to the line they trot, suddenly rejuvenated. The snap is quick, almost the moment Matt puts his hands below center. He pivots, hands to Maurice on the counter left. Like coal miners, Regalia, Sandie, and Briner have dug a tunnel to the end zone, on a diagonal running right between the smashing bodies, and Maurice flies down it going right past a defensive back who looks as if he's seen a ghost as the white jersey flits by. Darnell closes, but can't get a hand on him.

It's 27–15, De La Salle, with 6:57 to go. On the Poly sidelines the coaches, older players, and graduates nod, swallow their shock and sinking spirits, and take turns saying, "Okay, that just means we got to score two. Got to score two." They're right: two touchdowns and two extra points will still give Poly the win. Brandon's done it before; he took them the distance in less than a minute against Loyola.

Ladouceur is thinking the same thing. He's watching his main guys going down on their knees between plays, eyes rolling, skin flushed. Out comes the trick bag: it's time to go for two points on the conversion.

Kicker Bloomsburg stays on the sidelines. Two backs line up behind Matt, who rolls right after faking a left-side handoff and floats a ball to Alijah in the corner: 29–15. Now if Poly scores two touchdowns, they'll have to make both extra points just to tie. It's that De La Salle trademark: keep the pressure on.

How will Poly answer?

Twenty-three

SEND IN THE CLONES

Raul Lara stares down at his clipboard, thinking, *Well, we had our chances.*

It's clear that the game plan they've devised has been vindicated. The Poly coaches have noted the absence of Carlos, seen Landri cramping and puking on the sidelines, and noticed other Spartan players tapping their helmets, a sign they want to be rotated out. They've watched the fresh white jerseys trot onto the field, Dan Wright, Erich Faustman, Sean Matlock, Mike Pittore—the clones, someone called them, a few weeks ago in the film room.

In the third quarter, Poly's shift from a 4-4 defense to a 4-3, with different players dividing up the responsibility for the dive back off the veer, had confused De La Salle for its one offensive series. The Spartans had gained ten yards to Poly's eighty-five. They'd held the ball for all of two minutes, to Poly's ten minutes. They wore down. But, as Anthony Cobb said to Mark Carrier and Eugene Burkhalter on the sidelines, "We forgot to score."

Not scoring on the third-quarter drive had essentially put Poly behind the eight ball for the rest of the game, because Ladouceur and Panella would not be fooled twice. They'd had to wait to get the ball back until near the end of the third quarter, but when the Spartan offense took the field, they had the 4-3 figured out. *They countered us real well by trapping us,* Lara thinks, *and they trapped us real well.*

Now it was Poly's turn, once more. There was plenty of time, in the abstract. But they had to remember how to score.

On the last touchdown, Tyrone Jenkins had watched the white jersey, No. 21, streak past on its way to the end zone. It had all happened in an eye blink, hardly any time to react, but Drew had passed through Tyrone's territory and through his arms. That hurt. That's why, when Bloomsburg's kickoff came in Tyrone's direction, he took it and ran as if grateful for the chance to atone, juking, driving, spinning out of tackles, all the way up to the 45.

Just like that, Poly had a chance again. Score here, stop the Spartans, get the ball back, and score again—like old times. Brandon immediately threw to Rory on a flare, and the sweet-faced, strong-legged kid, the only Poly player who was playing big minutes both ways, tore through the right side of De La Salle's defense for eleven yards.

On the De La Salle 44-yard line, Brandon takes a pass drop, then low-fives the ball to Hershel on a draw. The defense isn't fooled, the clones maintain their spacing and responsibilities, closing in. Hershel takes it up the middle into heavy traffic, snakes in an S-curve, shakes his hip to the outside to freeze the oncoming defensive back, who's closing in for the tackle. It's a nice ten-yard gain.

Only Hershel isn't done. In midswerve he leaps and hurdles the defender, and as Cole Smith and Nate Kenion converge from the left, he stops dead. He must have been using his side mirror, because Alex Watson flies in from his wide-receiver spot to tag

Cole. Whirling to get his arms on Hershel, Nate comes face-to-face with . . . Rory? *Ka-pow!*

Hershel glides along, on cruise control, checking out the De La Salle defensive net and the remaining Poly blockers. The yard markers float by under his feet. He's veering left, setting up the last blocker, a wide receiver who's chest to chest with Damon Jenkins, all that's between Hershel and the goal. Damon isn't trying to fight his way to Hershel. He's stringing along the blocker, desperately interposing himself, trusting the chief tenet of defense, support from the backside defenders, the ones initially left out of the play. Trust and support: the chief articles of faith at De La Salle.

Hershel rides the blocker's slipstream right up to Damon, who spins backward trying for a grab. Nice move, but it's not going to work. Hershel high-steps free at the 12-yard line. He's been running for twelve straight seconds, much longer than a hundred-meter dash, but there's plenty of gas left in his tank. That's when the cavalry arrives, Nick Barbero and Willie Glasper, all the way from across and down the field, and in the thirteenth second Hershel goes out of bounds at the 10.

The run felt like an eternity, but in football, time starts up as soon as the ball is set on the hash by the ref. First and ten, Brandon gives it to Hershel out of the I formation up the middle. The hole opens, momentarily, but Brendan Ottoboni fills the gap for a one-yard gain. On second down, Poly comes out with an empty backfield, not even pretending to present a running option. De La Salle shows four players on the line, five spaced along the 5-yard line, and two safeties back—very tough to pass against. Brandon drops back, fires a pass left to Derrick, who's trying the same five-yard stop pattern Marcedes worked in the first half. The coverage is tight, and a diving defensive back gets a hand on the ball and deflects it just enough so that Derrick can't hold on.

Third and nine. There's a predictable feeling about the Jackrabbits's red-zone offense tonight. They've tried Hershel, they've tried Derrick—now it is Marcedes's turn. A quick slant over the middle or a deep corner fade can be a foolproof play even when anticipated, especially when the receiver has a serious height advantage. Marcedes starts from wide right and angles left, as if expecting a bullet. But De La Salle has a man shading in front, forcing Brandon, who's rolling under pressure, to loft a deep corner throw. Marcedes has the defensive back, Damon, in front of him, which should be to his advantage. But in the time it takes Marcedes to pivot and pursue the ball toward the darkness of the corner, Damon gathers himself and springs, a huge leap, floating above Marcedes, deflecting the ball an instant before landing on Marcedes's back.

Did Damon interfere with Marcedes? The back judge sweeps his hands back and forth above the grass. Incomplete, no penalty. Marcedes storms, jumps, pleads; he approaches the line judge, then thinks better of it, remembering his excessive-celebration penalty.

Fourth and nine; 5:30 left. Poly comes up showing triplets on the right side, with one back behind Brandon. At the snap the right defensive end, guessing correctly that Brandon will roll his way, blows in at top speed, untouched. Brandon has to rise up on his toes as he runs, throwing over the leaping end. Derrick cuts short his route at the three, instead of carrying it out to the end zone, a cardinal sin, but one perhaps justified by the low-velocity throw. The moment Derrick catches it Damon slams him down—he's going to be playing on Saturday, and maybe Sunday, someday.

With all the emotion and energy expended, the entire stadium crashes with Poly's hopes. Even the keening up in the stands, a long, low moaning, dies away. Faces are sagging, tired, the cheerleaders' cries grow faint and feeble. As Derrick slowly hauls himself up to his feet, though, someone is there with a hand to help and a pat on the shoulder pads: Hershel Dennis.

Yet it's still not over, not with over four minutes left. It wouldn't even take a miracle. In the Loyola game under similar circumstances, Marvin Simmons blocked a punt for a touchdown. But it's clear Poly has been gored. De La Salle comes out in a full-house backfield, runs a little misdirection; Alijah gets six yards. A delay penalty on De La Salle moves the ball back five yards. Alijah gets five more. Then there's another delay. Even if these are intentional, to run down the clock, De La Salle is playing it a little too fine; or else the Spartans are simply exhausted. Alijah runs a short pitch. Now the Spartans have to punt from their end zone.

Poly puts on a big rush and almost gets the block, but Bloomsburg's kick is high and long. If only the Jackrabbits had kept running the ball when they had it at the 10, this could be their winning touchdown drive coming up, plenty of time left on the game clock. Instead, Poly looks like an ox who's been culled but whose body hasn't gotten the message yet.

A draw to Hershel is stuffed. Brandon drops back and, in a mirror image of Poly's first offensive play of the game, launches the bomb to Derrick. He's not quite as open this time, but he does get a step on Damon, and the ball is again perfect, in his hands. He can't hold on.

On third down Brandon is sacked back to the 48. On fourth, a pass to Rory gets good yardage but falls well short of the first down.

Three handoffs for short yardage later, Matt Gutierrez takes a final snap to run out the clock. He's like a knight being dubbed, dropping to one knee, then rising up. His first act is to pat Poly tackle Ernesto Villasenor, who's been in his face all night, on the helmet. Then, as the Spartans surge onto the field in ecstasy, Matt walks up to Manuel Wright and shakes his hand.

Twenty-four

AFTER THE FALL

And then it was over. The players surged onto the field, pursued by the bright halogen suns of television crews. Many of the Poly kids could barely raise their eyes; many of the De La Salle kids could barely lift their arms in triumph. In the stands, a contingent of Poly fans with tears in their eyes joined the De La Salle fans in applauding the Spartan players.

Terry Eidson turned and took it all in. "The greatest victory in Spartan history."

Bob Ladouceur nodded, then, under a barrage of questions, began summing up. "Our biggest thing we had to do was get our kids rehydrated. Our two-way linemen, Landri and Briner, they were gassed at halftime. You got to hand it to Poly, they wore us down, even though Mike Blasquez does wonders with our kids. The second-stringers came in and did a job.

"Sometimes I would think this was just a high school game. If it turned out that the streak ended at one hundred and sixteen, I wouldn't have felt bad—losing to Poly tonight. In the end, it was a great day for high school sports."

Coaches and players were getting their handshakes, hugs, snapshots. Alijah Bradley grinned when asked if he had any particular impression of the game. "Bing," he said. "I kept meeting Bing. He just kept hitting me in my legs. I respect him. They're a good, tough team, but we kept bringing it."

Raul Lara made a beeline for a certain De La Salle student— No. 21, Maurice Drew. "You're a hell of a football player," Lara said. "Don't tell me you're a junior."

Drew smiled. "Yeah."

Lara threw his hands up.

Walking amid a crowd, he said, "We wore them down in the third quarter, but when we didn't execute on two long drives, we gave them new life. You can talk all you like about the missed passes, but those drives were what killed us."

Neither team had plans to stay around Vets for long, and so as soon as they could, the players staggered up to the tunnel, accepting congratulations and condolences, seeking out and meeting their opposite numbers from the game. Many observed it had been the quietest game they'd ever played in. "We thought Poly would trash-talk us," Matt said, "but they were absolutely silent. Well, except for Marcedes."

In the tunnel the Poly trainers worked on cutting tape and tending minor injuries, quietly weeping. When Kristen Cauldwell comforted a sorrowful Mark Washington with a hug, a dazzle of camera strobes went off, startling and then angering them. Poly was having a hard time dealing with the press, as cameras and microphones were thrust into glum faces. Nobody wanted to talk. A reporter cozied up to Marcedes and congratulated him; Marcedes only said, "Thank you, sir."

Darnell sat next to Manuel, whose lower lip hung low as he stared into space. "We played our best but we didn't accomplish our goals," Darnell said softly. "They played really good; I didn't think they would be able to stay with us all four quarters."

De La Salle tackle Eric Sandie's mother, Terry, concurred. "I was nervous, we were all on the verge of tears in the third quarter." Her son thought otherwise: "We knew if we could get a touchdown in the second half, the game would pretty much be over."

Over by the stadium railing, where players went to greet their family and friends, one father of a Poly player needed more consoling than his son. When the dad began to complain loudly about the offensive play selection, his son was on him in a flash: "No, that's not right. We play as a team, we lose as a team." The stunned father apologized.

Coach Lara and Marcedes reappeared outside, at the request of the media. Marcedes had conquered his disappointment and now faced the bright lights, subdued, but, as usual, still good for a quote: "We knew De La Salle was an excellent team from watching film. As far as taking it bad, well, we don't have our heads down. It's not like we played a Rooty-Poo team." The comment inspired a flurry of journalistic head-scratching: How to spell that word . . . Rudy-Foody? Rootie-Pootie?

Lara's expression was wry and relaxed again, as if he'd had a great weight removed. He extolled De La Salle, joked that he would ask Bob Ladouceur to sit him down and tell him the secret of Spartan bonding—although "I don't want to go on no camping trips!" He winked. "Remember, we *are* playing them next year."

Staff from both schools were herding the players across the field, toward their waiting buses. A dejected Rory Carrington was almost the last Poly player to leave the tunnel. Told that his play had been singled out by several of the De La Salle guys, he didn't smile, but he did vent a huge sigh. "Somebody had to lose," he said. "We had our chances, but they executed better. Now we'll just have to win CIF."

The stadium empty, a helicopter circled the field and parking lots, keeping an eye on things. Back at the tunnel an exhausted

Andy Briner held a finger in the air to oblige a photographer. He smiled giddily and said, "I think I'm going to faint."

The last press left. No more players came out of the tunnel. The last TV van pulled out of the back gate, and the scoreboard suddenly went black. Mike Blasquez came out, his cherubic features aglow. Everybody was fine, no major injuries, Carlos was up and about. "I've never been prouder," Blasquez said. "They left everything on the field. I am in awe of these average athletes who went up against these monsters and vanquished them. I'm just gonna relish it a bit. This is a great night for me tonight." Smiling, off he went under an almost full moon.

Then Bob Ladouceur came out. He looked up at the moon, then bowed his head to think. "At the end, I said to someone"—a faint smile—" 'And he took a stone from his pouch . . .' "

Twenty-five

POINTS AFTER

The Spartans went off to the Marriott, where the parents who had come down to Southern California had dozens of pizzas and soft drinks awaiting them in a meeting lounge, equipped with a big-screen television. They ate and watched a tape of the game one of the coaches had brought directly from the film booth. When Scott Regalia sat down and took his first bite of a slice of pizza, he winced in pain. His jaw was too bruised from the hit he had taken from Darnell Bing early in the game. Scott soon gave up trying to eat. Most of the players were dinged, many sprouting ice bags on their limbs, shoulders, and knees as they settled down to watch the tape.

Meanwhile, the coaches and school officials had their own adult party in an adjoining lounge. "We flipped on the TV," reported Brother Chris, "just in time to catch highlights of the game on Fox and ESPN."

The victors had a 4 A.M. wake-up call to catch an early-morning flight—airport security was in its worst post-9/11 phase—a prospect that had Ladouceur and the other coaches shuddering. But they made the bus, made the flight, and got home before noon. Life could resume, interrupted by phone calls. According to De La Salle president Bruce Shoup, Ladouceur received a congratulatory call from Steve Mariucci, coach of the San Francisco 49ers; Ladouceur himself never mentioned it.

On Sunday, the Spartans slept a lot and tried to do their homework. Matt slept, watched a little football on TV, then turned to his thesis paper on *Frankenstein*. "I tried to start it, then fell asleep for four hours. I woke at seven P.M. and typed it until midnight. I knew I'd get no mercy from the teacher."

Back in Long Beach, the Parrish family Sunday SAT class met as usual. "Eight out of ten boys came," said Freddie Sr. "Winston and Darnell had family commitments, so they didn't. I told Freddie Jr. that if he doesn't score twelve hundred on the SAT, the television goes."

Coach Lara went to church with his family and later, to celebrate his mother's birthday, took everyone to dinner at the Lakewood Hometown Buffet. Jeff Turley went to his son's baseball game, his first as a pitcher, then to church, then to his brother's house to escape the phone calls. Tim Moncure went to a nephew's fourth birthday party, took his daughter and son shopping, and "watched the war and a little bit of the USC-Washington game." Herman Davis said he "cut the grass, trimmed the edges, played with the dog, drank a few beers, and then watched the war. I didn't watch any football." Doc Moye did watch football, saying, "Nothing changed, it was just one game. My reason for coaching is to get kids into schools." Merle III slept in, having woken early on game day to take the Cal Basic Ed Test to qualify as a teacher. "I watched the afternoon game, didn't answer the phone, didn't answer my pager, didn't talk to my dad."

Marcedes slept until noon, went to his SAT class, then went out to Roscoe's Chicken & Waffles downtown. Afterward, he went home and "watched and watched the film of the game, over and over, to see how we could improve."

Sunday morning's newspapers all featured the game, and the reviews were good: "Lived up to the hype," "History was made last night," "The game of the century."

For De La Salle, the biggest game in high school history was now number 117 and counting. The Spartans would be moving on, as they always did, not to the next opponent as much as to the next repetition, next bench press, next self-correction.

For Poly, however, recovery after the first loss in four years was very much a worry for coaches, administrators, and players. Coprincipal Mel Collins addressed the team before practice Monday. "Usually after a championship game," he said, "come Monday you turn in your uniforms and pads. This time you can do something about it." Go out, he continued, and get better. Go out and win CIF.

Then it was time for practice. Coach Lara stood alone with a clipboard in the center of the field. As soon as the first play was run, there was a little break in tension, and several players laughed. Suddenly a voice was raised. "Hustle up! Let's go, let's go!" shouted Hershel. It was unlike him, but everyone recognized the act of a team leader, taking charge.

After the team broke into its units, the coaches discussed the inevitable changes that would occur in the wake of The Game. "In the beginning of the year we try to evaluate as many guys as we can," Lara explained. "Who's going to be a guy, who ain't gonna be a guy, and who could possibly be a guy." On Saturday night a few guys had emerged, but a couple had also lost their places on the pecking order. "Some players are going to get pink slips today," said Herman Davis. "That's football."

Ten minutes later voices were raised across the field, and a knot of players were struggling with each other. Apparently one player had exploded at his coach when told of his demotion. The angry player was escorted off by Junior and a couple of others for a cooldown talk. An emotional apology, then he returned to practice.

But the incident had shaken everybody, especially because a racial epithet had been used, directed at a white coach. When the short practice was over, Lara faced the biggest speech of his coaching career. He kept it low-key, but blunt: "The season is beginning right now. The hardest part is here. Are we going to fold up our tents and say forget it? Or are we going to go back to the championship.

"Guys, we *have* to go back to the championship. Either that, or you just had your championship. Seniors, nine more weeks. We're not even Moore League champs. In a couple of weeks we're gonna face J-town. You may be smacking your lips, but they are pointing for us."

Lara read from two letters, one from a former coach praising the team, one anonymous and taunting them. Then he said, "Time to watch film."

The Friday after the game, the top three coaches at USC, including head coach Pete Carroll, marched unannounced into the office of Poly coach Raul Lara. "Pete said they just wanted to get out of the office and decided to come check on our guys," recounted Lara. "It was pretty neat, I mean, wow! We just sat there for about twenty minutes and talked about the game. They're really interested in Hershel, they just love Hershel."

That evening Poly played Compton on a field that smelled, literally, of shit, thanks to broken sewer pipes underground. The players' uniforms were sopping with fetid water by the time the game was over, but they did not pause to change clothes. This was Compton, and Poly was playing under the lockdown rules it adopts for hostile territory. The Jackrabbits were a million miles away from the game of the century.

The morning after, Darnell Bing woke up partially paralyzed. He was taken to the emergency room, where testing determined he had suffered an attack of Bell's palsy, an obscure but treatable neurological disease. Darnell would be unable to play for the Moore League season.

When Poly played Jordan—"J-town"—its fiercest Moore League rival, the Panthers nearly ate the Jackrabbits. A new coach, an attacking attitude, and some talented athletes who'd decided to cast their luck with the insurgent school nearly pulled off the upset before falling short. The game was the wake-up call Poly had needed, and didn't get, before De La Salle.

Up north, the Spartans cruised through their season without incident. After the Poly game, Bob Ladouceur had reluctantly admitted that they would probably go unchallenged all the way for the rest of the year, play-offs included. A freak accident amidst the string of blowout victories was an injury to James Bloomsburg, who broke his kicking leg while demonstrating a wrestling move in the De La Salle parking lot. This would put an end to James's dream of a Division I scholarship, but not to his aim of kicking in the pros one day. "I just have to start over and work my way back," he said, like a true Spartan.

Poly's sense of playing a season under a cloud continued when defensive end Joshua Tauanuu's father died. Josh stayed out a week, then returned to the team that had become, even more than before, a kind of surrogate family. The week of the last game of the Moore League season, starting offensive lineman Charles Owens was found to have an uncontrollable blood-pressure condition and an irregular heartbeat. Given that his mother had passed away earlier in the season, Charles was invalided from the team, although he continued to come to practice and watch from the sidelines—and, remarkably, stayed cheerful.

When the play-off seedings for the Southern Section were announced, Poly was rated number one. Among the changes in the team makeup were the additions of Junior Lemauu as a blocking tight end and of junior linebacker Mark Washington, who had inexplicably been left out of the game against De La Salle. Darnell Bing also returned to action. Poly drew a tough bracket in the play-offs, but routed Fountain Valley, ground down Loyola, smacked rival Long Beach powerhouse Los Alamitos, and ended up in the title game against the Edison Eagles of Huntington Beach. It would be the first all-public-school CIF Southern Section championship in sixteen years.

With the season playing out according to form, the mood at De La Salle is mellow, sprinkled with humor and ample opportunities to reflect. The college recruitment season is in full swing, which ensures a stream of phone calls and visits. This was always happening at Poly, of course, the scouts and coaches coming by to grade the talent. In the two days before The Game, college-coach drop-bys at Poly included those from Oregon State, Wisconsin, Boise State, Idaho, Montana State, Washington, Cal Berkeley, and even Fordham.

At De La Salle, the hot prospects are Derek and Matt. Derek verbally committed to Notre Dame long ago, but since then the Irish have had one coach hired away and his replacement, George O'Leary, was forced to resign after only a week due to a falsified résumé. It's obviously a program in disarray, and so the college recruiters are back to persuade Derek to rethink his choice. Even De La Salle president Bruce Shoup is pressed by a PAC 10 supporter on the sidelines of a game, but no one who knows Derek believes he will change his mind.

Matt's future is also a topic of daily discussion among those in the college game. Oregon comes calling in the form of Spartan coach Joe Aliotti's brother Nick, the offensive coordinator. Matt has said he's decided on Michigan, a school known for producing NFL-prospect quarterbacks, but Oregon has just finished a terrific season and is in the running for a national championship. Plus, it's closer to home. "Matt's parents can watch his brother's De La Salle game on Friday night," says Aliotti, rehearsing his argument with his brother, "take a plane Saturday morning and be there by kickoff for the home games. It would be much harder to do that at Michigan."

A USC coach, Wayne Moses, is waiting just outside to take his turn to pitch Landri, whose Southern California roots are well known. It's not clear if either player will want to talk, but there's no sense of impatience or frustration in either Aliotti or Moses as they wait for a messenger to return with the word. This is the world of college athletics—grown men hanging on the decisions of high school seniors.

As usual, the most striking anomaly of a De La Salle football year—other than another undefeated season—is how few seniors are being solicited for scholarships. Other than Derek and Matt, Nick Barbero is the only other player with an offer, although everyone is certain Andy Briner will get something. Alijah Bradley could probably get a ride from a lower-division school, but, like Derek and Matt, he has one college in mind: Michigan. The Wolverines aren't going to use a scholarship on a 5'7", 167-pounder, even one as accomplished and courageous as Alijah, but they're more than happy to welcome him as a walk-on. Alijah does receive the NFL's Student Athlete Award, which includes a banquet February 20. His 3.7 GPA will earn him the equivalent of a football scholarship in financial aid.

De La Salle president Bruce Shoup nods approvingly at this: "Our coaches don't influence where kids should go as much as protect them from where they shouldn't go. There are an awful lot of negative influences, including some NCAA coaching and recruiting practices, out there."

The Poly players and coaches were surprised, and even a little miffed, to hear how few Spartans receive scholarships. Several Jackrabbits speculated that De La Salle's habit of blowing out opponents by an average score of 48–9 hurt the statistics of top players, thus making them less visible and attractive to recruiters. Ladouceur vehemently disagrees: "First of all, college recruiters don't care about stats at all. They can tell right off the bat after watching five minutes of film whether they like your player or not. And usually they can tell if he can play at a Division I level. They're going to look at how they move, how they throw, how they run against really good competition."

Later that week, the coach of the woeful Cal Berkeley Bears resigned. It has been a staple joke in Bay Area newspapers all season that the Bears team would have trouble beating De La Salle, so it only seems natural for Bob Ladouceur's name to surface among the job candidates. This is of grave concern to Spartan fans, but in fact the marketing of Ladouceur is Terry Eidson's idea. He's been pushing Bob Ladouceur for a couple of years to at least make what is called "an expression of interest" in college jobs. "I want him to go through the process," says Eidson, who is so fiercely protective of Ladouceur that he would welcome the loss to his athletic program if the right job came along. But Ladouceur remains immune to the charms of college coaching. As Eidson recounts the conversation:

"I asked him, 'What do you think the job pays?' And he says, 'Uh, two hundred?'

" 'This is the PAC 10,' I tell him. 'They'll pay five hundred thousand dollars, maybe seven hundred thousand—I don't think a million.' "

In the end, Ladouceur never says anything to give the impression he would ever leave De La Salle, at least for another coaching job. He once off-handedly remarked that he was ready to try something new: "Twenty-two years is a long time to do anything." But he is tempted by the prospect of coaching his son Dan, a freshman, and that would seem to guarantee the Spartans three more years of Ladouceur. It would also bring The Streak, if he stays undefeated, to 171 games—although there's nothing to say Terry Eidson and the rest of the coaches won't build on that for another few years.

But Ladouceur won't make any predictions about sticking around for his other son, six-year-old Michael. "God, I hope I'm not still here!" he says with a laugh.

EPILOGUE

De La Salle won its CIF Northern Sectional championship game, against San Leandro, 48–13, before three thousand spectators in a driving rainstorm. Maurice Drew scored three touchdowns on 154 rushing yards, and a third *USA Today* year-end number one ranking was assured. It was a low-key affair.

The real drama came after the game, when linebacker and tight end Brendan Ottoboni, who'd taken a big hit while stretching out for a pass, became ill at the celebration afterward in the school cafeteria. His parents took him to the hospital, where a CAT scan revealed a frightening amount of internal damage: bruised adrenal glands, stomach, liver, pancreas, and duodenum. The word was, if either of the adrenal glands had ruptured, he might have died. For the next two days, Ottoboni's health was foremost on the coaching staff's minds. Within a week he was on his way to a full recovery.

It was time for me to say good-bye, for now. I visited Brother Chris and congratulated him on the excellent season his nephew Tom Brady was enjoying with the New England Patriots. What was left to say about the Spartans? "I still think that when it happens—losing—it will be a good thing," he said. "It will get that monkey off our back. I don't know to what degree fear of losing drives us anymore.

"In one sense, it's unreal that a student can come to high school and play a varsity sport and never lose for ten years. That becomes the ever-growing challenge: to motivate the students for the right reasons. Even when we won, the coaches weren't satisfied with the performances of the team. That's what teachers do. They teach the game, not the outcome.

"Last year Lad, Terry, Joe Aliotti, and me, we talked over the schedule. Long Beach wanted the game. Our coaches said, 'We're the hunted. You come here.'

"But then we got practical. They said they couldn't afford to go north this year. And we said, 'It looks like they're a great team, they're gonna be ranked number one.' So we decided, 'What could be better? Number two De La Salle goes to number one Long Beach Poly and we lose to them in their house.' I said to Terry, 'That's going to be your call.'

"It turned out to be a wonderful story from the pregame hype to the game, a great story for prep sports. How often do prep sports get the front page of the sports page? The game had everything."

I had my farewell conversation with Bob Ladouceur at 8 A.M. in the House of Pain while he sweated away on the exercise bike. I finally asked him what I really wanted to know: about Teilhard de Chardin. "He brought heaven and earth together and made it make sense," he said, knees pumping. "I have his biography on the nightstand, but I don't know when I'll finish it." Pause. "The last real book, I mean novel, that I read was the *Leper Priest of Moloka'i*, the story of Father Damien." Longer pause. "Have you read Marianne Williamson's *Return to Love*? She's awesome. I love her stuff. My wife brings these books home, I read 'em. That's my job." He laughed, sweat pouring down his face.

When I return to Long Beach for the CIF Southern Section championship game and see the Poly boys again, several go out of their way to tell me they've come back all the way from their loss to De La Salle. Indeed, there's a focus and intensity, as well as a maturity, that was somewhat lacking in October. They're not as distractible, and their eyes are clear. It's impossible not to think about what might have been, but it's probably true, as one Poly parent said, that losing the game to De La Salle has been one of the greatest learning experiences these kids will ever have.

The Friday before the championship game I come to school to browse the glass cases of memorabilia in the Administration Building. I kneel and dig through ancient yearbooks—the *Caerulea*, as it's still called, was a fine-print literary journal back in the 1900s. I'm looking for an early reference to Poly football, perhaps a picture of my grandfather in his football togs, and one of my father with his black teammate, friend, and fellow end, J. D. McCowen.

Suddenly I'm staring at a name written in faded cursive on the cover of the yearbooks from '07, '08, and '09. The set once belonged to Maxwelton Wallace, my grandfather's older brother. There, buried in a page of period prose, is the story of Poly's first football team, in 1908; there is Uncle Max, nicknamed Ramrod, listed as being one of a half dozen on the practice squad. There aren't even twenty players on the entire team.

I've never heard a peep about Max all these years, and now I find out, today, that we Wallaces were there at the very beginning. It gives me a little more insight into the unrelenting pressure I felt, back when I was a child, to play Poly football.

I sit cross-legged on the polished linoleum I walked on as a youth. There's a sense of past and present meeting here, the world of my grandparents now represented by a few crumbling volumes of juvenilia. In the 1941 yearbook, there's Dad, tall and skinny at fifteen, posing next to McCowen. "He was much better than me," my father reminisced one day during this long season. "He went up and played for Oregon, where a lot of Poly boys went in those days." The roster of my father's teammates would make up a fine Hollywood platoon: Takahashi, DuBois, Shimazu, DeCoudres . . . the Japanese-Americans, of course, will shortly be interned, placed behind barbed wire for no reason other than their last names. In 1942 the "integrating symbol" that was football didn't work for everybody, under every situation.

Once a volume of promise, the yearbook now feels elegiac. I think about the future, too. Why didn't I come back to Long Beach? My son would be a sophomore Jackrabbit, the fifth generation of Wallaces to play ball at the Home of Scholars and Champions. I console myself with the thought that at 135 pounds Rory would have had his work cut out for him, going up against these deuce-and-a-half Poly linemen. Of course, knowing his stubborn will and character, and his athletic ability, superior to mine, I know he would've stuck it out, too. He would've found a way.

Poly's championship game is a thriller and, yes, another exorcism.

Before thirteen thousand fans at Edison Field, Poly falls behind, victim of a fake punt and Edison's pass attack, keyed by a 6'6" quarterback. Funny bounces go against Poly, kickoffs are fumbled. Yet the Jackrabbits catch up, take the lead, are tied, take the lead, and are tied again at 28–28. That's when the defense rises, led by Manuel, Junior, and Marcedes, who comes in at defensive end in passing downs and proves to be as terrifying as a pterodactyl to the Eagles. After stopping an Edison drive, Poly gives or throws the ball to Hershel in the last four minutes, and the young man who has always carried the football as if it contained the honor of his city goes to work, ripping off several of his trademark, electrifying long runs. The last, a thirty-four-yard touchdown, concludes the scoring at 42–28.

The Jackrabbits have won their third straight CIF Southern Section championship. They've become the first school ever to be in five championship games in a row. During one time-out the scoreboard at Edison Field flashes, "Poly's class of 2000 took 1,118 AP courses with a pass rate of 78 percent, compared to the national average of 50 percent."

In the locker room, Lara calls the team together. Everyone is present but Junior Lemauu, who played a dominating game with severe bronchitis. "Where's Junior?" asks Lara. A chorus replies, "In the shower!" Everyone laughs. "This is the last time I'm going to do this," Lara says. "This is hard for me right now, very hard. What's so neat about this championship is, we were fighting, we were struggling, we were trying to fix things. Listen: that's what family is all about.

"Sometimes your brother, your sister, or a family member is going to get on your ass. But when you get down, they'll back you up. This was definitely a family-unit thing. Now let's get our prayer."

The moment after the "Amen," senior Tyrone Jenkins shouts, "Juniors! Weight room on Monday! Whole team!" Next year's De La Salle game is going to be different.

The team leaves Edison Field a few minutes after midnight. The boys gaze sleepily out the bus windows at a snowcapped mountain, the Matterhorn, floating above palm trees: the Jackrabbits are passing Disneyland on the way home from their own roller-coaster ride.

In February, four of Poly's Top 5 recruits sign with USC: Darnell, Hershel, Winston, and Manuel. As he has promised, Marcedes signs with UCLA, insuring a crosstown rivalry for years to come.

A total of ten Jackrabbits will receive scholarship offers, including Rory (Idaho State), Chris Davis (New Mexico State), Pago Togafau (Idaho State), Ernesto Villasenor (Adams State), and John Williams (Adams State). At De La Salle, five players will get offers, including Derek, Matt, Nick Barbero (Montana State), Nate Kenion (St. Mary's) and Andy Briner, who gets a full ride at Cal Berkeley. Others will play as walk-ons or at junior colleges.

Derek Landri is the BVAL's player of the year, and makes the All-*USA Today* team; Darnell and Marcedes are second-teamers. Bob Ladouceur is *USA Today*'s Coach of the Year, for the third time. Down in the Southland, Raul Lara will be the *Long Beach Independent Press-Telegram*'s choice for coach of the year. Hershel Dennis—who else?—will be player of the year.

Also in February, Spartan principal Brother Chris's nephew Tom Brady leads his Patriots to an upset victory in the Super Bowl. Later that spring, reserve Spartan quarterback Brian Callahan's father becomes head coach of the Oakland Raiders. In March, the *New York Times* illustrates an article on the war in Afghanistan with a diagram of a football play that looks awfully familiar; it's 38 Power Pass Throwback, the perfectly timed throw to Maurice Drew that Matt Gutierrez executed for De La Salle's second touchdown. It looks as if someone leaked the play to the *Times*.

Spring is good to Long Beach, too. The LBUSD's superintendent of schools, Carl Cohn, wins the prestigious Harold W. McGraw Jr. Prize in Education, and the district is one of five nominees for a $500,000 Broad Foundation Prize for Urban Education, to be awarded to the district that "demonstrates the greatest overall improvement in student achievement while significantly closing the achievement gap." Approximately 73 Poly seniors are accepted to UC Berkeley and UCLA.

Then the fun starts up again. The two athletic directors, Joe

Carlson and Terry Eidson, agree to a plan that the Hawaii High School Athletic Association has long been pitching to West Coast football powerhouses: a doubleheader game between the two top California teams and the two top Hawaii teams. On September 21, 2002, the Jackrabbits will take on public school and state champion Kahuku, while De La Salle will play Catholic St. Louis, the state runner-up, at Aloha Stadium. The HHSAA will pay for everything, with the help of major corporate sponsorship. The Hawaii newspapers, of course, immediately start banging the war drums, predicting the largest crowd ever to attend a sporting event in Hawaii's history.

In June undersized center and monster-manhandler Scott Regalia begins taking part in spring practice over at Diablo Valley Community College. The coaches tell him he's too small, but after he handles all their top linemen in drills, outlifts them in the weight room, and surprises everyone with his speed and catching ability, they come up with a plan to suit his skills and character. "You're going to be a fullback," they tell him, handing him his playbook. From laboring at the most overlooked and least glamorous position in football, Scott has become a member of the glitterati—the backfield.

During the summer, Derek Landri breaks his leg fooling around on a bicycle, missing Notre Dame's practices and the beginning of the season; Andy Briner separates his shoulder while a passenger in a car accident, missing his first season at Cal Berkeley, but retaining his scholarship; Manuel Wright and Darnell Bing score below the SAT cutoff and can't enroll at USC; and Brandon Brooks is unrecruited and so goes off to Compton Junior College to prove himself all over again.

Reaction to The Game continues to be overwhelmingly positive. Fox Sports Television reports that it was the most-watched televised high school sporting event in history—and the 2.0

Nielsen rating did not include those who watched via satellite or took in one of the two replays Sunday, as well as other affiliate replays. Al Del Grande's delasallesports.com Web site would end up logging 856,706 hits for the month of the game; on October 8, the site got 61,557 hits, the largest ever for a single day. A month afterward, NFL Films aired its segment on the game, which ran for a week on ESPN and at halftime during pro games.

A new football season gets under way in August. Matt Gutierrez is third-string quarterback at Michigan, Hershel Dennis third-string running back at USC, and Winston Justice becomes a starting offensive tackle for the Trojans a few days after his eighteenth birthday.

Even before the season opens, Poly's Freddie Parrish IV emerges as the top-rated safety prospect in the country despite having seen only limited action behind Darnell Bing. With his sterling character and high SATs, Freddie is hot (and it doesn't hurt that his father pays a professional filmmaker and recruiting marketer $1,400 to create a video of Freddie working out in a combine). By September, Freddie has accepted a scholarship offer at Notre Dame, where he will join Derek Landri under new coach Tyrone Willingham.

Both high schools open with emphatic victories. De La Salle is ranked number one in the polls, Poly number six. Both teams win convincingly in their doubleheader games at the Hawaii Football Classic, September 21: De La Salle 31–21 over St. Louis, and Poly 42–16 over defending state champion Kahuku. That same weekend, Valdosta (Ga.) ties number two–ranked Tallahassee (Fla.) Lincoln, and by the following Tuesday the news is out: the Rematch on October 12 will be the second-ever national championship game in the history of high school football.

There would be no equaling the media frenzy and buzz attending the first game, but the star-making machinery belatedly kicks into gear. By the Friday before the match, National Public Radio is airing segments on the hour, John Madden is touting the match on his radio show, and chat rooms are ablaze across the land. Oddsmakers install the Jackrabbits as favorites, and Poly's coaches don't dispute them, talking openly of the family feeling this year's team shares. Coach Lara hints that they're glad to do without the distracting glare of the spotlight that always seemed to shine on the Top 5.

Poly has the core of a strong offensive line and defense: Kevin Brown, Charles Owens (his blood pressure stabilized), Junior Lemauu, Hercules Satele, Marlin Simmons, Joshua Tauanuu, and Mark Washington Jr. At quarterback, Leon Jackson has turned Poly into a passing juggernaut, finding receivers Derrick Jones—fresh off running a 10.34 hundred meters—and Alex Watson for sixty- and seventy-yard touchdown strikes. The running game is good, despite having graduated Hershel and Rory, due to the arrival of Lorenzo Bursey, a transfer from Beverly Hills High.

Meanwhile, aside from Maurice Drew, De La Salle seems less than formidable. The quarterback, Britt Cecil, hardly played last year. The game after the Hawaii Classic, the Spartans only won 14–0 (Maurice was out with an injured ankle). A rumor has been going around that allowing this year's undersized, untested bunch to take the field might be Ladouceur's way of orchestrating a fitting finale to The Streak.

If that is to be the case, then it's a lovely day for a new beginning. Fourteen thousand fans, most of them in the De La Salle section, hardly fill the seventy-thousand-seat stadium, and in the brilliant sunshine the ambience feels more like a day at the beach.

De La Salle wins the coin toss, takes the kickoff to the 28-yard line. On the first drive, Cecil throws eighteen yards to Cameron Colvin on a third and eight, then Maurice bursts up the middle for seventeen yards. After a Poly penalty, the ball is on the 15, and onlookers are getting a feeling of déjà vu—confirmed on the next play, when Maurice tears through tacklers on the left side, twisting his 5'7" body, now pumped up to 193 pounds, down to the 1. Cecil sneaks it over for the score.

After the kickoff, Leon Jackson moves the Jackrabbits with his passing, hitting Alex Watson for a twenty-seven-yard gain, but Poly has trouble running and has to punt. After holding De La Salle's offense to three plays, Poly again can't run the ball and punts. De La Salle receives on their 47, excellent field position, works down to the Poly 5 on a mix of runs and passes, then self-destructs with penalties. Pushed back to the 42, they march back down to the 27, where Poly finally holds on fourth and nine, after Ladouceur disdains going for the field goal.

Poly takes over. A Lorenzo Bursey run for six yards is negated by a sack of Jackson, who bounces back with an eighteen-yard pass to Alex Watson. Three plays bring up a fourth and one on the Spartan 49, and Jackson moves back to punt. At the snap, Jackson fakes as if the ball has sailed over his head, while Freddie Parrish from the blocking-back position takes the ball and passes to Bursey for the first down. With flair and grit, Poly appears to be headed for a tying score early in the second quarter. But an offside penalty is followed by an incomplete pass, a three-yard completion to Derrick Jones, and a sack of Jackson. Suddenly they have to punt again, and there will be no trick play this time.

After a couple of Drew runs, Cecil, the undersized, unheralded quarterback, runs the ball himself four straight times, moving the ball down into Poly territory. On second and nine from the 46, Cecil fakes a handoff to Maurice, wheels around to his right, and throws a long spiral that drops into a sprinting

Cameron Colvin's hands at the goal line—a touchdown that feels like a dagger in Poly's heart.

The Poly defensive back burned on the play, Kevin Massengill, blocks the ensuing extra point, but at 13–0 the nature of the game changes. The young, inexperienced, and perhaps over-matched De La Salle team that entered Memorial Stadium is no more. In its place is a fiery, precise, and battle-toughened group, worthy successors to the previous Ladouceur teams.

At halftime the statistics tell the story, and for Poly they are numbing: De La Salle totals 128 yards (48 passing, 80 running) to Poly's 39 (33 pass, 6 run).

In the third quarter, Poly takes the kickoff and introduces a new wrinkle in its offense, using junior running back Jeremiah Toloumu as a 6', 230-pound pass receiver to bring the ball down to the 39. Yet again the Spartans hold. Poly's punt is downed on the 1-yard line, however, opening the door to a decisive defensive stand, which could lead to good field position, if not a safety or blocked punt.

But a fourteen-yard pass to De'Montae Fitzgerald on third down gives the Spartans room to breathe, and five plays later Cecil passes to Fitzgerald again as he cuts underneath the defense. With the help of a crunching block from Aharon Bradley, Alijah's brother, Fitzgerald completes a seventy-four-yard touchdown play. A two-point conversion run by Cecil ups the lead to 21–0.

Poly keeps sputtering. Jackson can find Alex Watson, but no one else, and the runners can't make their tacklers miss. When the Jackrabbits go for it on fourth and seven on their own 45, it feels like a gesture of futility—and definitely premature, given that it's still the third quarter. De La Salle takes over and scores two plays later on a thirty-six-yard pass in which Spartan downfield blockers devastate Poly defenders once again.

The consequences of the fourth-down gamble become apparent on the next drive when Jackson passes Poly down to the 2-yard line. A score here, with the entire fourth quarter ahead, could have put the Jackrabbits within striking distance—but not at 28–0. In any event, Jackson fumbles, and Drew recovers. Yet Poly comes right back, driving down to score with over nine minutes to go in the fourth; they even manage to recover the ensuing onside kick.

This, however, is Poly's last gasp. Three straight incomplete pass attempts lead to a punt, and the Spartans go on cruise control the rest of the way. Britt Cecil, who in his first four games completed just 17 of 38 passes for 330 yards and no touchdowns, ends up throwing 12 for 17 and 237 yards; he has a hand in all four scores. Maurice Drew gains 161 yards, having often carried Jackrabbits on his back as he bulled and twisted his way. The undersized six-footers of the Spartan line blocked and tackled with crisp explosiveness. "In the end, it's the same story: The Athletes vs. The System," says Terry Eidson. "The System came through again."

The Streak now stood at 130, and counting. "I'm kind of emotional about it right now, but I think this is our greatest victory," said coach Ladouceur in the postgame press conference. "Nobody expected us to beat these guys and maybe we doubted ourselves a little bit, especially early in the season, that we wouldn't be able to pull this off. Give credit to our kids. They worked hard the last three or four weeks. They knew they weren't good enough. Everybody knew it. But they put their nose to the grindstone and worked hard to get ready for this game. Everything good that happened today they worked for."

So the rematch was a fizzle, despite the splendid weather, beautiful setting, and the unlikely fact that a number one and number two team were meeting for only the second time in 131 years.

Perhaps the second of anything can never equal the first.

But the game did have consequences, besides dropping Poly to number ten in the polls. A couple of weeks afterward, the California Interscholastic Federation announced it would explore the possibility of holding state championships in football. If such a thing came to pass, it would finally bring De La Salle and Southern California's best together at the end of the year—and put a stop to the growing impression that the fifth game of the preseason determined the true champion of California, and even the country. It might also negate De La Salle's advantage in strength and conditioning, because a fifteenth game, in mid-December, would put a premium on teams with lots of depth and, perhaps, favor those that play themselves into shape.

As Bob Ladouceur once said, "It's like we're their white whale."

In November of 2002, Darnell Bing got a qualifying SAT score and accepted his USC scholarship; he would start school in January. When USC and UCLA played each other for hometown bragging rights, both Hershel and Marcedes scored their first college touchdowns in the fourth quarter for their respective teams, long after the outcome was decided. USC would go on to finish fourth in the country.

Maurice Drew would be a *Parade Magazine* All-American, and the *Contra Costa Times* Player of the Year. He elects to go to UCLA, where, in company with Marcedes Lewis, he'll be assured of meeting plenty of Poly competition in the years to come. As for Bob Ladouceur, he is selected *USA Today*'s Coach of the Year for the fourth time, making it two in a row. In the spring of 2003 he finally amends his one-size-fits-all speech, dropping any references to De La Salle's critics, and adding this paragraph, among others:

Now for our biggest challenge: How do you teach sixteen-, seventeen-, eighteen-year-old boys how to love each other? I am not talking about getting along with each other, tolerating each other. I am talking about learning how to love. All of us are born with the desire to love and be loved—but the cruel irony of this innate desire is that the majority of us really don't know how to do this well. If we are to boil the purpose of existence down to its most common denominator, wouldn't this be it? To learn how to love and create a loveable self? If we are to reach for the stars, hit the high note, or strive for the highest ideal, then this is what we must do. This is the most important work any parent, teacher, coach, educator could ever do—teach love. You teach love by modeling love. By listening intently, understanding completely, accepting without judgment, separating achievement from self-worth.

As I was finishing the last chapter of this book in mid-June of 2002, I would often refer to the videotape of The Game. Late one night, while studying the fourth quarter and the De La Salle touchdown drive that sealed Poly's fate, I saw a ghost on the playing field.

It was a moment, on third down and three, on the 49-yard line of the Spartans, in the fourth quarter, when De La Salle seemed to run a passing play without any intermediate receivers. Suddenly, however, one appeared, out of thin air, and the resulting catch and run had moved the ball down to the 35, into scoring distance—leading to the touchdown that put Poly away. Something about the play haunted me. Gradually a memory returned of seeing the Poly coaches run and rerun film of this very play, on the melancholy morning following The Game.

Running the film back and forth, clicking off each frame on the remote, I was at first perplexed, then grudgingly admiring.

Matt seemed to look downfield, while the brawling duo of Landri and Ottoboni appeared to block their foe and run him out of the play. There's a Poly defensive back about five yards from them, backpedaling, keeping an eye on the duo because the tight end is his responsibility. He knows something strange is going on. He knows an offensive tackle can't be this far downfield on a pass play—it's illegal. Sometimes it happens accidentally and the refs overlook it. Sometimes they call it. But this is weird, two big guys growling and tussling, shoulder to shoulder, playacting: Ottoboni and Landri are blocking a ghost. There's no Poly player there, but they're fussing and fighting as if they've got a live one in front of them. Frame by frame the sleight of hand unfolds. Landri hesitates; Ottoboni, on the outside, slides behind his butt and, voilà, he's in the wide-open alley five yards downfield. Matt throws a dart that he snatches in stride.

There it is, the trick play that sealed the game, put it out of reach, and plucked the heart out of the kids from the inner city. It's not the keister-rooski, the bouncing self-blocked punt that turned the tide against Mater Dei for De La Salle. That was a fortuitous accident. It's not the fumble-rooski, the ancient and honorable lay-the-ball-down intentional fumble with which Loyola scored to take the lead on Poly with seconds to go in the 2000 championship. That was a great piece of daring and deception, and it was also completely aboveboard. No, this Ghost Dance is something different. It's a play designed to work through an illegal deception.

And Poly knew it. As I combed through my notes later that night, I found the relevant dialogue from the postgame film session for coaches and players: "Ahhhh!"—"Illegal man downfield"—"Shame on them." Then there was Herman Davis's basso profundo: "We will learn from that." And I remembered coach Lara's shake of the head, followed by a flat, what-can-you-do statement: "We didn't get the call." And they moved on.

Poly moved on: I checked my notes once again, including from my visit months later. There was no lingering over the moment, no cursing, no "We wuz robbed." Because they accepted that this, too, was part of football.

Besides, a check of the rules raised doubts that the play was a violation—an offensive lineman can go four, maybe five yards downfield on a passing down under certain circumstances, and so it's a discretionary call on the part of the ref. In fact, the longer I looked at Landri and Ottoboni, the more I had to give them the benefit of the doubt. It's a precisely run play, which is in its favor. Anyway, there's something so endearing and artful about this Ghost Dance that I believe it must be admitted to the canon. Landri and Ottoboni are like a pair of hugely muscled ballroom dancers doing a spirited, romping tango, like Bob Hope and Bing Crosby cutting up in a road movie. You can see them having fun. It may be the game of the century, but they're goofing, really selling the invisible defender they're pummeling. They're dancing the Spartans into the history books. They could have roses clenched between their teeth.

That's where this ends, not in controversy but acceptance.

In the movie, *The Man Who Shot Liberty Valence,* James Stewart plays a mild-mannered lawyer who thinks he's shot the villainous gunfighter when John Wayne actually did it. The final scene has two newspaper editors debate whether to write the truth. One of them says, "When it comes down to a choice between printing the truth and printing the legend, I always say, 'Print the legend.' "

With this game, I'm luckier than the newspaper editors. I can print both.

ACKNOWLEDGMENTS

In the reporting for this book I was honored by the trust and confidence of many people. While space does not permit me to individually thank each student, coach, teacher, parent, and administrator at every campus, I do wish to extend my congratulations to them for the tremendous vitality and character that they bring to their schools.

There is a small group of people without whose cooperation this story could not have been told in the depth it deserved. At De La Salle High School, principal Brother Christopher Brady and athletic director Terry Eidson first heard out my proposal and gave me a chance to prove my good intentions. Head coach Bob Ladouceur let me sit in on his deliberations and the team's most private meetings without any restrictions on what I could write. He also gave me permision to quote from his "What Is a Spartan?" speech. I cannot thank him, and them, enough.

At Long Beach Poly High School, coprincipals Shawn Ashley and Mel Collins couldn't have been more welcoming, allowing me access and tolerating my numerous drop-in visits. Long Beach Schools superintendent Carl Cohn gave me time from his exceedingly busy schedule for a long and illuminating interview about how the LBUSD turned Poly High around and into a beacon of the community. Former football coach Jerry Jaso and his successor, Raul Lara, were frank and forthcoming informants, to whom I owe much.

I also thank the following administrators and coaches: at De La Salle, President Bruce Shoup, Dean Joe Aliotti, Rudy Schulze, Mike Blasquez, Mark Panella and his wife Sue, Terrell Ward, Nate Geldermann, and Jason Alumbaugh; at Poly, Athletic Director Joe Carlson, Activities Director Terry Spier, PAAL principal Barbara Lindholm, Keith Anderson, Jim Barnett, Merle Cole II, Merle Cole III, Herman Davis, Ryan Downey, Darryl Garmon, Tim Moncure, Doc Moye, Don Norford, Ray Porter, Rob Shock, Keith Thompson, Jeff Turley, and Tim Wedlow.

Among the community of football coaches across the USA, I must thank Bruce Rollinson, head coach of Mater Dei; Jim Moxley, head coach of Buchanan High; Cal Lee of St. Louis High; and Jenks (Okla.) coach Allan Trimble—each of whom gave of his time and spoke candidly about the process of hunting a national championship. Thanks also to my unnamed Punahou School informants.

The sportswriting community also played a large role, both in the reporting they did, and which I acknowledge as a source, as well as for the camaraderie and insights offered on the sidelines: from the *Long Beach Independent Press-Telegram,* Ted Kian, Louis Johnson, Doug Kirkorian, and Dave Keisser; from the *Contra Costa Times,* Joe Stiglich, Neil Hayes, and Gary Peterson; from the *Los Angeles Times,* Eric Sondheimer, Ben Bolch, and Gary Klein; Mark Tennis of *Student Sports*; Stacey Kaneshiro, Wes Nakama, and Eugene Tanner of the *Honolulu Advertiser,* and Jason Kaneshiro of the *Honolulu Star-Bulletin;* also, Michael Arkush, Damon Esper, and Jennifer Allen. (If I have overlooked anyone else, please accept my apologies.)

Kudos to the excellent unofficial De La Salle Sports Web site run by Al Del Grande as a labor of love; as a clearinghouse of high school football information, as well as particulars about De La Salle, it is unparalleled. De La Salle documentarian Steve Lilly was a source of thoughtful discourse. I also enjoyed Long Beach Poly's student newspaper, *The High Life*, where I got my start. And, of course, my hand and heart go out to *USA Today*, without whose polls The Game could not have taken place.

Thanks to every single De La Salle player, but especially to Nick Barbero, James Bloomsburg, Alijah Bradley, Andy Briner, Pedro Cabrera, Brian Callahan, Maurice Drew, Ryan Eidson (and brother Shaun), Daniel and Steve Fujimoto, Matt Gutierrez, Nate Kenion, Derek Landri, Gino Ottoboni, Scott Regalia, and Dan Tobacco.

Thanks as well to every Poly player, again especially to Brian Banks, Darnell Bing, Brandon Brooks, Rory Carrington, Hershel Dennis, Jeff Hastings, Leon Jackson, Winston Justice, Junior Lemauu, Marcedes Lewis, Maurice Murray, Freddie Parrish IV, Art Vasoncelos, Mark Washington Jr., and Manuel Wright.

Poly community members or former players who contributed significantly included Kelvin Anderson of World Famous VIP Records, Larry Austin, Mark Carrier, Linda Carrington, Anthony Cobb, Hershel "Dino" Dennis, Rose Teofilo Dennis, Tom Ivey, Freddie Parrish III and Sylvia Parsons Parrish, Emerald Tapley and his son Mike, Philip Turner, Mark Washington Sr., Bertha Williams, Yvonne Withers, and Terrence Wright.

Thanks to Thom Simmons of the CIF Southern Section, who graciously allowed me sideline access to the CIF-SS championship game.

A very special thanks to Herman Davis, institutional historian, never at a loss for words.

On the professional level, thanks to Laurie Fox for her adept representation and timely cheerleading; Mitch Ivers; and Luke Dempsey, who helped trim a loose and baggy monster.

On the home front, love to Mindy and Rory, who cared for a football zombie and put up with his neglect; to my brother Alex, who videotaped everything; my father, who clipped everything; to my niece Jenny Hedley, who sent me the newspaper clipping that launched this project; football pals Charlie and Ned Perkins; football enablers Eric, Ann, and Max Margenau; and especially to Dell, Sandi, and Thomas Hutchinson, who put me up during my Northern California sojourns and on each return greeted me like a prodigal house pet.

Finally, I would be remiss not to thank my own football coaches: Shin Matsutani, Don Reynolds, Rex Burrell, Hank Mobley, Junji Nakamura, Ernest Radford, Mike Giers, Al Matz, and Jon Meyer. You did what you could.